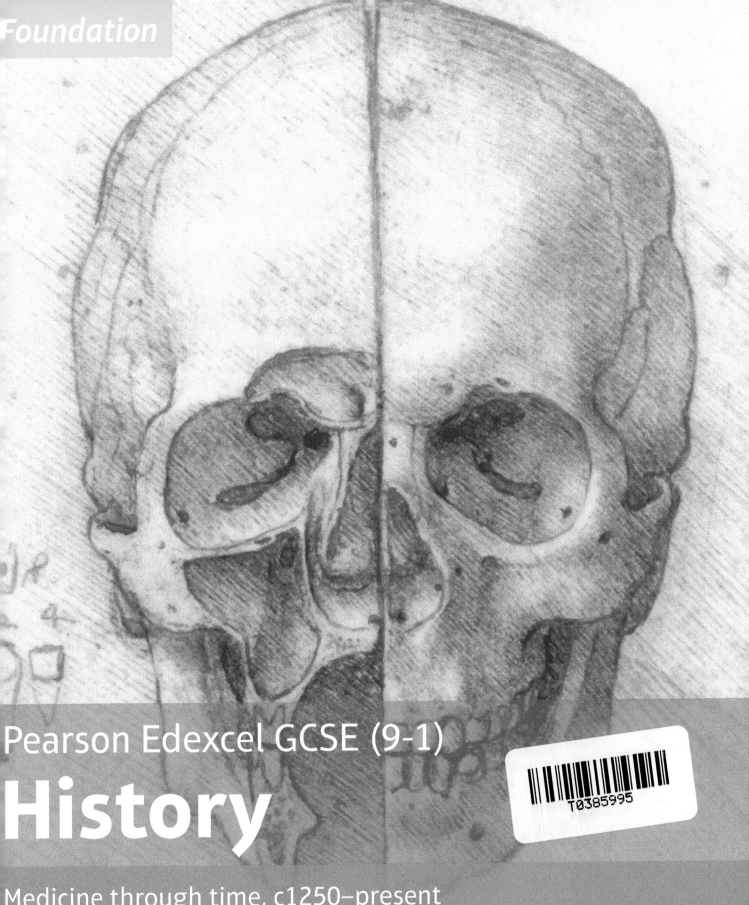

Foundation

Pearson Edexcel GCSE (9-1)

History

Medicine through time, c1250–present

Series Editor: Angela Leonard   Authors: Sally Thorne   Hilary Stark   Laura Goodyear

Pearson

Published by Pearson Education Limited, 80 Strand, London, WC2R 0RL.

www.pearsonschoolsandfecolleges.co.uk

Copies of official specifications for all Edexcel qualifications may be found on the website: www.edexcel.com

Text © Pearson Education Limited 2018

Series editor: Angela Leonard
Designed by Colin Tilley Loughrey, Pearson Education Limited
Typeset by QBS Learning
Original illustrations © Pearson Education Limited
Illustrated by KJA Artists Illustration Agency, Phoenix Photosetting, Chatham, Kent, and QBS Learning.

Cover design by Colin Tilley Loughrey
Cover photo © Science Photo Library / Sheila Terry

The rights of Hilary Stark, Sally Thorne and Laura Goodyear to be identified as authors of this work have been asserted by them in accordance with the Copyright, Designs and Patents Act 1988.

First published 2018

23
10 9 8 7 6 5 4

British Library Cataloguing in Publication Data
A catalogue record for this book is available from the British Library.
ISBN 978 1 292 25834 8

A note from the publisher
1. While the publishers have made every attempt to ensure that advice on the qualification and its assessment is accurate, the official specification and associated assessment guidance materials are the only authoritative source of information and should always be referred to for definitive guidance.

Pearson examiners have not contributed to any sections in this resource relevant to examination papers for which they have responsibility.

2. Pearson has robust editorial processes, including answer and fact checks, to ensure the accuracy of the content in this publication, and every effort is made to ensure this publication is free of errors. We are, however, only human, and occasionally errors do occur. Pearson is not liable for any misunderstandings that arise as a result of errors in this publication, but it is our priority to ensure that the content is accurate. If you spot an error, please do contact us at resourcescorrections@pearson.com so we can make sure it is corrected.

Websites
Pearson Education Limited is not responsible for the content of any external internet sites. It is essential for tutors to preview each website before using it in class so as to ensure that the URL is still accurate, relevant and appropriate. We suggest that tutors bookmark useful websites and consider enabling students to access them through the school/college intranet.

Acknowledgements

Acknowledgements

Picture credits

The publisher would like to thank the following for their kind permission to reproduce their photographs.

(Key: b-bottom; c-center; l-left; r-right; t-top)

Cover: Science Photo Library/Sheila Terry.

Alamy Stock Photo: Prisma Archivo 28, Everett Collection 82, Photo Researchers/Science History Images 102, Bruce McGowan 118l, Everett Collection Historical 147l, Ernest Brooks/GL Archive 147r, Windmill Books/Universal Images Group North America LLC 149, Imperial War Museum, London,UK/Derek Bayes/Lebrecht Music & Arts 155, Lebrecht Music & Arts 156, Chronicle 161, **Getty Images:** De Agostini Picture Library/De Agostini 6 & 13, Italian School 19, Dea/A. Dagli Orti/De Agostini 40, Science & Society Picture Library 55 & 171, Ann Ronan Pictures/Print Collector/Hulton Archive 56, Lordprice Collection 63, Universal History Archive/Universal Images Group 68 , 86, 91 & 92,Hulton Archive 72, GL Archive 77, Peter Purdy/BIPs/Hulton Archive 100 & 118r, BSIP/Universal Images Group 103, Keystone/Hulton Archive 114, Paul Popper/Popperfoto 151, Popperfoto 162, **©IWM:** Ernest Brooks (Lieutenant) 140 &147, John Warwick Brooke 160t, Albert Roberts 172, **Public Health England:** 115, **Robert Knox:** 168 &178, **Science Photo Library:** Otis Historical Archives/National Museum of Health And Medicine 143, **TopFoto.co.uk:** 113, **The Bridgeman Images:** French School (15th century)/Musee de l'Assistance Publique,Hopitaux de Paris, France/Archives Charmet 10b & 30, English School (15th century)/ British Library, London, UK/British Library Board 10t & 14, Universal History Archive/UIG 12 & 44, Vein or Blood-letting Man/ British Library, London, UK/British Library Board 24; English School, (14th century)/Private Collection 32, Vesalius, Andreas (1514–64) (after)/ Bibliotheque des Arts Decoratifs, Paris, France/Archives Charmet 53r, Private Collection/Christie's Images 93, English School,(20th century)/Private Collection/The Stapleton Collection 136-137, **The Great War and the R.A.M.C.:** Brereton, F. S. (Frederick Sadlier) 158, **The Royal Society:** Antoni van Leeuwenhoek 46, © **Wellcome Collection Licensed under Creative Commons CC-BY:** 50, 53l, 58, 78, 79, 81, 94l, 94r.

Text credits

We are grateful to the following for permission to reproduce copyright material.

23 Simpkin, Marshall Ltd: Advice from John of Gaddesden's medical book, the Rosa Anglica; **30 Margaret Paston:** Extract from a letter sent from Margaret Paston to her husband, John Paston, in 1464; **35 Oldcastle Books:** Sean Martin, A Short History of Disease (2015); **45 Winterdown Books**: Thomas Sydenham's Observationes medicae (London, 1676) and his Medical observations, 1991;

49 Nicholas Culpeper: The English Physician: Or An Astrologo-Physical Discourse of the Vulgar Herbs of This Nation (1652) **57 Deborah E. Harkness:** An article in the Bulletin of the History of Medicine (2008) **62 Nicholas Culpeper:** From Complete Herbal, a 17th-century version of medieval theriaca; **71 British medical association:** British Medical Journal: BMJ, Volume 1, 1875; **73 Cambridge scholars publishing:** Disease, Class and Social Change (2012), Marc Arnold; **78 Dover publication:** Extract from Notes on Hospitals, published in 1859; **92 Times Newspapers Limited:** This letter was printed in The Times in 1849; **103 The Mirror:** In this 2013 news article, Angelina Jolie explains why she chose to have a mastectomy; **108 The Telegraph:** 'Too much of a good thing', was published in The Telegraph in 2013, by Joe Shute; **111 St. Martin's Press:** Health and Medicine in Britain since 1860 by Anne Hardy (2001); **111 Crown copyright:** Former Labour Prime Minister Tony Blair wrote this at the start of a document about the modernisation of the NHS. It was published in 1997 contains public section information licensed under the Open Government license v3.0; **118 The Noble foundation:** An extract from Alexander Fleming's acceptance speech; **119 Patricia Alice Harding:** In this study of the role of science in science education, published in 1996, Patricia Harding sets out an alternative point of view; **125 Crown copyright:** A 2012 Department of Health consultation (when a group of people meets to discuss an idea or issue) on smoking, which sets out the reasons why the government has taken action to limit visibility of cigarettes contains public section information licensed under the Open Government license v3.0; **138 Ebury Press:** From an interview with Gunner William Towers in 1989; **138, 159, 161 The Echo Library:** From Pat Beauchamp's autobiography, Fanny Goes to War, published in 1919; **150 Dover Publications:** From 'The General', a poem written by Siegfried Sassoon in 1918; **150 Boolarong press:** From Edward Munro's Diaries of a Stretcher Bearer; **151 Crown copyright:** From a speech made by Walter Roch in Parliament, 23 June 1915 Contains Parliamentary information licensed under the Open Parliament Licence v3.0; **154 Random house:** From an interview with Captain Maberly Esler in 1974; **155 Wilfred Owen:** From 'Dulce et Decorum Est', a poem written by Wilfred Owen in 1917; **155 Praeger:** From the notebook of Lance Sergeant Elmer Cotton, who served in the 5th Northumberland Fusiliers in 1915; **156 Clarendon Press:** From the autobiography of Geoffrey Keynes, The Gates of Memory (1981); **158 Hachette Livre:** From F. S. Brereton, The Great War and the RAMC, published in 1919; **159, 166 Simpkin, Marshall, Hamilton, Kent & Company, Limited:** From Ward Muir's Observations of an Orderly, published in 1917; **163 W.G.Macpherson:** From Major-General Sir W. G. Macpherson, Medical Services General History, published in 1924; **164 Telegraph:** From The Daily Telegraph, a British newspaper, 29 April 1915; **166 Pan books:** From the diary of B. C. Jones, 1915–16; **168 Macmillan:** From Radiography and Radiotherapeutics, by Robert Knox, published in 1917; **170, 172 Hachette Book Group**: From A Surgeon's Journal 1915–18, by Harvey Cushing, published in 1936.

Contents

Timeline 10

Chapter 1: c1250–c1500: Medicine in medieval England **12**

1.1 Ideas about the cause of disease and illness 13

1.2 Approaches to treatment and prevention 22

1.3 Dealing with the Black Death, 1348–49 32

Recap page c1250–c1500 37

Writing Historically 38

Chapter 2: c1500–c1700: The Medical Renaissance in England **40**

2.1 Ideas about the cause of disease and illness 41

2.2 Approaches to prevention and treatment 49

2.3 William Harvey 58

2.4 Dealing with the Great Plague in London, 1665 61

Recap page c1500–c1700 65

Writing Historically 66

Chapter 3: c1700–c1900: Medicine in18th- and 19th-century Britain **68**

3.1 Ideas about the cause of disease and illness 69

3.2 Approaches to prevention and treatment 76

3.3 Fighting cholera in London, 1854 91

Recap page c1700–c1900 97

Writing Historically 98

Chapter 4: c1900–present: Medicine in modern Britain **100**

4.1 Ideas about the cause of disease and illness 101

4.2 Approaches to prevention and treatment 107

4.3 Fleming, Florey and Chain's development of penicillin 117

4.4 The fight against lung cancer in the 21st century 122

Recap page c1900–present 127

Writing Historically 128

Thematic: Preparing for your exams 130

Chapter 5: The British sector of the Western Front, 1914–18: injuries, treatments and the trenches **136**

Sources and the examination 138

5.1 The historical context of medicine in the early 20th century 142

5.2 The context of the British sector of the Western Front 146

5.3 Conditions requiring medical treatment on the Western Front 153

5.4 The work of the RAMC and FANY 158

5.5 The significance of the Western Front for experiments in surgery and medicine 165

Recap page 174

Historic Environment: Preparing for your exams 176

Answers to Medicine Recap 182

Index 183

How to use this book

What's covered?

This book covers the Thematic study on Medicine through time and the Historical Environment, c1250 to present. These units make up 30% of your GCSE course, and will be examined in Paper 1.

Thematic studies cover a long period of history, and require you to know about change and continuity across different ages and aspects of society. You will need to know about key people, events and developments and make comparisons between the different periods studied.

Linked to the thematic study is a historic environment that examines a specific site and its relationship to historical events and developments.

Features

As well as a clear, detailed explanation of the key knowledge you will need, you will also find a number of features in the book:

Key terms

Where you see a word followed by an asterisk, like this: Salient*, you will be able to find a Key Terms box on that page that explains what the word means.

> **Key term**
>
> **Salient***
> An area of a battlefield that extends into enemy territory, so that it is surrounded on three sides by the enemy and is therefore in a vulnerable position.

Activities

Every few pages, you'll find a box containing some activities designed to help check and embed knowledge and get you to really think about what you've studied. The activities start simple, but might get more challenging as you work through them.

Summaries and Checkpoints

At the end of each chunk of learning, the main points are summarised in a series of bullet points – great for embedding the core knowledge, and handy for revision.

Checkpoints help you to check and reflect on your learning. The Strengthen section helps you to consolidate knowledge and understanding, and check that you've grasped the basic ideas and skills.

The Challenge questions push you to go beyond just understanding the information, and into evaluation and analysis of what you've studied.

Sources and Interpretations

This book contains numerous contemporary pictorial and text sources that show what people from the period, said, thought or created. You will need to be comfortable examining sources to answer questions in your Paper 1 exam.

Although interpretations do not appear in Paper 1, the book also includes extracts from the work of historians, showing how experts have interpreted the events you've been studying.

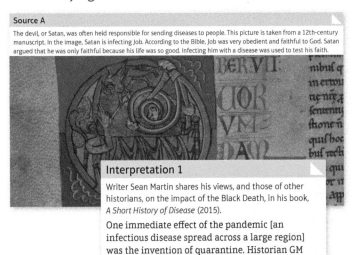

> **Source A**
> The devil, or Satan, was often held responsible for sending diseases to people. This picture is taken from a 12th-century manuscript. In the image, Satan is infecting Job. According to the Bible, Job was very obedient and faithful to God. Satan argued that he was only faithful because his life was so good. Infecting him with a disease was used to test his faith.

> **Interpretation 1**
> Writer Sean Martin shares his views, and those of other historians, on the impact of the Black Death, in his book, *A Short History of Disease* (2015).
>
> One immediate effect of the pandemic [an infectious disease spread across a large region] was the invention of quarantine. Historian GM Trevelyan argued that the Black Death was at least as important as the industrial revolution, while David Herlihy argued that the Black Death was "the great watershed", [an important turning point] without which there would have been no Renaissance, and with no Renaissance, no industrial revolution.

Extend your knowledge

These features contain useful additional information that adds depth to your knowledge, and to your answers. The information is closely related to the key issues in the unit, and questions are sometimes included, helping you to link the new details to the main content.

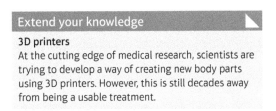

> **Extend your knowledge**
>
> **3D printers**
> At the cutting edge of medical research, scientists are trying to develop a way of creating new body parts using 3D printers. However, this is still decades away from being a usable treatment.

Exam-style questions and tips

The book also includes extra exam-style questions you can use to practise. These appear in the chapters and are accompanied by a tip to help you get started on an answer.

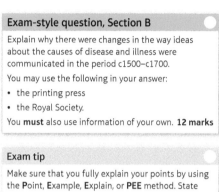

Exam-style question, Section B

Explain why there were changes in the way ideas about the causes of disease and illness were communicated in the period c1500–c1700.

You may use the following in your answer:

- the printing press
- the Royal Society.

You **must** also use information of your own. **12 marks**

Exam tip

Make sure that you fully explain your points by using the **P**oint, **E**xample, **E**xplain, or **PEE** method. State your argument, then add some examples from your own knowledge to back it up. Finish off by explaining how that evidence relates to the question.

Recap pages

At the end of each chapter, you'll find a page designed to help you to consolidate and reflect on the chapter as a whole. Each recap page includes a recall quiz, ideal for quickly checking your knowledge or for revision. Recap pages also include activities designed to help you summarise and analyse what you've learned, and also reflect on how each chapter links to other parts of the unit.

At the end of most chapters is a spread dedicated to helping you improve your writing skills. These include simple techniques you can use in your writing to make your answers clearer, more precise and better focused on the question you're answering.

The Writing Historically approach is based on the *Grammar for Writing* pedagogy developed by a team at the University of Exeter and popular in many English departments. Each spread uses examples from the preceding chapter, so it's relevant to what you've just been studying.

Preparing for your exams

At the back of the book, you'll find a special section dedicated to explaining and exemplifying the new Edexcel GCSE History exams. Advice on the demands of this paper, written by Angela Leonard, helps you prepare for and approach the exam with confidence. Each question type is explained through annotated sample answers at two levels, showing clearly how answers can be improved.

Pearson Progression Scale: This icon indicates the Step that a sample answer has been graded at on the Pearson Progression Scale.

This book is also available as an online ActiveBook, which can be licensed for your whole institution.

THINKING HISTORICALLY

These activities are designed to help you develop a better understanding of how history is constructed, and are focused on the key areas of Evidence, Interpretations, Cause & Consequence and Change & Continuity. In the Thematic Study, you will come across activities on both Cause and Change, and in the Historical Environment on Evidence, as these are key areas of focus for these units.

The Thinking Historically approach has been developed in conjunction with Dr Arthur Chapman and the Institute of Education, UCL. It is based on research into the misconceptions that can hold students back in history.

THINKING HISTORICALLY Change and continuity (2a-b) — conceptual map reference

The Thinking Historically conceptual map can be found at: www.pearsonschools.co.uk/thinkinghistoricallygcse

About change

This course is about two things: it is about the history of medicine, and it is about **change**. You are going to look at a long period of time – over 750 years. Medicine is the theme you will follow through these years. Concentrating on just one part of British life means you can also focus on how and why things change (and sometimes how and why they don't.)

This introduction is to help you understand the language and concepts historians use when they discuss change.

- **Change** – this is when things become different than they were before.
- **Continuity** – this is the opposite of change, when things stay the same, sometimes for a very long time.
- Change isn't always the same as **progress** – which is when things get better.
- The **rate of change** – change doesn't always happen at the same pace – sometimes things change very quickly, but sometimes they change slowly. Historians are interested in why this is.
- A **trend** is when there are a number of similar and related changes, continuing in the same direction, over a period of time – for example, the fact that there were 35 million people with smartphones in the UK in 2014 is part of the trend in the growing use of mobile phones.

- A **turning point** is when a significant change happens – something that is different from what has happened before and which will affect the future. For example, it was a turning point when Michael Harrison made the first ever mobile phone call in Britain on 1 January 1985.
- Historians are very interested in the **factors** that affect change. Some of them can be quite obvious, but others are more surprising. For example:
  - developments in science and technology, particularly around miniaturisation, have affected the development of the mobile phone
  - people's attitudes have also affected the development of the mobile phone. For example, text messaging (SMS) was not originally designed to be used – it was built in to help scientists test the first networks and phones. But users found out about it, liked it, and it has now become part of our world
  - less surprisingly, government has affected the development of mobile phones – with regulations about networks, laws about using them, and planning control of phone masts.

Look out for plenty more factors that affect change throughout the course.

Activities ?

1. Write your own definitions for each of the words in bold above, and explain your own example of each one.

2. Graphs can be a useful way to show change. Study the graph opposite.
   a. Where would you put these two factors affecting change on the graph? i) Worries about the health effects of butter are common. ii) Government campaigns to get people to reduce the fat in their diet.
   b. At the same time, bread sales fell by about 50%. Is this a factor affecting spread sales?

3. Study the table summarising Katy and Mel's journeys to school.
   a. Draw a line graph, with two lines, showing Katy and Mel's independence in their journeys. On the x-axis have the school years from 1 to 11. On the y-axis, plot their independence. For each of them, score their two journeys (to and from school) and add the scores together. Going with a parent: scores 1 mark; using public transport: 2 marks; going by themselves: 3 marks. (Use half marks when they sometimes do one thing, and sometimes another: e.g. in Year 8 Katy scores 1½ for her journey to school, because she sometimes goes by car and sometimes goes by bus.)
   b. Explain which period of time on the graph is the best example of continuity.
   c. Does the rate of change vary? Explain your answer.
   d. Is there a trend? If so, explain what it is.
   e. Is there a turning point for either of them? If so, explain what it is.
   f. Explain what factors you think affected the changes in their journeys to and from school.

4. Make a timeline or a graph to show change in your life over time. Show any trends or turning points, and places where the rate of change increases. Explain what factors have influenced these changes.

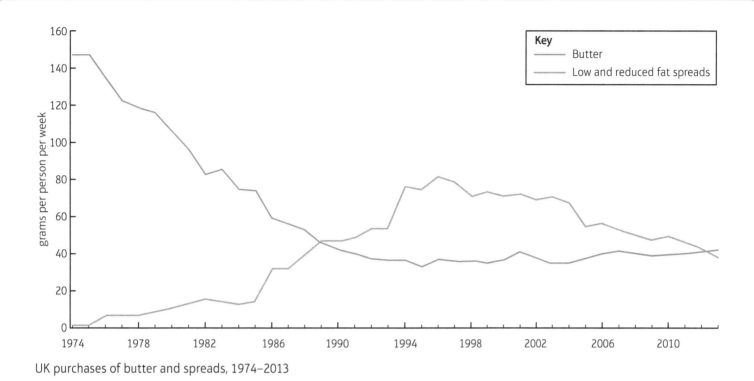

UK purchases of butter and spreads, 1974–2013

Journeys to and from school

School year	Katy	Mel
Years 1–6	Mel and Katy are twins; they went to a primary school that was about 10 minutes walk from home. Their Dad walked with them to school in the morning, and their Mum met them and walked home with them at the end of the day.	
Year 7	They now moved to a secondary school which was about three miles away. Their Mum took them to school in the car in the morning. They went to an after school club, and then their Dad picked them up in the car at about 5 o'clock.	
Year 8	Going to school, usually got a lift from her Mum in the car, but sometimes caught the bus with Mel and her friends. Stayed at the after school club until Dad picked them up in the car.	Caught the bus to school with her friends. Stayed at the after school club until Dad picked them up in the car.
Year 9	Cycled to school with her mates Aarav and Claire. Often stayed to do sport after school, and then cycled home.	Caught the bus to school with her friends. Usually stayed at the after school club until her Dad picked her up in the car. In the summer sometimes went home on the bus with her friends.
Year 10	Cycled to school with her mates. Often stayed to do sport after school, and then cycled home. In the summer developed a crush on one of Mel's friends, Callum, and started going in on the bus with Mel and her friends.	Caught the bus to school with her friends. Went home on the bus with her friends.
Year 11	Started going out with Callum. Usually met him on the bus in the mornings, and walked home with him after school.	Caught the bus to school with her friends. Went home on the bus with her friends.

Timeline: Medicine

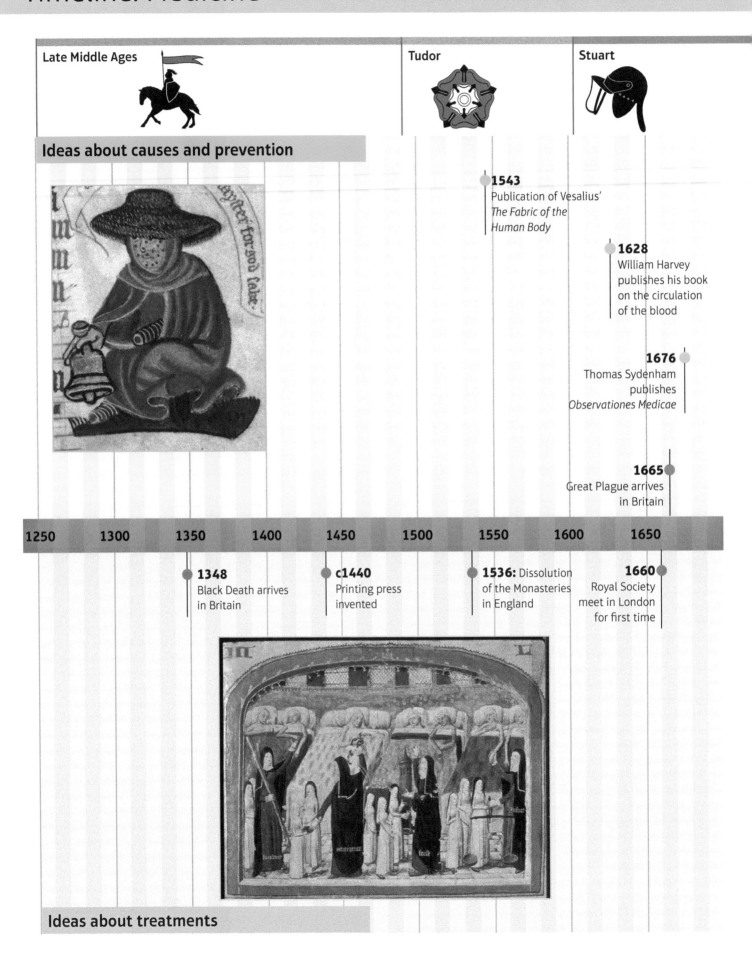

| Late Middle Ages | Tudor | Stuart |

Ideas about causes and prevention

1543
Publication of Vesalius'
*The Fabric of the
Human Body*

1628
William Harvey
publishes his book
on the circulation
of the blood

1676
Thomas Sydenham
publishes
Observationes Medicae

1665
Great Plague arrives
in Britain

| 1250 | 1300 | 1350 | 1400 | 1450 | 1500 | 1550 | 1600 | 1650 |

1348
Black Death arrives
in Britain

c1440
Printing press
invented

1536: Dissolution
of the Monasteries
in England

1660
Royal Society
meet in London
for first time

Ideas about treatments

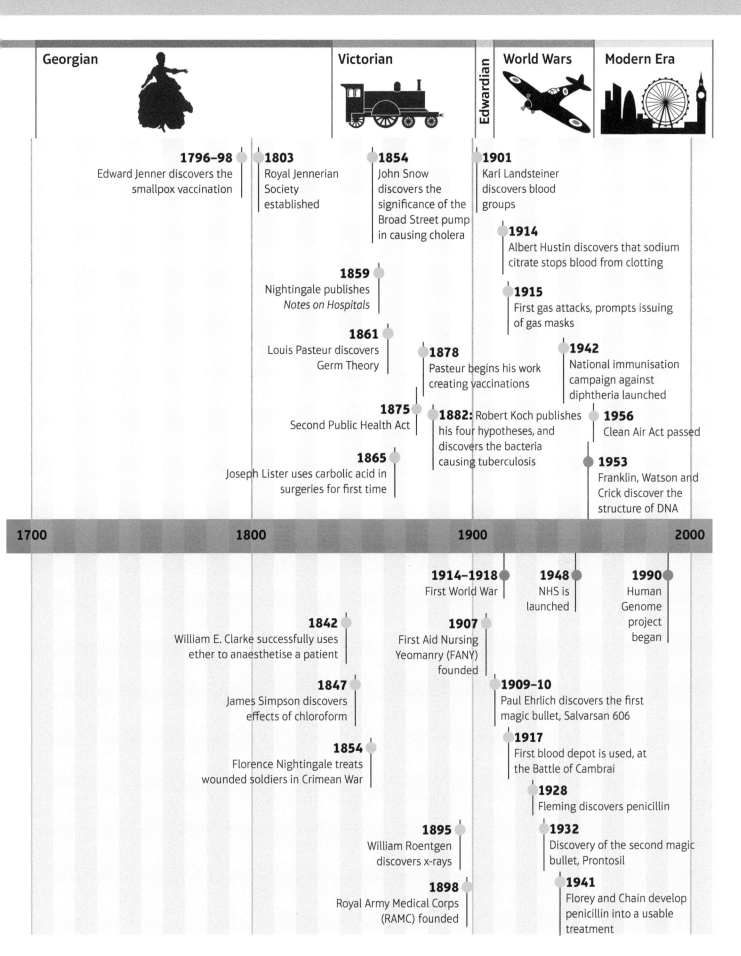

Georgian

1796–98
Edward Jenner discovers the smallpox vaccination

1803
Royal Jennerian Society established

1842
William E. Clarke successfully uses ether to anaesthetise a patient

1847
James Simpson discovers effects of chloroform

1854
Florence Nightingale treats wounded soldiers in Crimean War

Victorian

1854
John Snow discovers the significance of the Broad Street pump in causing cholera

1859
Nightingale publishes *Notes on Hospitals*

1861
Louis Pasteur discovers Germ Theory

1878
Pasteur begins his work creating vaccinations

1875
Second Public Health Act

1882: Robert Koch publishes his four hypotheses, and discovers the bacteria causing tuberculosis

1865
Joseph Lister uses carbolic acid in surgeries for first time

1895
William Roentgen discovers x-rays

1898
Royal Army Medical Corps (RAMC) founded

Edwardian

World Wars

1901
Karl Landsteiner discovers blood groups

1914
Albert Hustin discovers that sodium citrate stops blood from clotting

1915
First gas attacks, prompts issuing of gas masks

1942
National immunisation campaign against diphtheria launched

1956
Clean Air Act passed

1907
First Aid Nursing Yeomanry (FANY) founded

1909–10
Paul Ehrlich discovers the first magic bullet, Salvarsan 606

1917
First blood depot is used, at the Battle of Cambrai

1928
Fleming discovers penicillin

1932
Discovery of the second magic bullet, Prontosil

1941
Florey and Chain develop penicillin into a usable treatment

Modern Era

1953
Franklin, Watson and Crick discover the structure of DNA

1914–1918
First World War

1948
NHS is launched

1990
Human Genome project began

1700   1800   1900   2000

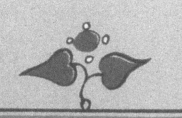

01 | c1250–c1500: Medicine in medieval England

Medieval England was a hard place to live in. Most people worked in the fields, growing crops for wealthy landowners. Poor diets, especially when there was not enough food to go around, meant that sickness and disease were never far away. Some people lived in towns and cities, but this was not much better than the countryside: the crowded streets and lack of drains meant diseases spread easily. Nearly half of the population died before reaching adulthood.

There wasn't much scientific knowledge in medieval England. Instead, the books promoted by the Catholic Church relied on advice from leading doctors who lived long ago, such as Hippocrates and Galen, to explain why people caught diseases. Sometimes people believed God could send disease as a punishment for bad behaviour.

Most of the time, people accepted this. Only in times of terrible disease, such as during the Black Death in 1348, did they start to question what the Catholic Church was telling them about medicine.

Learning outcomes

By the end of this chapter, you will:

- understand what ideas people in medieval England had about the causes of disease and illness
- understand what methods medieval people tried in order to prevent and treat disease
- complete a case study on the Black Death, including approaches to its treatment and attempts to prevent it from spreading.

1.1 Ideas about the cause of disease and illness

Learning outcomes

- Understand different ideas about the cause of disease before 1500, including the Theory of the Four Humours.
- Know the different influences on ideas about the cause of disease before 1500.

Supernatural and religious explanations of the causes of disease

What medieval England was like	How this affected medical ideas
People were very religious and went to church regularly.  The Catholic Church was the only accepted religion. It owned many churches, monasteries and convents. These buildings became important centres of the community.	The Church provided some medical care. People were expected to give a sum of money to the Church each month. This was known as a tithe*. The Church used the tithes to pay for the care given to people in need. 
There were often famines* and a lack of food.	Malnutrition* meant people were more likely to fall ill.
There was a lack of scientific knowledge.	The lack of knowledge meant that the causes of disease and illness were unknown.
	The Church often told people that illness was sent by God.
Ordinary people didn't go to school. Most people could not read or write.	People received most of their education from the Church. They learned from the stories they heard, or the paintings they saw in their church.
The Church taught that sin was very dangerous.	The Church taught that those who committed a sin could be punished by God with illness. The devil could also send disease to test someone's faith, as seen in Source A.

Source A

The devil, or Satan, was often held responsible for sending diseases to people. This picture is taken from a 12th-century manuscript*. In the image, Satan is infecting* Job. According to the Bible, Job was very obedient and faithful to God. Satan argued that he was only faithful because his life was so good. Infecting him with a disease was used to test his faith.

Key terms

Famine*
Food shortage, usually due to bad harvests.

Tithe*
A sum of money given to the Church by individuals each month.

Malnutrition*
Illness caused by lack of food.

Manuscript*
A book or text written by hand before the invention of printing.

Infecting*
Giving somebody a disease.

The Church often explained famine and illness by saying they were sent by God to punish people for their sins*. If, after people had prayed, they became well or famine went away, then the Church could say a miracle from God had happened. This, the Church said, was proof that God existed, and reinforced the idea that God controlled everyone and everything that happened.

Leprosy

The Bible said that leprosy was sent by God as a punishment. Leprosy usually began as a painful skin disease, followed by paralysis* and death. Fingers and toes would fall off, body hair would drop out and ulcers would develop both inside and outside the body.

There was no cure for leprosy, so lepers were sent away from their home towns. They usually had to move to leper houses or to island communities far away from other people. If they were allowed to stay in their home towns, they had to wear a cloak and ring a bell to warn people they were there. This was because it was believed their breath was contagious*. Although this was not true, it shows that medieval people had some correct ideas about how some diseases were transmitted.

Key terms

Sin*
Breaking a religious law.

Paralysis*
Being unable to move either all or part of your body as a result of illness, poison or injury.

Contagious*
A disease which can be caught through contact with an infected person.

Source B

A painting of a leper from around 1400. Lepers were made to wear a cloak to cover their diseased bodies and ring a bell to warn people when they were nearby. The bell would also have acted as a way to ask for money. The words say, 'Some good, my gentle master, for God's sake'.

Astrology

Along with the role of God, the position of the planets and stars was also thought to be very important when diagnosing* illness. A physician* would use star charts, looking at when the patient was born and when they fell ill, to help decide what was wrong.

Astrology was a **supernatural*** explanation for disease. It could be traced back to Hippocrates (see page 17), who had been a leading physician from Ancient Greece.

The Theory of the Four Humours

Another very popular idea used to explain disease was the **Theory of the Four Humours**. The theory said that the body was made up of four liquids known as humours. These were:

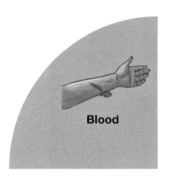

Blood

Yellow bile – this was seen in pus or vomit*

The Four Humours

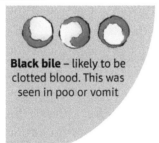

Phlegm – watery substance coughed up or sneezed out of the nose

Black bile – likely to be clotted blood. This was seen in poo or vomit

Figure: The Theory of the Four Humours

It was believed that all the humours must be balanced and equal. If the mix became unbalanced, a person became ill. The Theory of the Four Humours was a **rational** explanation of disease – it was based on observing patients and using reasoning to suggest a treatment.

Activities

1   Give at least three reasons why many people in the Middle Ages believed that the main cause of illness and disease was punishment from God.

2   Draw an illustration in the style of a medieval manuscript to explain The Theory of the Four Humours.

Activity ?

Create a paper fortune teller to help you remember the different parts of the Theory of the Four Humours.

a On the outside, write the names of the Four Humours.

b On the first layer inside, write the qualities of each humour – hot, cold, wet, dry.

c On the next layer, write anything else that is related to the humour – seasons and/or elements.

Key terms

Symptoms*

Signs of an illness, for example a temperature or a rash.

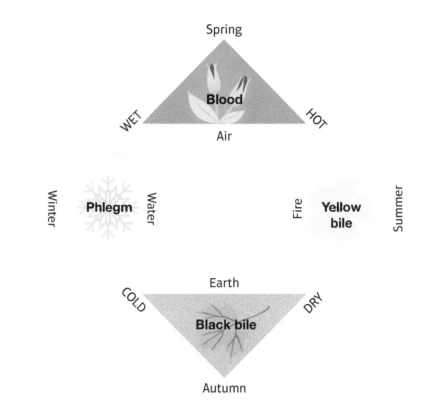

Figure 1.1 The Four Humours.

Humour	Season	Element	Qualities
Blood	Spring	Air	Hot and wet
Yellow bile	Summer	Fire	Hot and dry
Black bile	Autumn	Earth	Cold and dry
Phlegm	Winter	Water	Cold and wet

The Four Humours of the body were linked to the Earth's elements – air, fire, earth and water and to different qualities such as hot and wet. To be able to diagnose* a patient the physician would look for symptoms*. For example, a person suffering from a fever had a temperature, causing the skin to become hot and red. This was seen as a sign of too much blood. A person suffering from a cold was thought to have too much phlegm, which was cold and wet.

The humours were also linked with the seasons. For example, in winter, which is cold and wet, it was thought that the body produces too much phlegm, causing coughs and colds.

The humours were also linked with the personality. For example, in medieval times a person with depression was thought to have too much black bile. The humour of blood was linked to happiness.

The origins of the theory

The Theory of the Four Humours comes from an Ancient Greek physician named **Hippocrates** in the 5th century BCE. Hippocrates looked very carefully at his patients' symptons and recorded them. The Theory of the Four Humours was developed from what he saw.

Galen, a physician in Ancient Rome during the 2nd century CE, developed the ideas of Hippocrates. Galen put forward the idea of balancing the humours by using the **Theory of Opposites**.

For example:

* too much phlegm, which was linked to water and the cold, could be cured by eating hot peppers
* a patient with a fever, which was linked to too much blood and heat, could be cooled with cucumber.

Why was the theory so popular?

The Theory of the Four Humours could be used to explain almost any kind of illness – physical or mental. This was important because there was no other scientific explanation for the cause of disease.

If you are suffering from too much...

phlegm   blood

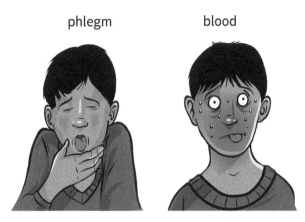

...then treatment is something...

hot and dry   cold and wet

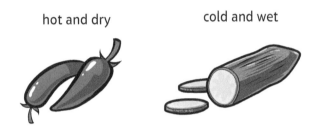

Figure 1.2 Examples of the Theory of Opposites.

Activities	?

1 Create an advice poster to explain how the Four Humours led to illness. Select **two** of the Four Humours and give examples of the different illnesses that were caused by having too much of each humour.

2 Briefly explain how Galen built on the work of Hippocrates. Using the Theory of Opposites, suggest some cures for the Four Humours.

Why were the Four Humours popular in the Middle Ages?

Galen's influence

The ideas of Galen were very important in the Middle Ages for three reasons:

The role of the Church

- Galen and Hippocrates wrote that the body was clearly designed for a purpose. Galen also believed in the idea of the soul*. These ideas fitted in very well with the ideas of the Church, so the Church agreed with Galen's teachings.
- At this time, books were produced by the Church, so the Church could control what physicians read.

The importance of book learning

- Few people could read in the Middle Ages. Physicians who could read were thought to be clever.
- Physicians read as many books as possible, so people would think they were good at their job.
- Galen's books were widely read by physicians. No one questioned what these ancient books said.

Why were the Four Humours popular in the Middle Ages?

The lack of alternatives

- There was no scientific evidence to show that the Four Humours were wrong.
- Dissections* were not allowed, because the Church taught that the body needed to be buried whole in order for the soul to go to heaven. This meant physicians could not find out the cause of diseases.
- Sometimes a barber surgeon* might carry out minor surgery or dissect the body of a criminal. When this happened, the physician would sit far away from the body, reading Galen's books.

Figure: Why Galen's ideas about the Four Humours were so popular in the Middle Ages.

Key terms

Soul*

The spiritual part of a person.

Dissection*

Cutting open a dead body to study it.

Key term

Barber surgeon*

Barbers worked with sharp knives, so as well as giving people haircuts, they also carried out medical treatments such as blood-letting (see page 23). Over time, they started to carry out minor surgery.

Exam-style question, Section B

Explain why there was continuity in ideas about the cause of disease during the period c1250–c1500.

You may use the following information in your answer:

- the Church
- Galen.

You **must** also use information of your own.   **12 marks**

Source C

A picture of a medieval dissection. The physician is sitting high up, away from the body. He is reading aloud from the works of Galen. The body is being dissected by somebody else. This painting appeared in the first illustrated anatomy* book to be printed – the *Fasciculus Medicinae*, written by Johannes de Ketham, an Austrian professor of medicine, in 1491.

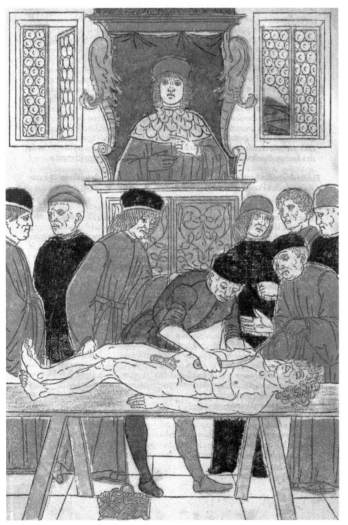

Exam tip

There are **six marks** available here for your knowledge and **six marks** available for how well you explain your answer. The knowledge you include should focus on the question.

- The focus is on 'continuity'. This means explaining why things stayed the **same** between c1250 and c1500.
- You should also focus on people's beliefs about the cause of disease (rather than treatments or care).

Other ideas about the cause of disease

Miasma

A **miasma** was bad air that was believed to be harmful. Hippocrates and Galen both wrote about miasmata (which is the plural of miasma) and suggested that people might get a disease from swamps, corpses and other rotting things.

Smells were also linked with God. A clean and sweet-smelling home was a sign of religious cleanliness. Incense* was burned in churches to make the air clean. Homes that smelled badly suggested sinfulness. If a person was unwashed, other people would avoid them, in case they breathed in the bad miasma and got a disease.

Miasma was another **rational** explanation of the cause of disease.

Key terms
Anatomy*
Knowledge of the body and how it works.
Incense*
Sweet-smelling spices.

Urine charts

Medieval physicians carefully examined a patient's urine* in order to make their diagnosis*. It was thought to be one of the best ways to check on the balance of the humours inside the body. The physician would carefully check the urine on a urine chart. He would check the colour, thickness, smell and even taste of the urine before making his diagnosis.

Influences on ideas about the cause of disease

The Middle Ages was a time when there was **continuity*** in ideas about the cause of disease. There were only a few small changes. For example, astrology became more popular, but it did not add to Galen's work. On the whole, ideas remained the same.

Key terms

Urine*

Wee

Diagnosis*

Physician's suggestion about what illness the patient is suffering from.

Continuity*

Things stay the same.

Individuals and the Church

- The Church did not like change and wanted ideas to stay the same.
- The Church produced all the medical books, so they had control over who read them and what people read.
- The Church liked the Theory of the Four Humours because it fitted with their teachings about the world. Therefore, the Church only let people read Hippocrates and Galen's work.

**Influencing beliefs:
The cause of disease**

Science and technology

- During the Middle Ages, scientists explained any new discoveries using old ideas.
- The most important piece of new technology was the printing press*, which was invented in around 1440. This made it easier to print medical textbooks, so more people could learn about ideas such as the Four Humours.
- Science and technology did not change medical ideas during the medieval period.

Attitudes in society

- People in the Middle Ages had a strong belief in God. They thought that if a person criticised the Church they would be sent to hell* when they died.
- Physicians* who questioned the ideas of Hippocrates and Galen were seen to be criticising the Church. People did not want them as their doctors.
- Many people saw no reason to change the way medicine was done.

Figure 1.3 The three main factors that influenced what people believed caused disease in the Middle Ages.

Activity ?

This activity will help you to decide the importance of each key idea about the cause of illness in the years c1250–c1500.

- Write on slips of paper, the key ideas about the causes of illnesses at this time: God; the Four Humours; miasma; position of the planets/stars. Draw a triangle like the one shown below.

- Which of these four ideas do you think was the most important? Put this idea at the top of your pyramid. Which was the least important? Put this idea at the bottom of your pyramid. Now place the other two ideas in the remaining positions on the pyramid. Discuss your ideas with another person or in a small group.

Key terms

Printing press*

A machine used to print words and pictures. This was much quicker than copying books out by hand.

Hell*

A place of suffering that Christians believe people go to when they die if they have committed sins.

Physician*

Someone who practises medicine.

Summary

- Many people believed that disease was a punishment or test from God because of sin.
- The Theory of the Four Humours was very popular. It said that the humours had to be balanced, otherwise a person could become ill.
- Other ideas about the causes of disease and illness included miasma (bad air) and the position of the planets or stars.

Checkpoint

Strengthen

S1 Create a spider diagram or a bullet point list to show the different ideas people had between c1250 and c1500 about what caused illness and disease.

S2 Select one of the Four Humours, then list its properties – (the season, the element and the quality).

Challenge

C1 Explain **how** the Church had an impact on medieval medicine.

If you are not confident about this question, form a group with other students, discuss the answer and then record your conclusion. Your teacher can give you some hints.

1.2 Approaches to treatment and prevention

Learning outcomes

- Understand different approaches to treatment and prevention before 1500.
- Understand how people cared for the sick, including treatments in hospitals and in the home before 1500.

Religious and supernatural treatments

As the Church taught that disease was sent by God as a punishment for sin, it followed that the cure should also involve the supernatural*. Religious treatments included:

- praying
- fasting (going without food).

Pilgrimages* to the tombs of people famous for their healing powers also became popular. Figure 1.4 shows some ways in which pilgrims tried to cure their illnesses.

The reputation of a tomb for healing the sick was important as it encouraged more pilgrims to visit, who gave money to the church.

Key terms

Supernatural*
Something which cannot be explained by science or nature.

Pilgrimage*
A journey to an important religious place.

Touching holy relics – objects believed to be of special religious importance.

Presenting a gift at a shrine, as an offering to God. These were often in the shape of the body part that needed healing.

Lighting a candle.

Praying for God to help heal your wound or illness.

Figure 1.4 Pilgrims suffering from disease visit a holy place.

If prayers and offerings did not work, there were other supernatural remedies* available, although the Church did not approve of them. Many people tried reading out spells or wearing lucky charms to cure or prevent disease.

Sometimes the sick were stopped from looking for a cure. After all, if God had sent the disease as a punishment for sin it was important for the disease to run its course. Taking medicine to cure the disease might keep you alive, but it would mean that your soul would still be damaged. This meant the person might not go to heaven* when they died.

Astrology

Another supernatural idea about the cause of disease was the position of the planets and stars. Physicians checked star charts when diagnosing illness. These were also important when prescribing* treatment. The position of the planets was checked at every stage of the treatment.

> ## Key terms
>
> **Remedies***
> Treatments for symptoms.
>
> **Heaven***
> A place where the good are believed to go after death.
>
> **Prescribing***
> When a physician (doctor) advises what treatment to use.
>
> **Lethargy***
> Extreme tiredness.
>
> **Extremities***
> Outer parts of the body such as hands and feet.
>
> **Enema***
> When liquid is put into a person's bottom to flush out the contents.
>
> **Hindering***
> Preventing something from happening.

Humoural treatments

Today, when we fall ill, doctors see what symptoms we have, make a diagnosis of what is wrong with us and give us treatment that tackles the cause of the symptoms. They don't just treat the symptoms.

Medieval physicians did not work in the same way. Each symptom was treated separately, as they believed each symptom represented an imbalance in the humours. An example of a doctor using humoural treatments for each symptom in turn can be seen in Source A.

> ## Source A
>
> Advice from John of Gaddesden's medical book, the *Rosa Anglica*. John, a very well-respected English physician, wrote this very popular medical text in the 14th century. Here, he explains how to cure lethargy*.
>
> *It is necessary for lethargics that people talk loudly in their presence. Tie their extremities* lightly and rub their palms and soles hard; and let their feet be put in salt water up to the middle of their shins, and pull their hair and nose, and squeeze the toes and fingers tightly, and cause pigs to squeal in their ears; give them a sharp clyster [an enema*] at the beginning… and open the vein of the head, or nose, or forehead, and draw blood from the nose with the bristles of a boar [a wild pig]. Put a feather, or a straw, in his nose to compel [force] him to sneeze, and do not ever desist from hindering* him from sleeping; and let human hair or other evil-smelling thing be burnt under his nose…*

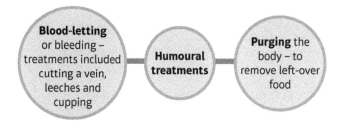

Blood-letting

Blood-letting/bleeding, was the most common treatment for an imbalance in the humours. The idea behind it was that bad humours could be removed from the body by removing some of the blood.

Blood-letting was usually done by barber surgeons and wise women, rather than physicians. Demand was so high that even some people with no medical background offered the service.

Bleeding was carried out in several different ways.

Type	Method	Uses
Cutting a vein*	A vein near the elbow was usually cut into using a knife, letting blood out.	Cutting was the most straightforward method of bleeding. Blood-letting charts like the vein man (see Source B) were used to show points in the body where bleeding could be used for different illnesses.
Leeches*	Freshwater leeches were placed on the skin. The leeches sucked blood from the patient. Bleeding might continue for many hours.	Used for people whose age or illness made cutting a vein too dangerous.
Cupping	The skin was pierced with a knife or a pin, to make the patient bleed. A heated cup was then placed over the cuts to draw blood out of the body.	Used for women, children and the very old. People believed cupping in different areas of the body treated different illnesses. See Source B.

Sometimes patients died from being bled for too long. Records from the time suggest that this happened quite often. It was thought that the benefits of being bled were better than the chances of dying from being bled too much.

Source B

A vein man, or phlebotomy* chart. This picture was printed in a manual belonging to the York Barbers in the late 15th century. It shows points on the body where blood-letting should happen, matching different ailments with different places on the body. For example, if a patient was suffering from depression, the recommendation was to bleed them from a vein in the back.

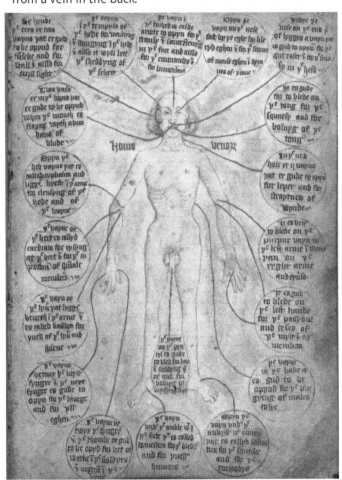

Purging

Because it was believed that the humours were linked to foods eaten, a common treatment was getting rid of any left over food from the digestive system*. This was called purging. The patient was either given an emetic* to make them vomit or a laxative* to make them poo. Sometimes emetics contained poisonous plants like black hellebore, so it was best to vomit them up quickly. Laxatives were also made from herbs.

Sometimes people needed a bit more help to purge, and the physician would give them an enema. For example, water mixed with honey, oil, wheat bran, soap and herbs such as mallow and camomile. The physician would squirt the enema into the patient's anus* using a greased pipe fixed to a pig's bladder. This would clear out any stubborn blockages of food that might be there.

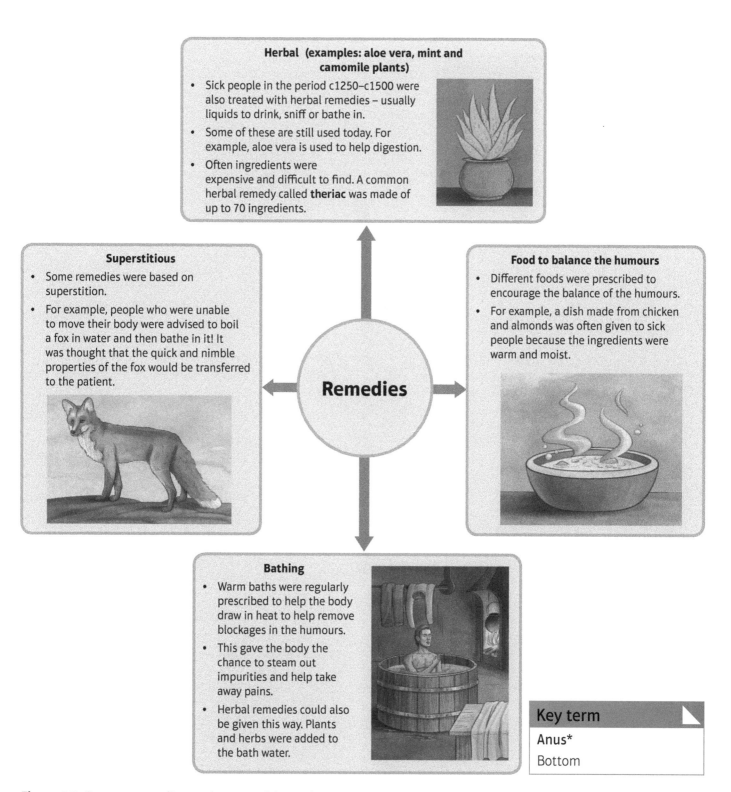

Herbal (examples: aloe vera, mint and camomile plants)

- Sick people in the period c1250–c1500 were also treated with herbal remedies – usually liquids to drink, sniff or bathe in.
- Some of these are still used today. For example, aloe vera is used to help digestion.
- Often ingredients were expensive and difficult to find. A common herbal remedy called **theriac** was made of up to 70 ingredients.

Superstitious

- Some remedies were based on superstition.
- For example, people who were unable to move their body were advised to boil a fox in water and then bathe in it! It was thought that the quick and nimble properties of the fox would be transferred to the patient.

Remedies

Food to balance the humours

- Different foods were prescribed to encourage the balance of the humours.
- For example, a dish made from chicken and almonds was often given to sick people because the ingredients were warm and moist.

Bathing

- Warm baths were regularly prescribed to help the body draw in heat to help remove blockages in the humours.
- This gave the body the chance to steam out impurities and help take away pains.
- Herbal remedies could also be given this way. Plants and herbs were added to the bath water.

Key term

Anus*

Bottom

Figure 1.5 Common remedies used to treat sick people, c1250–c1500.

Preventing disease

Although a physician could expect to be paid a lot more money for providing treatments for diseases than preventing them, people were encouraged to help themselves not to fall ill. This was seen as far safer than cures and treatments that might not work.

Key term
Dysentery*
Very severe diarrhoea.

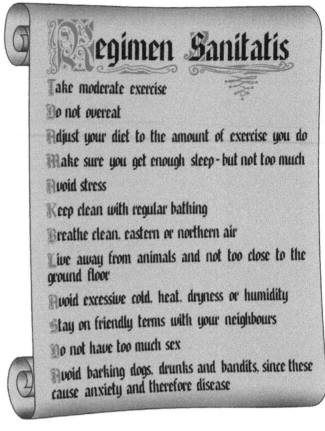

Regimen Sanitatis

Take moderate exercise

Do not overeat

Adjust your diet to the amount of exercise you do

Make sure you get enough sleep - but not too much

Avoid stress

Keep clean with regular bathing

Breathe clean, eastern or northern air

Live away from animals and not too close to the ground floor

Avoid excessive cold, heat, dryness or humidity

Stay on friendly terms with your neighbours

Do not have too much sex

Avoid barking dogs, drunks and bandits, since these cause anxiety and therefore disease

Figure 1.6 Physicians gave patients the *regimen sanitatis* to help them look after their health.

Hygiene

- People believed that cleanliness was next to godliness, so it was important to stay clean. The Church offered advice on how to keep the body clean. This was a set of instructions called *regimen sanitatis* (see Figure 1.6).
- Wealthy people were given their own personal set of instructions to stay healthy. A physician would give advice based on the patient's humours and lifestyle. This was very expensive.
- Only the wealthy had private baths. Public baths could be used if you were able to pay. The poor bathed in rivers.

The Church

Most people believed that the best way of preventing disease was to lead a life free from sin.

Preventing disease

Diet

- Since the humours were thought to be produced from food, what and when you ate were both thought to be important in keeping the humours in balance.
- Eating too much was discouraged. Some medieval people claimed several kings had died as a result of eating too much.
- Fear of digestive problems leading to death was so great that many people purged themselves, either by making themselves vomit or by using laxatives. Edward I died of dysentery*, an infection in the digestive system.

Purifying the air

- Medieval people attempted to keep the air free from miasmata (bad airs) by purifying it.
- They did this by spreading sweet herbs, such as lavender. This might be carried as a bunch of flowers (a posy) or placed inside a pomander (a large locket which would be worn around the waist).
- Local authorities tried to keep towns clean. For example, they tried to remove rotting animals left lying around and pulled down or cleaned very smelly public toilets.

Figure: Ways to prevent illness and disease.

Medieval 'medics'

Most people in the Middle Ages would have been treated at home by a female family member. Women cared for the sick, mixing remedies themselves. Women also acted as midwives.

Asking for medical advice cost a lot of money. Most people could not afford it. For people willing to pay, advice was available from physicians, apothecaries and surgeons.

Key terms

Faeces*

Poo

Alchemy*

The process of changing one substance into another, such as ordinary metal into gold.

Physicians

How were they trained?
- During the Middle Ages, new universities were set up across Europe to train physicians.
- It took 7–10 years to train to be a physician.

What was their role?
- To diagnose illness and recommend treatment.
- Physicians didn't give the patient the treatment.

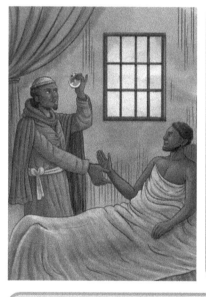

Were they expensive?
- Physicians charged a lot to be seen. They could charge high fees because there weren't very many of them. There weren't very many because the training took so long.
- Royalty and the very wealthy often employed a physician full time. Others paid for them when they needed them.

What did they do?
- The physician looked at a sample of the patient's urine, faeces* and blood.
- He also looked at the astrological charts to see the position of the planets both when the patient was born and at the time they became sick.
- Based on this, and the humours of the patient, he recommended treatment.

Figure: The role of the physician.

Apothecaries

How were they trained?
- They studied herbal manuals (books) to find out about the healing power of herbs and plants.
- They mainly learned from experience. Knowledge was sometimes passed down from family members.

Were they expensive?
- A physician usually prescribed the treatment – the apothecary only mixed it, so they cost much less than a physician.
- Because apothecaries were less expensive, people often went straight to an apothecary instead of a physician. Apothecaries were seen as a threat to trained doctors.

What did they do?
- They mixed and sold herbal remedies and poisons.
- Many practised alchemy*.
- Some sold charms to prevent disease.

Figure: The role of the apothecary.

Source C

A picture of an apothecary's shop taken from an Italian medical text published in the 14th century. The shelves are filled with large, ornate jars, which held theriac*.

Olei amigdala:. Coplo chare cā mē. bu. mp. Electō meōs dulce. muam. pretum sto. rullī. secundum mscenb; debiluy. Remō neri cā mastice. Quio gūar bũotei tepatī Conuer mag tpano adolesenab; neri ouenuliy.

Surgeons

How were they trained?

- Some surgeons were highly trained: in Europe, some physicians were encouraged to study surgery alongside medicine, so they learned their skills at university.
- Barber surgeons were probably the least qualified medical professionals in England. They learned their skills by watching other barber surgeons, rather than through academic training.

What was their role?

To perform surgical treatments.

Were they expensive?

- As they were untrained, barber surgeons were much cheaper than physicians.
- Skilled surgeons would be as expensive as seeing a trained physician.

What did they do?

- Barber surgeons had sharp knives and steady hands as their job was originally to cut hair and shave. They regularly performed small surgeries, such as pulling teeth and bleeding patients.
- A skilled surgeon could set a broken limb or remove an arrow.

Figure: The role of the surgeon.

Key term

Theriac*

An ancient herbal mixture used as a remedy.

Activities

1 Draw a cartoon stick figure to represent each different medical professional: physician, apothecary, surgeon. Add labels to explain what sort of treatments each person carried out.

2 Complete the table below to show what each medical professional did.

Medical Professional	Did they diagnose illnesses?	Did they treat illness?	Did they provide herbal remedies for symptoms?	Did they give advice or remedies to prevent illness?
physician				
apothecary				
surgeon				

3 What was the main factor in deciding the type of medical professional a patient might use? Factors might include the following:

- The professional's role
- The cost
- The type of illness.

Talk about this with a partner.

Caring for the sick: hospitals and the home

Hospitals

The number of hospitals in England increased during the Middle Ages. By 1500, there were 1,100 hospitals, ranging in size from a few beds to hundreds. Bury St Edmund's, for example, had at least six hospitals to look after lepers, the sick and the old. However, many hospitals did not actually treat the sick. Instead, they offered hospitality* to travellers and pilgrims, which is how hospitals got their name.

About 30 per cent of hospitals were owned by the Church in the Middle Ages, and run by the monks and nuns who lived in nearby monasteries. The rest were funded by an endowment*, where a wealthy person had donated money for the setting up of a hospital.

The Church was in charge of running many of these hospitals, too.

Medieval hospitals that did treat the sick were not the same as the hospitals we have today.

Medieval hospitals were good places to rest and recover. They would have been kept very clean and the bed sheets and clothing of the patients changed regularly. This meant that, for people not suffering from a deadly disease, hospitals were probably quite successful because they were safe, clean places for people to get well in.

Key terms
Hospitality*
Welcoming someone and giving them food and shelter.
Endowment*
Money given to a person or organisation.

Patients with mental illness or those who were pregnant were often not allowed to enter hospitals.

Patients would share beds.

Patients were often cared for by monks and nuns.

The focus was caring for the sick, rather than curing disease. As the Church believed that diseases had been sent by God, they believed that only prayer might cure them.

Figure 1.7 Common features of medieval hospitals.

Source D

A picture of a medieval hospital, from 1482. Some of the patients are sharing beds, which was normal at this time. The only patient allowed their own bed was a dying woman. Henry VII's famous hospital, the Savoy, opened in 1512. It was unique in offering all patients their own beds.

The Church wanted patients to recover: this was further proof that God existed and the importance of prayer in their recovery.

Many European hospitals employed physicians and surgeons, but there is no evidence to suggest that English hospitals did the same. Since priests and monks were forbidden from cutting into the body, treatment was very limited.

Infectious or terminally ill patients were often banned from hospitals, as prayer and penance* could do nothing for these people. However, patients who had a chance of recovery were able to take part in Church services from their beds, to pray for recovery.

Key term

Penance*

A punishment inflicted on yourself to show that you are sorry for your sins.

The home

Although many hospitals were established in medieval England, the vast majority of sick people were cared for at home.

> **Who treated the sick?**
> It was expected that women would care for their own families.

> **How did women care for the sick?**
> - They kept the patient clean and comfortable.
> - They prepared food and mixed herbal remedies for the patient.
> - They tended the garden in which the herbs were grown to make the remedies.

> **What were the limitations of this form of care?**
> - Women were not medically trained.
> - However, some sources hint that they were well respected and perhaps even more trusted than trained physicians.

Figure: The role of women in caring for the sick

Source E

An extract from a letter sent from Margaret Paston to her husband, John Paston, in 1464. The Pastons were wealthy landowners living in Norfolk. At the time that this letter was written, John Paston was staying in London.

For God's sake beware of any medicine that you get from any physicians in London. I shall never trust them because of what happened to your father and my uncle, whose souls God forgive.

Exam-style question, Section B

'Hospital treatment in England in the period from 1250 to 1500 was very rare.'

How far do you agree? Explain your answer.

You may use the following information in your answer:

- charity hospitals
- care in the home.

You **must** also use information of your own. **20 marks**

Exam tip

Look carefully at the topic the question asks you to focus on. For this question, it is 'hospital treatment 1250–1500'. You must show a detailed knowledge of this topic, so take some time to consider what you know first.

Four of the marks for this question are for good spelling, grammar and punctuation, and the use of specialist terms. Take extra care over things like capital letters and spelling key words.

Summary

- Religious treatments included prayer, fasting and pilgrimages.
- Supernatural treatments included saying spells or carrying charms.
- There were a large number of treatments aimed at rebalancing the humours. This was normally done by eating a particular food, taking herbal remedies or by bleeding or purging the body to remove bad humours.
- Medieval people were advised to avoid getting ill by living a healthy lifestyle and keeping clean.
- Physicians, apothecaries and barber surgeons all provided different treatments.
- Hospitals followed religious teachings. Patients were cared for and prayers were said, but they rarely received any medical treatment. Most sick people were cared for in the home by a female family member.

Checkpoint

Strengthen

S1 What were the three different types of blood-letting?

S2 List the different ways people tried to prevent disease in medieval England.

S3 List the different sources of help sick people had in medieval England.

Challenge

C1 You need to show links between the treatments and remedies used in the Middle Ages, and the ideas people had about what caused disease. Make a list of treatments and remedies and a list of ideas about the causes of disease. Draw as many links as you can between the two lists. Now write sentences explaining three of the links you have made.

If you do not feel confident answering any of these questions, discuss them with a partner or in a group.

1.3 Dealing with the Black Death, 1348–49

Learning outcomes

- Understand what the Black Death was and how it affected people in England during the years 1348–49.
- Understand the disputed causes, treatments and preventative measures used during the time of the Black Death.

In 1348, a new disease reached England. It had spread from the Far East across the whole of Europe. It was a new plague* called the Black Death. It was unfamiliar to ordinary people or to English physicians. Within months, it had spread across England, killing thousands of people. It didn't matter if you were rich, poor, lived in a town or in the countryside. Those who caught it usually died within days.

The disease still occurs every so often in modern times, but it is easily treated with antibiotics* and patients usually make a full recovery. In the Middle Ages, treatments like antibiotics did not exist.

Source A

This engraving from the 14th century shows somebody suffering from the Black Death.

Key term

Plague*

An infectious disease that spreads very quickly and kills a large number of people.

Antibiotics*

A medication that kills the bacteria infecting the body without killing the patient.

Bubonic plague*

The disease that caused the Black Death. It caused fever and swellings (or buboes) to grow on the victim's body.

Groin*

Area at the top of the thigh.

Source B

In this extract from a report on the Black Death written in 1347, Italian chronicler Marchionne di Coppo Stefani describes how helpless people felt in the face of the epidemic (outbreak).

Neither physicians nor medicines were effective. Whether because these illnesses were previously unknown or because physicians had not previously studied them, there seemed to be no cure. There was such fear that nobody seemed to know what to do.

The Black Death

The Black Death was an outbreak of the bubonic plague*. The disease was carried in the digestive system of fleas. It was probably spread by flea bites, and possibly also spread in the air. The main symptom was buboes, which were swellings in the armpit or groin*, filled with pus.

Accounts from the time estimate that a third of the population of England died.

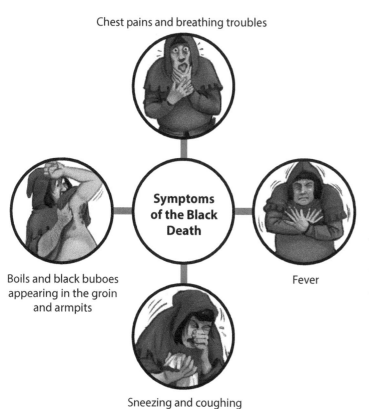

Chest pains and breathing troubles

Boils and black buboes appearing in the groin and armpits

Fever

Symptoms of the Black Death

Sneezing and coughing up blood

Figure 1.8 Symptoms of the Black Death.

The Black Death is the name given to the outbreak of the plague in 1348. After this, the plague returned every 10–20 years, although it killed fewer people with each outbreak. People used the same knowledge they had about the causes of disease and illness to deal with the Black Death. New treatments appeared and advice on how to avoid catching the disease spread quickly.

Causes and treatments of the Black Death

A lack of medical knowledge about what caused the Black Death meant that people did not know how to treat it. Their attempts to explain and treat the disease are shown in the table below.

	Religious and supernatural	Natural causes	Common beliefs
Causes of the Black Death	• Many people believed that the Black Death was a punishment for all of the sin in the world. • In 1345, there was an unusual positioning of the planets. Astrologers saw this as a sign that something wonderful or terrible was about to happen.	• The main natural cause of the Black Death was believed to be bad air (miasmata). • People believed that breathing this bad air caused the body's humours to become out of balance.	• For ordinary people, the spread of the Black Death was terrifying as nobody really knew what caused it.
Treatments for the Black Death	• Tell a priest about your sins and God will forgive you. • Pray to God for his forgiveness. • Offer gifts to God to show your loyalty. • Many people felt that catching the disease showed that God had judged them, so there was nothing they could do to get better.	• Bleeding and purging to make sure people had the right amount of each humour. • Smelling herbs to avoid breathing bad air. • Some surgeons tried to cut into or burst the buboes. • Apothecaries sold remedies but these did not cure the plague.	• People were willing to try anything to survive the Black Death. They prayed, as well as seeking cures like bleeding. • However, it became clear that neither priests nor physicians could stop the disease.

Activity ?

In groups of four, use the information on the causes and treatments of the Black Death to create a television news report about the possible causes of the Black Death and what treatment people were given. One of you should play the part of a journalist, while the others take on the roles of priest, physician and an everyday person. Remember to give advice on both how to treat the disease and how to prevent it.

The journalist should ask each person the same questions:

1 What do you think is the one **main** reason for the Black Death?

2 What would be the best treatment to attempt to cure the plague?

3 Do you have any recommendations for how a healthy person can stop themselves from catching the Black Death?

Key terms

Fast*

Give up food for a period of time.

Chanting*

Saying something over and over again.

Posy*

A bunch of flowers or herbs.

Quarantine*

Separating the sick from the healthy to stop the spread of a disease. Those who are sick are not allowed to leave the quarantined area.

Enforce*

To make sure the thing happened.

Preventing the Black Death

Supernatural means

The main advice given by priests was for people to:

- pray to God and fast*
- go on a pilgrimage and make gifts to God
- show God how sorry you are by whipping yourself. Large groups of people wandered the streets of London, chanting* and whipping themselves.

Natural means

Escaping areas where there was plague was the best advice for prevention. It was essential to escape the bad air to stay healthy.

If travel was impossible, people believed it was helpful to carry a posy* of flowers or fragrant herbs and hold it to your nose. This helped to avoid breathing in the miasma. Unlike the usual advice on preventing disease, people were advised to avoid taking a bath. It was believed that water would open the skin's pores to the bad air.

Common beliefs

People did not know how to prevent the disease. However, they did stop visiting family members who had caught the plague – there was a common belief in the need to avoid those with the disease.

Government action

Local authorities attempted to take action to prevent the plague from spreading. New quarantine* laws were put in place to try to stop people from moving around too much. People new to an area had to stay away from everybody else for 40 days, to make sure they were not carrying the disease. However, since the local government did not have a great deal of power at this time, they could not fully enforce* these laws: rich people, for example, moved around quite freely and the Church continued to run as normal.

Because of the belief in bad air causing disease, the local authorities also stopped cleaning the streets. They believed that the foul stench of the rubbish and rotting bodies would drive off the miasma causing the plague.

Interpretation 1

Writer Sean Martin shares his views, and those of other historians, on the impact of the Black Death, in his book, *A Short History of Disease* (2015).

One immediate effect of the pandemic [an infectious disease spread across a large region] was the invention of quarantine. Historian GM Trevelyan argued that the Black Death was at least as important as the industrial revolution, while David Herlihy argued that the Black Death was 'the great watershed', [an important turning point] without which there would have been no Renaissance, and with no Renaissance, no Industrial Revolution.

THINKING HISTORICALLY Cause and Consequence

The language of causation

Study these words. They are useful in describing the role of causes.

motivated	precondition (*creates a situation in which something can happen*)	prevented	determined the timing	deepened the crisis	led to
exacerbated (*made worse*)	allowed	triggered	impeded (*creates an obstacle to something happening*)	catalyst (*causes something to happen*)	developed
underlying	created the possibility	influenced	enabled	accelerated	sparked

1   Create a table with the following column headings: 'word', 'meaning', 'timing'. Write out each word or phrase in a separate row of the 'word' column.

2   Discuss the meaning of each word or phrase with a partner. For each word or phrase, write a short definition in the 'meaning' column.

3   Is each word or phrase more likely to describe a short-term, medium-term or long-term cause? In the 'timing' column, write 'short', 'medium' or 'long'.

   Short-term cause – A cause which has immediate effect, for example, for a successful football club, this might be a player scoring the winning goal in a match.

   Medium-term cause – A non-immediate impact, for example for a successful football club, this might be the regular training of the team leading up to the match.

   Long-term cause – A cause which creates the opportunities for something to happen later on, for example a football club might buy new players to help them win trophies the following season.

4   Look at the following incomplete sentences. Write three versions of each sentence, using different words and phrases from the table to complete them. You can add extra words to make the sentences work. For each sentence, decide which version is the best.

   a   The power of the Church … the development of medical understanding.

   b   Following a *regimen sanitatis* (the set of instructions for keeping the body clean and healthy) … the prevention of disease.

   c   The lack of medical understanding … the spread of the Black Death.

5   You can also describe the importance of causes. Place the following words in order of importance. You should put words that suggest a cause is very important at the top, and words that suggest a cause is less important at the bottom of your list.

necessary	contributed to	added to	marginal	fundamental	influenced	supported	negligible

Summary

- Causes of the Black Death were thought to be supernatural – either as a result of the position of the planets, or a punishment from God – or caused by a bad air.
- Treatments included prayer and herbal remedies.
- To begin with, physicians tried bleeding and purging, but this made patients worse.
- Prevention was better than treatment: once you caught the Black Death, it was very likely that you would die.
- People tried to avoid catching the Black Death by avoiding people who had the plague.
- Local authorities tried to stop the spread of the plague by quarantining people.

Checkpoint

Strengthen

S1 Draw a spider diagram of the different things people believed caused the Black Death.

S2 Name four ways people tried to treat the Black Death.

S3 List three reasons why the local authorities were not very successful in the methods they used to try to halt the spread of the Black Death.

Challenge

C1 Look again at people's beliefs about the causes of the Black Death, and ideas to prevent it. Create a chart to match up ideas. An example is shown below.

Beliefs about what caused the Black death	How to prevent disease
God sent disease as a punishment	Prayer, fasting, pilgrimage, whipping oneself

How confident do you feel about your answers to these questions? Ask your teacher for some hints if you are stuck.

Recap: c1250–c1500: Medicine in medieval England

Recall quiz

1 Give two reasons why people believed God sent diseases.
2 Name two physicians from before the Middle Ages whose teachings were used in medieval times.
3 What were the Four Humours?
4 What had to happen to the Four Humours to cause disease?
5 Name two other things people in the period c1250–c1500 believed caused disease.
6 What was theriac?
7 What was the name for religious advice on how to maintain a healthy lifestyle?
8 What was the main job of the apothecary?
9 Roughly how many hospitals were there in England by 1500?
10 What proportion of people in England died of the Black Death?

Exam-style question, Section B

Explain why there was little change in the care provided by hospitals in the period c1250–c1500.

You may use the following information in your answer:

- ideas in the Church
- herbal remedies.

You **must** also use information of your own. **12 marks**

Exam tip

Use the following sentence starters to help plan your answer:

Hospital care changed little in the period 1250–1500 as most care was carried out by monks and nuns who believed illness was caused by…

There was also little change in the treatments given in hospitals in the period 1250–1500. For example, herbal remedies…

Activity ?

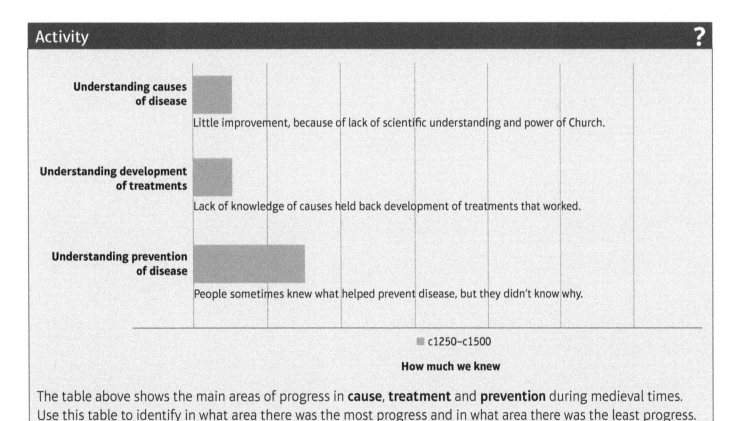

Understanding causes of disease
Little improvement, because of lack of scientific understanding and power of Church.

Understanding development of treatments
Lack of knowledge of causes held back development of treatments that worked.

Understanding prevention of disease
People sometimes knew what helped prevent disease, but they didn't know why.

■ c1250–c1500

How much we knew

The table above shows the main areas of progress in **cause**, **treatment** and **prevention** during medieval times. Use this table to identify in what area there was the most progress and in what area there was the least progress.

Writing historically: a clear response

Every response you write needs to be clearly written. To help you achieve this, you need to clearly show that your response is relevant to the question you are answering.

Learning outcomes

By the end of this lesson, you will understand how to:

- use key noun phrases from the question to make sure you give a direct answer
- write short statements to express your ideas and opinions clearly.

Definitions

Noun: a word that names an object, idea, person, place, etc. (e.g. 'disease', 'the Four Humours', 'Galen', 'Greece').

Noun phrase: a phrase including a noun and any words that modify its meaning (e.g. 'Galen the Greek physician.').

Verb: words that describe actions ('Galen <u>developed</u> a theory'), incidents ('The disease <u>spread</u>') and situations ('Galen's theory <u>lasted</u> for centuries').

How can I make sure I am answering the question?

Look at this exam-style question in which key nouns, noun phrases and verbs are highlighted:

> Explain why there was continuity in ideas about the cause of disease during the period c1250–c1500. **(12 marks)**

Now look at the first two sentences from two different responses to this question below.

Answer A

> Although the Church controlled medical learning, Galen's ideas on the cause of disease were accepted. Galen's ideas fitted in with the ideas of the Church.

Answer B

> Galen developed the Theory of Opposites. He also believed in the idea of a soul.

1. Which answer shows most clearly that it is going to answer the question?

2. Now look at this exam-style question:

> Explain **one** way in which people's reactions to the plague were similar in the 14th and 17th centuries. **(4 marks)**

a. Which are the key nouns, noun phrases and verbs in this question? Note them down in the table below. Then check and compare with a partner.

noun	noun phrase	verb

b. Which of the following two answers includes the most nouns, noun phrases and verbs from the question? Use your table like a checklist.

Answer C

> People believed that both the Great Plague and the Black Death were caused by bad air.

Answer D

> People's reaction to the plague in the 17th century was similar to people's reactions in the 14th century, in that they continued to avoid bad smells. This is because people still thought the plague was caused by miasma.

How can I clearly express my ideas?

One way to introduce your opinions and ideas clearly and briefly is by making short simple statements. Clear statements are often structured like this:

> Galen developed the Four Humours into the Theory of Opposites. The Theory of Opposites and his ideas were in harmony with those of the Church.

The verb tells you what happened.
The noun tells you who or what is the subject of the sentence.

3. Look again at Answer A's opening sentences:

> Although the Church controlled medical learning, Galen's ideas on the cause of disease were accepted. Galen's ideas fitted in with the ideas of the Church.

a. What verbs have they used to tell you what happened?

b. What nouns have they used to tell you what the subjects are?

The writer could have written:

> Because Galen's ideas on the cause of disease fitted in with the ideas of the Church, who controlled medical learning, they were accepted.

or

> Galen's ideas on the cause of disease were accepted as they fitted in with the ideas of the Church, even though the Church controlled medical learning.

Which version do you prefer? Discuss your opinion with a partner. Do you agree?

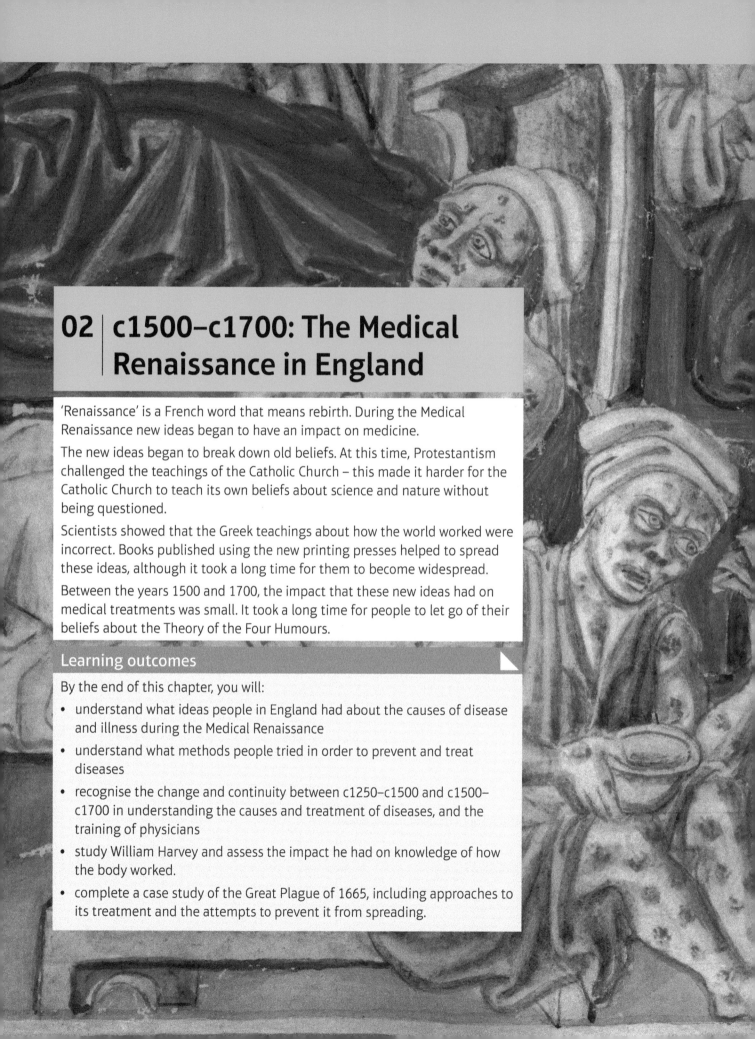

02 | c1500–c1700: The Medical Renaissance in England

'Renaissance' is a French word that means rebirth. During the Medical Renaissance new ideas began to have an impact on medicine.

The new ideas began to break down old beliefs. At this time, Protestantism challenged the teachings of the Catholic Church – this made it harder for the Catholic Church to teach its own beliefs about science and nature without being questioned.

Scientists showed that the Greek teachings about how the world worked were incorrect. Books published using the new printing presses helped to spread these ideas, although it took a long time for them to become widespread.

Between the years 1500 and 1700, the impact that these new ideas had on medical treatments was small. It took a long time for people to let go of their beliefs about the Theory of the Four Humours.

Learning outcomes

By the end of this chapter, you will:

- understand what ideas people in England had about the causes of disease and illness during the Medical Renaissance
- understand what methods people tried in order to prevent and treat diseases
- recognise the change and continuity between c1250–c1500 and c1500–c1700 in understanding the causes and treatment of diseases, and the training of physicians
- study William Harvey and assess the impact he had on knowledge of how the body worked.
- complete a case study of the Great Plague of 1665, including approaches to its treatment and the attempts to prevent it from spreading.

2.1 Ideas about the cause of disease and illness

Learning outcomes

- Understand the different ideas about the causes of disease that changed and stayed the same, c1500–c1700.

Ideas about disease and illness: change and continuity

Figure 2.1 Change and continuity surrounding the causes of disease and illness, c1500–c1700.

People who fell ill during the period 1500 to 1700 were likely to believe the same things about the cause of their illness as people in the Middle Ages. Very little had changed in the practice of medicine during this period.

However, all across Europe, enormous changes were taking place in other areas of daily life, especially in art and religious beliefs. Scientific discoveries meant that people were getting a better understanding of the world.

These changes meant that ordinary people began to become more interested in medicine. Across Europe people were wanting answers to questions about what caused disease. Epidemics* of the plague and other killer diseases, such as smallpox and the Great Pox (syphilis), could not be cured using treatments based on the Theory of the Four Humours such as blood-letting and purging*.

There was still a widespread belief in miasmata* as a cause of disease. A miasma could be the product of rotten vegetables, decaying bodies of humans or animals, excrement* or any swampy, smelly, dirty place.

Key terms

Epidemic*
When a disease spreads quickly through a whole community.

Purging*
A remedy designed to make a person vomit or poo.

Miasmata or Miasma*
Bad air.

Excrement*
Animal or human poo.

However, people did not understand why they still became ill even when they took care to avoid miasma.

Some people came up with new ideas about the causes of disease and illness. They included new ideas based on alchemy* and new discoveries about the body. Some of these new ideas are shown in the timeline below, together with the name of the scientist or doctor who discovered them.

New ideas and discoveries in the period c1500–c1700

Timeline

New ideas about disease and illness	Important individual
1500 onwards — In the 16th century, the Theory of the Four Humours began to be rejected by some physicians. New chemical treatments started to appear.	**Paracelsus,** a Swiss scientist and medical professor.
1546 — A new text called *On Contagion* put forward the idea that disease was caused by seeds spread in the air.	**Girolamo Fracastoro,** an Italian physician.
1628 — A new theory suggested that blood went around the body instead of being made in the liver, as taught by Galen.	**William Harvey,** an English scientist.
mid-1600s — Improved understanding of the digestive system* meant that people began to understand that disease was not caused by eating the wrong things.	**Jan Baptista van Helmont,** a Flemish physician (from modern-day Belgium).
1665 — New microscopes were being developed. These allowed tiny details to be magnified and clearly seen. A new book called *Micrographia* included a close-up drawing of a flea, copied from a magnified image.	**Robert Hooke,** an English scientist and head of experiments at the Royal Society (see page 46).
1676 — The medical textbook *Observationes Medicae* put forward the idea that illness was caused by factors outside of the body, rather than the Four Humours.	**Thomas Sydenham,** an English physician (see page 44).
1683 — More powerful microscopes allowed tiny 'animalcules' or little animals to be observed. The images were not very clear. This was the first recorded observation of bacteria.	**Antony van Leeuwenhoek,** a Dutch scientist (see page 46).

Figure: Ideas and discoveries that helped change the way people understood disease and illness, 1500–1700.

Due to all these new discoveries and ideas, by c1700:

- the Theory of the Four Humours was being questioned by physicians – however, it was still being followed by ordinary people in Britain
- other ideas about causes of disease had been put forward (for example, 'animalcules' or bacteria).

Even though some of these ideas were almost correct, they had very little impact at the time. This was mainly due to a lack of scientific proof. Without proof it was very hard to persuade people to change their beliefs about what caused disease.

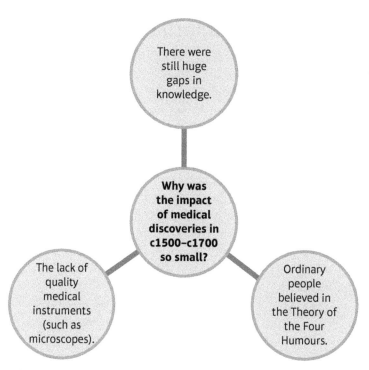

Figure 2.2 Why was the impact of scientific discoveries up to 1700 so small?

Change (completely different ideas)
· Disease came from outside the body, not caused by the Four Humours inside the body.
· Improved knowledge of anatomy*.

Old ideas that were a little different
· Physicians started to use their own observations* as well as medical books.
· People were still religious but they began to question what the Church was telling them.

Continuity (ideas that were the same as old ideas)
· Miasmata. People continued to believe disease was spread by bad smells.

Because the general public believed in the Theory of the Four Humours, most physicians* stuck to the old methods. Patients did not want to pay physicians to experiment on them. They just wanted them to make them better.

Changing ideas

The key point here is that, while the **practice** of medicine did not change much at this time, **ideas** were starting to change. By the end of the 17th century, doctors and scientists had lots of new ideas about the causes of illness and disease – they just weren't used in everyday medical practice.

Some ideas about the causes of disease and illness changed a lot during the Medical Renaissance, others stayed the same.

Figure: Change and continuity in ideas about the causes of disease and illness, c1500–c1700.

Key terms

Physicans*
People who have received training to be a doctor.

Anatomy*
Knowledge of the structure of the body and how it works, inside and out.

Observations*
To look at the patient and note any symptoms.

Activity ?

Draw two columns and label the first one 'Old ideas', and the second one 'New ideas'. Using the information in this chapter, and things you have already learned in Chapter 1, make brief notes on ideas about the cause of illness and disease in the years c1500–c1700 that were the same as c1250–c1500, and the ideas that were different.

Exam-style question, Section B

Explain **one** way in which ideas about the cause of disease and illness were similar in the 14th and 17th centuries. **4 marks**

Exam tip

This answer should not be very long, but it does need to have specific information for each time period. Try to make a general point that covers both time periods – for example, the idea of miasmata – and then give a specific example for each time period.

Source A

A drawing of Thomas Sydenham, by an unknown artist, after his death.

A scientific approach to diagnosis

One of the key changes during the Renaissance was the rise of **humanism***. Humanists believed that human beings could make up their own minds when it came to discovering the truth of the world around them.

Humanism was also a break with some of the old ideas. Humanists didn't believe that God was responsible for everything that happened, but they hadn't yet worked out an alternative explanation. People continued to make and use new copies of books by Hippocrates and Galen.

During the 17th century, there were more medical experiments. This, in part, was because the Church had less authority in everyday life. Proof that Galen had been wrong about human anatomy was becoming more widespread, thanks to the work of Vesalius (see pages 52–55). New ideas were starting to gain more support, although it would be a long time before this had an impact on everyday medical treatment.

Key term

Humanism*

People who believe in the importance of science to help understand how the world works. They do not accept supernatural or religious ideas.

Name: Thomas Sydenham

Job: Doctor

Nationality: English

Period of work: 1660s and 1670s

Big idea:

- He didn't rely on the ideas of Hippocrates and Galen. Instead, he observed his patients' symptoms to work out what illnesses they had. He then treated the disease instead of the individual symptoms.
- He studied disease and decided that, like plants, there were many different types which could be categorised into different groups (see Source B).
- According to the Theory of the Four Humours, a patient's disease was personal to them – it was caused by factors such as diet and the person's own balance of humours. This meant that treatments varied from person to person. Sydenham believed that treatments should be based on what disease had been identified by the physician, not the Four Humours or the type of person.

Work: He encouraged his students to observe the patients, note down their symptoms and choose treatments based on their disease.

Limitations: He could identify that measles and scarlet fever were different diseases, but he did not have scientific knowledge necessary to prove they were caused by different micro-organisms*.

Source B

Thomas Sydenham published his theories about disease and his observations of various epidemics in a book called *Observationes Medicae* in 1676. In this extract from the introduction, he explains that doctors should devote as much time to identifying different types of disease as botanists spend identifying different types of plant.

In the first place, it is necessary that all diseases be reduced to definite and certain species, and that, with the same care which we see exhibited by botanists [specialists in the scientific study of plants]; since it happens, at present, that many diseases... are... different in their natures, and require a different medical treatment. We should have known the cures of many diseases before this time if physicians, whilst with all due good-will they communicated their experiments and observations, had not been deceived in their disease, and had not mistaken one species for another.

Activities ?

1 List the effects humanism had on medicine during the Medical Renaissance.

Consider how it changed the following:

- Ideas about what caused disease.
- How doctors practised medicine.

2 Draw a stick figure to represent Thomas Sydenham. Add thought bubbles to detail his ideas about medicine.

3 Investigating the causes of disease and identifying different types was very important in the fight against disease. Imagine you are a doctor in the 17th century. Write a letter based on Sydenham's ideas, using these starter sentences.

Dear Doctor

For too many years now, the medical profession has relied on the old ideas of the Four Humours to...

It is time we looked to Thomas Sydenham's work on identifying diseases and started to...

Improved communications

One of the changes across Europe during the Medical Renaissance was that more people than ever before were able to read and write. This meant new ideas could spread further and more quickly.

The influence of the printing press

In around 1440, Johannes Gutenberg, a German goldsmith, created the world's first printing press*. It didn't take long for the popularity of his new invention to grow: by 1500, there were hundreds of presses in Europe.

Key terms

Micro-organisms*

A living organism so small it can only be seen under a microscope.

Printing press*

A machine for printing text or pictures. It had movable letters so that many copies of the same text could be printed.

The new printing press enabled information to be spread accurately and quickly. This meant that scientists could publish their work and share it much faster than when the work had to be copied by hand.

The printing press also took book copying out of the hands of the Church. This meant that more subjects were written about. The Church was no longer able to prevent ideas they disapproved of being published. For example, physicians could now publish works disagreeing with Galen.

The work of the Royal Society

Scientists wanted to talk to each other about their new discoveries and share new ideas. This led to the founding of the **Royal Society**.

The motto of the Royal Society means 'Take nobody's word for it'. This showed the Society's purpose – to find new scientific discoveries through experimenting and uncovering evidence.

The Royal Society met for the first time in London, in 1660. Its aim was to carry out experiments to further the understanding of science.

In 1665, the Society began publishing a scientific journal called *Philosophical Transactions*. It included letters, book reviews and summaries of experiments and observations carried out by scientists. The journal was written in English rather than Latin so that more people could read it.

Figure: The scientific work of the Royal Society.

Source C

This picture of 'animalcules' was drawn to go with a letter Antony van Leeuwenhoek had published in *Philosophical Transactions* in 1702. The letter was titled 'Concerning green weeds growing in water, and some animalcula growing about them'.

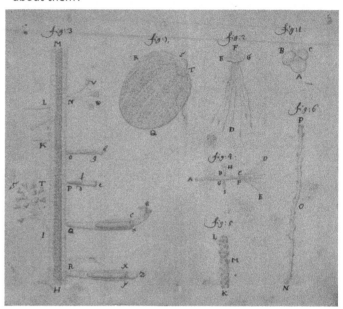

In 1662, the society received the support of King Charles II, who had an interest in science. The support of King Charles made people feel that the society was doing something important, so more scientists sent in their findings to the Society. This also encouraged people to donate money to the work of the Society.

Through its journal, the Society made it possible for scientists to see each others' research. This helped new ideas to spread. For example, Leeuwenhoek's study of 'animalcules' (see Source C) was read by the scientist Robert Hooke, who used a microscope to confirm Leeuwenhoek's findings.

THINKING HISTORICALLY **Change and continuity (2a)**

Identifying change and continuity

Change is happening all the time. Every day, things change slightly in lots of different ways. For example, ten more people in the country might be unemployed today compared to yesterday, or mobile phone batteries might have become 1% more powerful. Most of these changes are small, and not important enough to be called 'change' by historians.

The timeline below shows changes in understanding the causes of disease between 1526 and 1683.

1526 Paracelsus suggested that disease was caused by problems with chemicals inside the body

1546 Fracastoro wrote a text called *On Contagion*, suggesting that disease was caused by seeds that spread in the air

1628 Harvey proved that blood circulates around the body

1648 Van Helmont said that digestion happened because of stomach acid, rather than anything to do with the Four Humours

1665 Hooke developed a more powerful microscope and published a book of images from his observations

1676 Thomas Sydenham put forward the idea that diseases were separate from the patient, rather than being caused by something the patient did

1683 Leeuwenhoek developed a microscope and observed 'animalcules', or 'little animals'

1   Using only two events in the timeline, write a short paragraph explaining how understanding about the causes of disease changed during this period. Think carefully about which events you include.

A period of 'continuity' is a period of time when very little (if anything) changes.

2   Can you identify any periods of continuity in the timeline when looking at ideas about the causes of disease?

3   If you identified a period of continuity, write down:

   a   what it was that stayed the same over that period

   b   what, if anything, changed.

4   Write your own definitions of 'change' and 'continuity'.

Exam-style question, Section B

Explain why there were changes in the way ideas about the causes of disease and illness were communicated in the period c1500–c1700.

You may use the following in your answer:

- the printing press
- the Royal Society.

You **must** also use information of your own. **12 marks**

Exam tip

Make sure that you fully explain your points by using the **P**oint, **E**xample, **E**xplain, or **PEE** method. State your argument, then add some examples from your own knowledge to back it up. Finish off by explaining how that evidence relates to the question.

Make sure you first identify the focus of the question topic (ideas about the cause of disease c1500–c1700) and the 'concept' (change). Your answer should use these terms.

Summary

- There was very little change in medical practice. Methods of diagnosing illness remained similar to medieval times.
- Lots of new ideas about the causes of disease and illness started to appear, but they were slow to have an impact on patients.
- By the end of the 17th century, most doctors no longer believed that the Four Humours caused disease, although they still referred to the Theory of the Four Humours when diagnosing disease.
- There was a new fashion for careful observation and believing what you saw over what you read. Thomas Sydenham was important in promoting this method in England.
- The invention of the printing press made it easier for physicians to share their work.
- From the middle of the 17th century onwards, the Royal Society promoted experiments in science, funded research and helped to spread ideas and discoveries.

Checkpoint

Strengthen

S1 What new ideas about the causes of disease and illness started to appear at this time?

S2 Who was Thomas Sydenham and what new ideas did he have?

S3 How did the Royal Society encourage the development of medical ideas?

Challenge

C1 How important was new technology in helping scientists develop new ideas about the causes of disease and illness?

If you are not confident about any of these questions, form a group with other students, discuss the answers and then record your conclusions. Your teacher can give you some hints.

2.2 Approaches to prevention and treatment

- Understand the different approaches to prevention and treatment that changed and stayed the same between c1500–c1700.

Treatment: change and continuity

New herbal remedies

There was some change in how herbal remedies were used. It was believed that the colour or shape of the remedy should match the disease.

- Yellow herbs, such as radish and saffron, were used to treat jaundice (a disease which turns the skin yellow).
- Smallpox, which causes a red rash, was treated with the 'red cure' – drinking red wine, eating red foods and wearing red clothes.

Continuity (same old treatments)

Change (new treatments)

Keeping the Four Humours balanced

Since people continued to believe that disease was caused by the Four Humours being out of balance, bleeding and purging were still used to treat illness (see page 23).

Herbal remedies

These continued to be popular, but with some changes.

Transference

There was a new belief that an illness could be moved – transferred – to something else. For example, people believed that they could get rid of warts by rubbing the wart with an onion – the warts would 'transfer' to the onion!

New remedies

New plants and herbs started to appear from countries in the New World*. Some physicians believed that plants would treat the diseases that came from the country where they were found. For example:

- sarsaparilla was used to treat the Great Pox (syphilis)
- ipecacuanha (ipecac for short) from Brazil was used to treat dysentery*
- cinchona bark from Peru was used to treat malaria.

Tea, coffee, cinnamon and tobacco were also tested for healing properties.

Figure: Some illnesses were treated the same as they had been in the Middle Ages. There were also new treatments.

Source A

In 1652, Nicholas Culpeper published his book *The English Physician: Or An Astrologo-Physical Discourse of the Vulgar Herbs of This Nation*. Culpeper brought together all the information from the medieval *Materia Medica* and wrote it in English to make it available for everybody.

Vervain [a type of plant] is hot and dry, opening obstructions, cleansing and healing. It helps the yellow jaundice [when the skin turns yellow; usually due to a problem with the liver], the dropsy [when fluid collects in the cells of your body causing swelling] and the gout [a painful disease, caused by swelling in the joints]; it kills and expels worms in the belly, and causes a good colour in the face and body, strengthens as well as corrects the diseases of the stomach, liver and spleen; helps the cough, wheezings and shortness of breath, and all the defects of the veins and bladder, expelling the gravel and stone.

Key terms

New World*

North and South America. Europeans were only aware of the existence of these places from 1492.

Dysentery*

A stomach bug that causes very bad diarrhoea.

Chemical cures

The growth of alchemy* had an impact on medical treatments. People began to look for chemical cures for diseases instead of relying on herbs and blood-letting. This new science was known as **medical chemistry***, and it was very popular in the 17th century.

Medical chemists experimented with metals as cures for common illnesses. In 1618 the College of Physicians published a manual of remedies. Among its 2,140 remedies were 122 different chemical preparations*, including mercury and antimony*. In small doses, antimony causes sweating, which cools the body down. This fitted in with the idea of purging the body of disease. In larger doses, antimony was used to cause vomiting – another type of purge.

Key terms

Alchemy*

This was an early form of chemistry. Alchemists tried to turn one material into another: mostly, they were trying to discover a way of making gold.

Medical chemistry*

Using science to find chemical cures for diseases.

Source B

This woodcut, published in a French medical textbook by Hannibal Barlet in 1657, shows a patient vomiting after being given antimony as a purge.

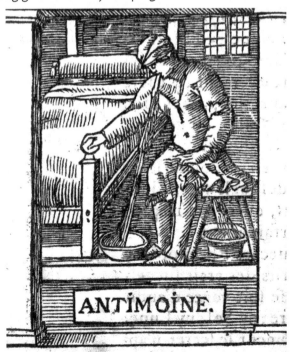

ANTIMOINE.

Syphilis

Syphilis, also known as the Great Pox, probably arrived in Europe with sailors who had travelled to the New World.

Sores and spots would appear on a person's genitals and around their mouth. Later, the patient would suffer from tiredness, headaches, a fever and aches. In the final phase of the disease sufferers could develop tumours and sores, blindness, become unable to move or even go insane.

Doctors were unable to treat syphilis. Many different remedies were tried, including guaiac wood from the West Indies and mercury. However, nothing worked.

Prevention: change and continuity

Preventing disease was still thought to be the best way to avoid dying from it, since treatments weren't much better than they had been in the Middle Ages.

People believed you could avoid disease by having a balanced lifestyle, as well as avoiding draughts, becoming too tired, avoiding rich and fatty foods and strong alcohol and being too lazy. How a baby was at birth was also important – being born small or weak might be used to explain death from an illness in adulthood. People were said to naturally have a weak or strong 'constitution*'.

Cleanliness was still important – both the home and the body needed to be kept free from bad smells.

Key terms

Preparation*

A medicinal substance created to treat a specific problem.

Antimony*

A chemical element with some metallic properties.

Constitution*

How strong a person's body is naturally, and how well they recover.

However, bathing had become less popular since the arrival of syphilis in England. This was because syphilis had spread quickly among people who regularly visited public bathhouses. However, the spread of syphilis at these places was probably due to the fact that many bathhouses were also brothels*. But the link between syphilis and bathhouses was not easily forgotten. People in the 16th and 17th centuries kept clean by rubbing themselves down with linen and changing their clothes regularly rather than by going to public baths.

People continued to try to avoid catching diseases by practising **regimen sanitatis***. However, by the end of the 17th century, avoiding diseases was as much about moving away from an area with a disease as it was about looking after yourself. The idea that certain weather conditions spread disease was becoming more popular. New instruments like **thermometers** were used to measure and record weather conditions.

More steps were also taken to remove miasmata from the air. Removing sewage and picking up rubbish from the streets was a task given to minor criminals.

Key term

Brothel*

A place where prostitutes work.

Regimen sanitatis*

A set of instructions for keeping clean (see Chapter 1, page 26).

Activities

1   Write your own definitions for:
    - alchemy
    - transference
    - chemical cure
    - constitution
    - miasma.

2   **a** Make a list of at least five treatments mentioned in this chapter. Sort them under two headings: 'Old treatments' and 'New treatments'.

    b Next to the new treatments you have identified, write an explanation of why you think people started to use this new treatment.

Exam-style question, Section B

Explain **one** way in which ideas about the treatment of disease were different in the 17th century from ideas in the 13th century.   **4 marks**

Exam tip

Ensure the details you use are relevant by checking the 'focus' of the question (treatments), the 'concept' (difference) and the 'time periods' (13th and 17th centuries) before selecting your facts. Make sure you give a fact that relates to each time period.

Preventing disease: things that were the same (continuity)	Preventing disease: things that were different (change)
People still believed there were many factors that could prevent disease, including superstitions and prayer…	…but people also started to believe that other things could help people avoid disease, such as having a balanced lifestyle and how strong you were at birth.
Cleanliness was still very important…	…but bathing had become less popular in England since the arrival of syphilis. People now kept clean by changing their clothes more often.
People continued to practise regimen sanitatis…	…but, by the end of the 17th century, people also began to think that disease was also related to other factors (for example, the weather).
Miasma was still believed in…	…but more steps were now taken to remove miasma from the air (for example, removing sewage and picking up rubbish from the streets).

Medical care: change and continuity

From c1500–c1700 as in the period c1250–c1500, people still went to trained physicians, apothecaries* and surgeons for treatment. However, there were some changes.

Key terms

Apothecaries*

People who made and sold remedies.

Apprenticeship*

Apprentices are young men taken on and trained by a 'master' in their chosen profession for a number of years.

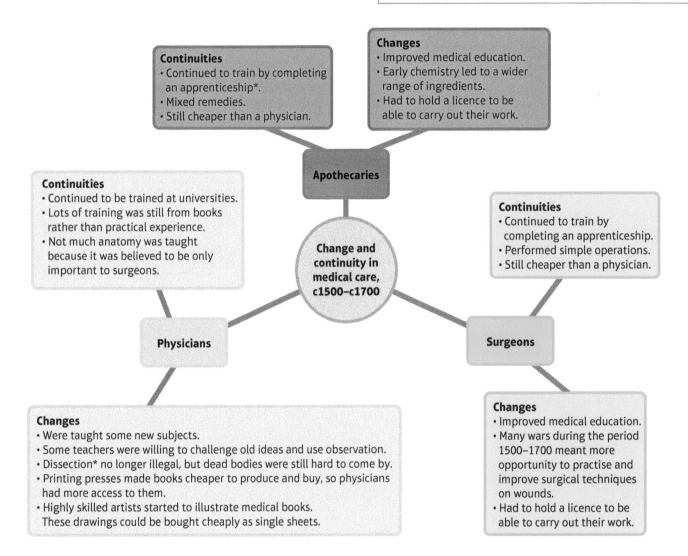

Continuities
- Continued to train by completing an apprenticeship*.
- Mixed remedies.
- Still cheaper than a physician.

Changes
- Improved medical education.
- Early chemistry led to a wider range of ingredients.
- Had to hold a licence to be able to carry out their work.

Apothecaries

Continuities
- Continued to be trained at universities.
- Lots of training was still from books rather than practical experience.
- Not much anatomy was taught because it was believed to be only important to surgeons.

Change and continuity in medical care, c1500–c1700

Continuities
- Continued to train by completing an apprenticeship.
- Performed simple operations.
- Still cheaper than a physician.

Physicians

Surgeons

Changes
- Were taught some new subjects.
- Some teachers were willing to challenge old ideas and use observation.
- Dissection* no longer illegal, but dead bodies were still hard to come by.
- Printing presses made books cheaper to produce and buy, so physicians had more access to them.
- Highly skilled artists started to illustrate medical books. These drawings could be bought cheaply as single sheets.

Changes
- Improved medical education.
- Many wars during the period 1500–1700 meant more opportunity to practise and improve surgical techniques on wounds.
- Had to hold a licence to be able to carry out their work.

Figure: Change and continuity in medical care.

Andreas Vesalius

The most famous anatomist* of this period was Andreas Vesalius. He studied medicine in Paris in 1533. Paris was a centre for the new humanist* ideas about medicine. From there he went to the famous university in Padua in Italy, where he became a lecturer in surgery. Vesalius had a serious interest in the human body and was keen to share his discoveries with the rest of the world.

Key terms

Dissection*

Cutting up a dead body in order to study how it works.

Anatomist*

Person who studies the human body and how it works inside and out.

Humanist*

Someone who follows humanism (see page 44).

Source C

A fugitive sheet printed in 1566 as an addition to an anatomical book by Valverde, a Spanish doctor.

Fugitive sheets were prints of anatomical drawings that were made for medical students. They usually had extra layers of paper that could be lifted to show the body during various stages of dissection.

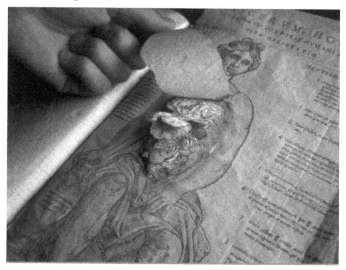

Name: Andreas Vesalius

Job: Physician and anatomist

Nationality: Flemish (from Belgium) but studied in France and taught in Italy

Period of work: 1530s and 1540s

Big idea:

- Used his own observations during dissections to understand the human body and encouraged all physicians to do the same.
- Noted that Galen had made some errors. He put this down to the fact that Galen dissected animals instead of people.
- In all, Vesalius found around 300 mistakes in Galen's original work on anatomy. These included:
  - the human lower jaw was in one part, not two
  - the main vein leading out of the heart did not lead to the liver
  - the human liver did not have five separate sections.

Work:

- He published his first book in 1537, called *Six Anatomical Tables*.
- In 1543, Vesalius published the book for which he is most famous: *On the Fabric of the Human Body*.
- He had been able to carry out a large number of dissections, using the bodies of executed criminals.

Limitations: Although physicians began to accept Vesalius' criticisms of Galen's work, they still used Galen's books instead of doing their own dissections and observations.

Source D

This illustration is from Vesalius' book, *On the Fabric of the Human Body*. It is titled *'Fourth Muscle Dissection'*. There are 14 muscle dissection pictures in total: eight drawn from the front and six drawn from the back. In each one, Vesalius has stripped back another layer of muscle from the human body to reveal what is underneath. The final picture in each sequence shows the body supported by walls or blocks, as the substance of the limbs is cut away.

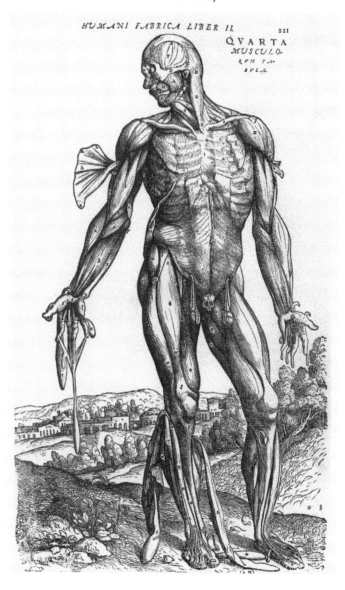

Made the study of anatomy not only acceptable, but fashionable. Doctors and medical professors now carried out dissections* themselves, rather than a surgeon.

His work was frequently copied. Versions of the drawings from the *Fabrica* appeared in other medical texts.

A lot of traditional physicians were angry that he had criticised Galen. They said that the differences Vesalius had found were down to the fact that there had been changes in the human body since the time of Galen.

Inspired other anatomists, some of whom went on to correct Vesalius' mistakes.

He influenced other physicians. After Vesalius died, Fabricius discovered valves in human veins. Fabricius shared this work with his students at Padua – one of whom was William Harvey, who went on to discover the circulation of the blood.

Vesalius

Figure 2.3 The impact of Vesalius.

Activities ?

1   Which individuals had an impact on changes in medical care between 1500 and 1700?

2   Draw a table to show changes and continuities in medical training during the 'Medical Renaissance'. Describe at least two changes and two continuities.

3   Vesalius is a key individual in the development of anatomy. Can you explain why he had an impact?

Exam-style question, Section B

'Individuals had the biggest impact on medical training in the 16th and 17th centuries.'

How far do you agree? Explain your answer.

You may use the following information in your answer:

• Vesalius

• the printing press.

You **must** also use some information of your own.

16 marks

Key term

Dissection*

Cutting up a dead body in order to study how it works.

Exam tip

This question asks you to consider the impact of one factor on medical training – individuals. However, you also need to consider what other factors might have had a big impact too. The bullet point is giving you a hint here by mentioning the printing press, a technological impact.

Plan to include two PEE paragraphs – one about individuals and one about technology.

Make your **p**oint – how the factor had an impact on medical training in the Renaissance.

Support with **e**vidence – give an example to support your point.

Explain – why do these details support your argument?

Source E

This is the first page of *Fabrica*. In it, Vesalius is dissecting a body whilst surrounded by a large crowd of people, including Galen. When his book was published, Vesalius dedicated it to the Holy Roman Emperor*, Charles V, and presented him with a hand-coloured copy. By doing this he hoped that his book would be more respected by the wider medical community. Charles V must have liked what he saw, because he later offered Vesalius the job of personal physician!

Caring for the sick: change and continuity

Hospitals

Some changes had begun to take place in English hospitals by the early 16th century. Whereas before, travellers, pilgrims*, the elderly, and a few sick people would have gone to hospitals for food, shelter and prayer, this had begun to change. Many people started to go to hospital with wounds, fevers and skin conditions. They didn't spend very long in the hospital before being discharged: this suggests that they got better.

A patient in a 16th-century hospital could expect:

- a good diet – this was still important, as many people didn't have access to good quality, healthy food
- a visit from a physician – doctors would visit the patients, sometimes as often as twice a day, to observe the symptoms and prescribe treatments
- medication – many hospitals had their own apothecary to mix the medicines.

However, the dissolution of the monasteries* in England in 1536 greatly changed how much hospital care was available in England.

Since most hospitals were connected to the Church, very few were able to stay open after the dissolution of the monasteries and nuns and monks were no longer available to give care. Some smaller hospitals opened, funded by charities, but it took a long time for the Church-run hospitals to be replaced.

Key terms

Holy Roman Emperor*

The Holy Roman Empire was an area of central Europe, where the different regions were ruled over by one 'Emperor' (leader).

Pilgrim*

The name given to a person on a pilgrimage (a journey to an important religious place).

The dissolution of the monasteries*

Henry VIII split from the Catholic Church in 1533 and created the Church of England. In 1536, he closed down monasteries and convents, and took their wealth and land.

Pest houses

One change in hospital care in this period was the start of hospitals that specialised in one particular disease. In the Middle Ages, there had been lazar houses for people suffering from leprosy*. There was a growing understanding that disease could be transmitted from person to person. This meant that new types of hospital began to appear that were only for people suffering from plague or pox. These were known as **pest houses**, **plague houses** or **poxhouses**.

These new types of hospital provided a much-needed service. Traditional hospitals would not allow patients who were contagious* in.

Community care

In spite of changes to hospitals, most sick people continued to be cared for at home.

Women continued to play an important role in the care of the sick. This included rich ladies, but also poor women working in big cities to support their families. They usually mixed and sold simple herbal remedies to purge the body or cure a particular problem. Records suggest that they were very popular, probably because they were cheaper than going to a physician or apothecary.

> **Key terms**
>
> **Leprosy***
>
> A disease that begins as a painful skin condition, followed by paralysis and eventually death.
>
> **Contagious***
>
> Having a disease which can be easily passed on to others.

Saint Paul's converted into a Pest House.

Figure 2.4 This 19th-century English engraving of St Paul's Cathedral shows it being used as a pest house during the Great Plague of London. St Paul's became a pest house during many outbreaks of disease in the city of London.

Interpretation 1

In this extract from an article in the *Bulletin of the History of Medicine* (2008), Deborah E. Harkness describes the attitudes of male medical professionals towards female healers in the 16th century. She suggests that we can see they were popular because male physicians at the time were very critical of them.

The view of women's medical work in London that emerges from urban records… stands in stark contrast to the view conveyed… at the same time by male medical practitioners – namely, the records of proceedings at the College of Physicians, the reports of the Barber-Surgeons' Company, and various printed works. In 1566, for example, physician John Securis surveyed the medical practitioners available to eager Elizabethan consumers – and he did not like what he saw… 'presumptuous' [overconfident] women offended his sense of proper medical order. Securis was not alone in his opinion that women and medical work were a problematic combination. A year earlier, John Hall, an eminent [famous] Maidstone surgeon who moved to London in the 1560s, described in print how the 'true minister' of surgery and the hard-working physician had to compete in the streets with the 'smiths, cutlers, carters, cobblers, coopers, curriers of leather, and a great rabble of women' for the attention of potential patients.

Summary

- Methods of treatment mainly stayed the same between 1500 and 1700. Bleeding, purging and other treatments based on the Four Humours were still popular. Herbal remedies were very common.
- New herbal remedies appeared. Exploration to places previously unknown, like the New World, meant that new plants were available.
- There was a new focus on chemical cures. This reflected a new interest in minerals and chemicals in society.
- People still believed in the importance of cleanliness and tried to avoid miasmata.
- Apothecaries and surgeons continued to treat the sick, and received more formal training.
- By 1700, physicians studied anatomy and botany as part of their medical courses.
- Vesalius, an anatomy professor, published an anatomy textbook called *On the Fabric of the Human Body*. It corrected many of Galen's mistakes and encouraged physicians to carry out their own dissections.
- Hospitals were more focused on medical treatment by the end of this period, but there were fewer of them in England because of the dissolution of the monasteries. However, the vast majority of sick people continued to be treated at home by women.

Checkpoint

Strengthen

S1 Describe the changes in the way that physicians were trained between c1250–c1500 and c1500–c1700.

S2 List three of the mistakes Vesalius found in the works of Galen.

S3 Describe the different places that sick people could seek medical treatment between 1500 and 1700.

Challenge

C1 Attitudes in society had a large impact on the amount of change in treatment during this period. Identify three ways that people's beliefs helped medical development and three ways that they held them back.

How confident do you feel about your answers to these questions? Share your answers with a partner and see if you can improve them together.

2.3 William Harvey

- Understand the importance William Harvey's research had on anatomical knowledge.

Name: William Harvey

Job: Physician to James I and Charles I. Famous anatomist.

Nationality: English (also studied in Padua, Italy)

Period of work: 1600s and 1610s

Big idea:

- Used his own observations during dissections to understand the human body and encouraged all physicians to do the same.
- Was particularly interested in blood.
- Had been shown Vesalius' idea that the veins contained valves, suggesting blood was flowing towards the heart. He proved this theory was correct by performing experiments like the one shown in Source A.
- Galen had suggested that blood flowed from one side of the heart to the other through invisible pores in the walls of the ventricles*. He also said that veins carried both blood and pneuma*, which was picked up in the lungs, while arteries carried just blood. Harvey's theory criticised both of these ideas. He showed that the veins carried only blood. He proved that the heart acted as a pump.
- This idea was influenced by new technology such as machines that could pump water.

Work:

- Harvey dissected reptiles as they are cold blooded and therefore their hearts beat slower, making it easier to study the movement of the blood while they were still alive.
- Harvey published illustrated books of his findings such as *An Anatomical Account of the Motion of the Heart and Blood in Animals*.

Source A

This source shows an illustration from Harvey's book, *An Anatomical Account of the Motion of the Heart and Blood in Animals*. In it, he is showing an experiment that proved blood flowed only in one direction.

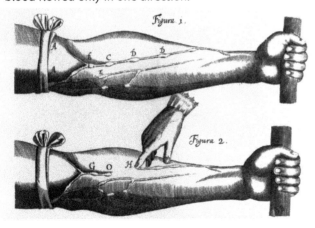

Key terms

Ventricles*

Chambers or spaces inside the heart.

Pneuma*

Means 'breath of life'. Galen thought it was both the air that you breathe and your life force, or soul.

Harvey made two particularly important discoveries.

- Harvey proved that **blood flows from arteries to veins** through tiny passages that cannot be seen by the naked eye. These passages are known as **capillaries**.
- Harvey also discovered that **blood was not made in the liver** as a product of what a person ate and then used up, as Galen had believed.

Factors enabling Harvey's discoveries

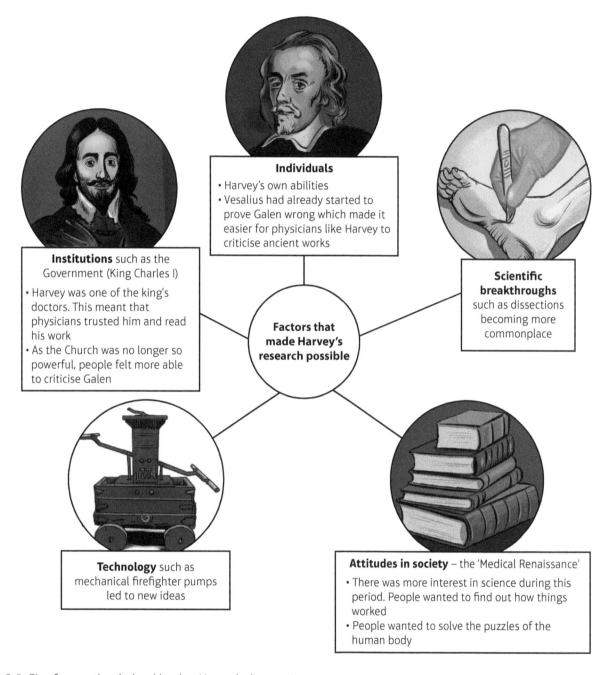

Individuals
• Harvey's own abilities
• Vesalius had already started to prove Galen wrong which made it easier for physicians like Harvey to criticise ancient works

Institutions such as the Government (King Charles I)
• Harvey was one of the king's doctors. This meant that physicians trusted him and read his work
• As the Church was no longer so powerful, people felt more able to criticise Galen

Factors that made Harvey's research possible

Scientific breakthroughs such as dissections becoming more commonplace

Technology such as mechanical firefighter pumps led to new ideas

Attitudes in society – the 'Medical Renaissance'
• There was more interest in science during this period. People wanted to find out how things worked
• People wanted to solve the puzzles of the human body

Figure 2.5 Five factors that helped lead to Harvey's discoveries.

The impact of Harvey

Observations of anatomy

- Harvey's arguments relied on the careful observations of human and animal anatomy.
- He encouraged other scientists to observe and experiment on actual bodies.

Harvey's ideas

- Harvey had proved that the liver did not create blood.
- He proved that blood circulated around the body.

This led other scientists to question how the body got its nourishment (energy). If the liver did not create blood, what did it do? If the body did not absorb blood, where did it get energy from? Scientists continued to observe and experiment to answer these questions.

Limitations

- Understanding the circulation of the blood had little practical use in medical treatments.
- As there were few practical uses for Harvey's work, many doctors ignored him.

Activities
1 Draw an outline of a person. Label it with the different discoveries that Harvey made about the human body and blood.
2 Give two reasons why Harvey's work did not have much impact when it was first published.

Summary

- William Harvey discovered that blood circulated around the body, instead of being made in the liver and absorbed into the body, as Galen thought.
- Harvey also proved that the heart acted as a pump, sending blood around the body.
- Harvey's work had little impact at first, because it couldn't be used to improve medical treatments.
- Harvey encouraged other scientists to carry out further experiments, building on his discoveries about blood and circulation.

Checkpoint

Strengthen

S1 Name three discoveries that Harvey made.

S2 Describe the factors which influenced Harvey's work.

S3 What was Harvey's biggest impact in the short term?

Challenge

C1 Who had the biggest impact on ideas about the human body - Vesalius or Harvey? Use information from the chapter to support your decision.

To help structure your answer to C1, you might find it useful to create a 'For' and 'Against' list for both individuals.

Learning outcomes

- Understand what the Great Plague was and how it affected people in England during the year 1665.
- Understand ideas about the causes of the Great Plague, and treatments and preventions used on those suffering, or at risk, from the Great Plague, and how these differed from the Black Death.

In 1665, there was a serious outbreak of the plague in England from June until November. The rate of infection* of the Great Plague peaked in September, when 7,000 deaths from the disease were recorded in one week. In total, 100,000 Londoners died – one in five people. This was the last serious outbreak of plague in England. However, as during the Black Death 300 years before, people still had little understanding about the disease. As with previous epidemics, the disease was spread by fleas carried on rats.

Ideas about the causes of the Great Plague

By 1665, it was still not known what caused disease in general. Most people blamed the same things for the Great Plague in 1665 as they had during the Black Death in 1348.

Extend your knowledge

Eyam, Derbyshire

The village of Eyam in Derbyshire was infected by the Great Plague in 1665 from fleas on cloth that had been shipped from London. The village was quarantined* to stop the disease from spreading.

Food was brought over by people from nearby villages and left at the edge of the town. The villagers left money in vinegar to make sure that they did not spread the Great Plague.

At least 273 people died from the Great Plague, out of a population of around 350. However, the quarantine worked: the plague did not spread outside of Eyam.

Key terms

Rate of infection*

The speed at which the disease was spreading.

Quarantined*

Not allowed to have contact with other people.

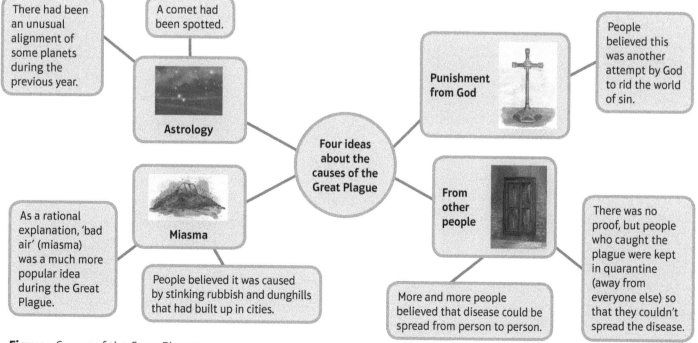

Figure: Causes of the Great Plague.

Approaches to treatment of the Great Plague

We don't know a great deal about treatments that were given to plague victims in 1665.

However, we do know that some of the new ideas about treatment of diseases had an impact on plague treatments. Physicians advised that patients be wrapped in thick woollen cloths and laid by a fire so that they could sweat the disease out. Transference* was also a popular idea – methods such as strapping a live chicken to a bubo*, was meant to draw out the poison and help the patient to recover.

Recipes for herbal remedies continued to be popular.

Quack doctors* took advantage of the general panic. They mixed remedies and advertised them as fabulous cures, hoping to make some easy money.

Key terms

Transference*

A disease moving from one living thing to another by putting them alongside one another.

Bubo*

A swollen lump on a person.

Quack doctor*

Somebody who did not have any medical qualifications, but who sold their services as a doctor or apothecary.

Source A

This recipe from Culpeper's *Complete Herbal* is for a 17th-century version of medieval theriac*. It was known as London treacle and was a popular treatment for, and preventative against, the plague.

Take ... the seeds of citrons, sorrel, peony, basil, of each one ounce; scoridum, coraliana, of each six drams; the roots of angelica, tormentil, peony, the leaves of dittany, bay-berries, juniper berries, of each half an ounce; the flowers of rosemary, marigolds, clove, gilliflowers, the tops of St John's wort, nutmegs, saffron, of each three drams; the roots of gentian, zedoary, ginger, mace, myrrh, the leaves of scabious, devil's-bit, carduus, of each two drams; cloves, opium, of each a dram; Malaga wine as much is sufficient ... mix them according to art.

People still did not understand the cause of the Great Plague and therefore could not treat it effectively. The best advice was the same as it had always been: make sure you don't catch it in the first place.

Approaches to preventing the Great Plague

Advice from physicians

The Royal College of Physicians advised the following.
1. Pray
2. Quarantine anyone who has the Plague.
3. Carry around a sweet-smelling pomander*
4. Eat a special diet.
5. Physicians should wear a special costume with a bird-like hood to attract the disease out of the patient. Sweet-smelling herbs should be placed in the 'beak'. The cloak should be treated with wax to protect the physician from infection.

Figure: Advice on preventing the plague given by physicians.

Advice from other healers

1. Drink 'plague water', a herbal remedy made up by apothecaries.
2. Smoke tobacco.
3. Catch syphilis*. It will prevent you getting the plague. (There is no link between syphilis and the plague and catching one would not prevent you catching the other.)

Figure: Advice on preventing the plague given by other healers.

Key terms

Theriac*

An ancient herbal mixture used as a remedy.

Pomander*

A large locket containing perfumed substances.

Syphilis*

A sexually transmitted infection sometimes known as 'the Great Pox'.

Government action

By order of King Charles II, people must fast* regularly and all local authorities must obey the following.

1. All public meetings, fairs and large gatherings to be banned.
2. Theatres to be closed.
3. All streets and alleyways to be kept clean.
4. All cats, dogs and pigeons to be killed if seen on the streets.
5. All known plague victims to be quarantined in their house or taken to a pest house.
6. Searchers and wardens must be appointed to go house to house checking for plague victims.
7. Red crosses to be painted on the door of any infected house.
8. The local authorities must bring plague victims food.
9. Carts to collect the dead bodies every day.

Figure: What the government did to try to prevent the spread of the plague.

Key term

Fast*

Eat no food.

Figure 2.6 A 17th-century street showing different methods used to prevent the Great Plague.

Many people believed the best way to avoid the Great Plague, was the same as it had been in 1348: run away. Since there was no known cure for the disease, people tried hard to stop the disease from spreading, or escape it completely.

Exam-style question, Section B

Explain **one** way in which ideas about preventing the plague were different in the 14th and 17th centuries.

4 marks

Exam tip

The Black Death of 1348 and the Great Plague of 1665 are both case studies for this unit. That means the examiner will want to see that you recognise the similarities and differences between these two specific outbreaks. This question is asking you to focus on the topic of 'preventions' to the plagues and the concept of change or the 'differences' between the two plagues.

Source B

In this engraving from 1665, you can see how people reacted to the Great Plague: by fleeing London and burying the dead.

THINKING HISTORICALLY Change and continuity (2b)

Events or historical change?

Change makes a situation different from before. Events are when something happens.

Sometimes a situation can be very different before and after an event – this event **marks a change**.

However, sometimes a situation is the same before and after an event, and sometimes a situation changes without a specific event taking place at all.

Study the following events and changes:

Vesalius published *On the Fabric of the Human Body*.	The Royal Society was founded in 1660.	The ideas of Galen slowly became less accepted.
Careful observation of patients became more important when diagnosing disease.	Thomas Sydenham published *Observationes Medicae*	Improved communications enabled scientists to study each other's research.

1 Sort the above into 'events' and 'changes'.

2 Match each event to the change that it marks.

3 In your own words, write a definition for the words 'event' and 'change'.

Summary

- Causes of the Great Plague were thought to be supernatural – either to do with the planets or as a punishment from God – or caused by a miasma.
- Most people now knew that the plague was spread from person to person.
- Methods to prevent the plague often involved creating a strong smell to ward off the miasma.
- The local government in London took a lot more action than in previous outbreaks.

Checkpoint

Strengthen

S1 Create a mnemonic to help you remember what people thought caused the Great Plague – Astrology, God, Miasma and Other People.

S2 What did quack doctors do during the Great Plague?

Challenge

C1 Identify three changes and three continuities between the case studies of the Black Death and the Great Plague.

If you are not sure, go back to the text in this section to find the details you need.

Recap: The Medical Renaissance in England, c1500–c1700

Activity ?

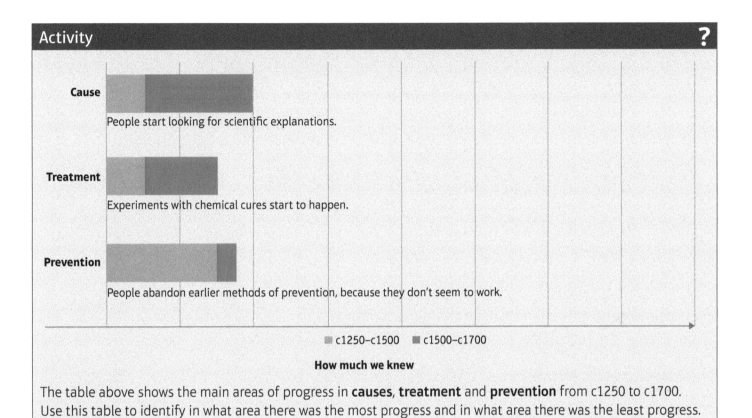

How much we knew

Legend: ▪ c1250–c1500   ▪ c1500–c1700

- **Cause**: People start looking for scientific explanations.
- **Treatment**: Experiments with chemical cures start to happen.
- **Prevention**: People abandon earlier methods of prevention, because they don't seem to work.

The table above shows the main areas of progress in **causes**, **treatment** and **prevention** from c1250 to c1700. Use this table to identify in what area there was the most progress and in what area there was the least progress.

Recall quiz

1 Name three doctors who came up with new ideas about the causes of illness in this period.

2 Why was Thomas Sydenham important to medical progress in the 17th century?

3 What was invented in around 1440 that helped the spread of scientific knowledge?

4 What was the name of the Royal Society's science journal?

5 What is medical chemistry?

6 Why did people take fewer baths in the 1500s?

7 Roughly how many mistakes did Vesalius find in the works of Galen?

8 Where were plague victims sent for treatment?

9 Who proved that blood circulated within the body?

10 List two ways in which people attempted to prevent the spread of the Great Plague.

Exam-style question, Section B

Explain why there was continuity in the way disease was treated in the period c1500–c1700.

You may use the following information in your answer:

- the Great Plague
- attitudes in society.

You **must** also use information of your own. **12 marks**

Exam tip

Allow about 15 minutes to write your answer to this type of question. You are given two information points. You do not have to use these ideas and you will not lose marks by leaving them out, but they are there to help you. Remember to look carefully at the topic and concept in the question, to ensure that all the ideas you use are relevant.

Writing historically: selecting vocabulary

The best historical writing uses carefully selected vocabulary to put forward ideas formally, clearly and accurately.

Learning outcomes

By the end of this lesson, you will understand how to:

- select nouns and verbs that can help you to express your ideas clearly
- use expanded noun phrases to help you put across information clearly and briefly.

Definitions

Noun: a word that names an object, idea, person, place, etc. (e.g. Medical books, bubo, Thomas Sydenham, Padua)

Verb: words that describe actions, incidents and situations (e.g. Sydenham <u>developed</u> a theory)

Modifiers: words that add to the meaning of verbs and nouns, e.g. adverbs, adjectives, etc. ('Sydenham <u>strongly</u> disapproved of <u>out-of-date</u> medical textbooks.').

Clause: a group of words or unit of meaning that contains a verb and can form part or all of a sentence ('Vesalius wrote the *Six Anatomical Tables*').

How can I add detail to my writing?

> Explain why there were changes in the way ideas about the cause of disease and illness were communicated in the period c1500–c1700. **(12 marks)**

Look at the first sentence of one answer to the above exam-style question. The key nouns, verbs and modifiers in the sentence have been highlighted:

> The microscope showed small 'animalcules', which helped to question the thoughts of others.

1. Rewrite the sentence using more precise nouns, verbs and modifiers. You could use the thesaurus extracts below to help you.

showed	small	helped	question	thoughts	others
revealed	tiny	assisted	disprove	theories	contemporaries
unmasked	microscopic	allowed	challenge	ideas	conservatives
discovered	miniscule	enabled	test	wisdom	rivals
demonstrated	miniature	facilitated	contest	explanations	other doctors

Now look at the next two sentences from the same answer.

> Better pictures meant that more and more things could be found. These findings could be shared in books by other people.

a. Identify all the nouns, verbs and modifiers.

b. For each noun, verb or modifier, note down two or three alternative choices.

c. Rewrite the sentences above, choosing more formal, precise nouns, verbs and modifiers.

How can I make the information in my writing clear and concise?

Compare these two versions of the same sentence from an answer to the exam-style question on the previous page.

> The microscope showed small 'animalcules' and challenged previous theories.

> The microscope's images were a challenge to previous theories.

The second sentence expresses the same ideas and information much more concisely.

2. Look at another sentence from this answer to the exam-style question on the previous page:

> The Royal Society held meetings of fellow scientists and this encouraged greater sharing.

a. Rewrite this sentence to make the highlighted text more concise, in the same way as the example does.

b. Compare your rewritten sentences with the original version. Which version do you prefer? Write a sentence or two explaining your decision.

Did you notice?

3. In the examples above, the shorter version has been created by turning a verb into a noun. Copy and complete the table below, turning the verbs into nouns. The first one has been done to help you.

Verbs	Nouns
to challenge	challenge
to introduce	
to create	
to submit	
to accept	

Improving an answer

4. Now look at the next section of this response:

> The society published its book in 1665. It contained ideas written by other people. This helped to share what they did and did lots for spreading ideas. They also turned other books into English so everyone could read them. They put their work together in a library. This meant people could read each other's work and was therefore good for starting new ideas.

Now try different ways of rewriting the sentences to make the nouns, verbs and modifiers more precise. Once you've changed the verbs, see whether you can convert any of them to nouns to make your writing more concise.

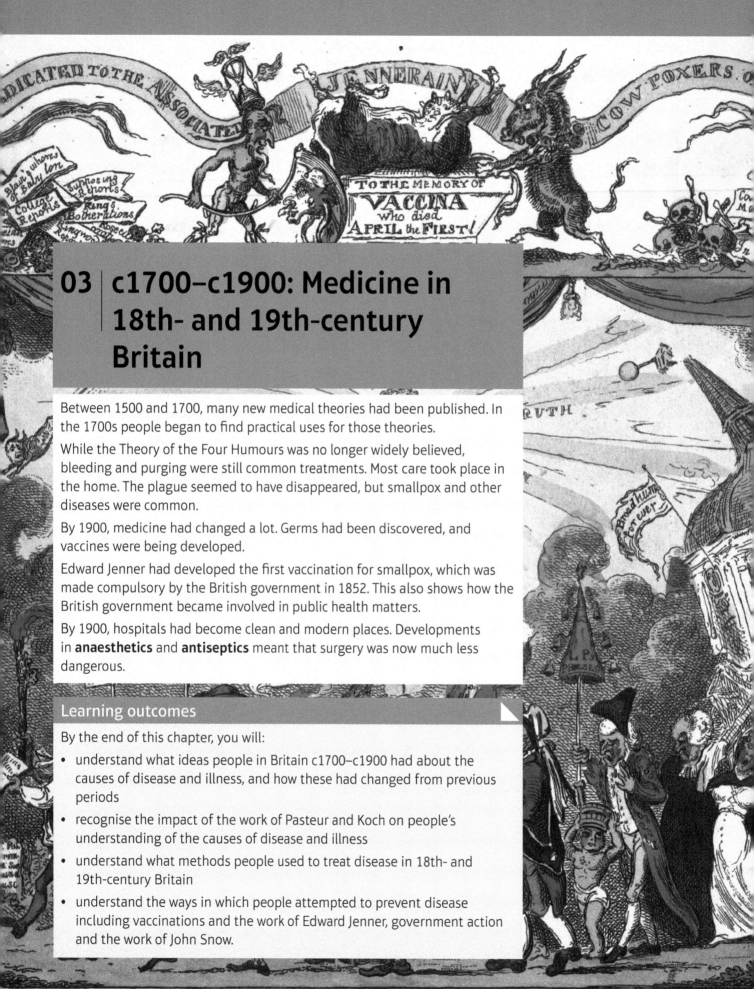

03 | c1700–c1900: Medicine in 18th- and 19th-century Britain

Between 1500 and 1700, many new medical theories had been published. In the 1700s people began to find practical uses for those theories.

While the Theory of the Four Humours was no longer widely believed, bleeding and purging were still common treatments. Most care took place in the home. The plague seemed to have disappeared, but smallpox and other diseases were common.

By 1900, medicine had changed a lot. Germs had been discovered, and vaccines were being developed.

Edward Jenner had developed the first vaccination for smallpox, which was made compulsory by the British government in 1852. This also shows how the British government became involved in public health matters.

By 1900, hospitals had become clean and modern places. Developments in **anaesthetics** and **antiseptics** meant that surgery was now much less dangerous.

Learning outcomes

By the end of this chapter, you will:

- understand what ideas people in Britain c1700–c1900 had about the causes of disease and illness, and how these had changed from previous periods
- recognise the impact of the work of Pasteur and Koch on people's understanding of the causes of disease and illness
- understand what methods people used to treat disease in 18th- and 19th-century Britain
- understand the ways in which people attempted to prevent disease including vaccinations and the work of Edward Jenner, government action and the work of John Snow.

3.1 Ideas about the cause of disease and illness

Learning outcomes

- Understand how ideas about the cause of disease changed and stayed the same, 1700–1900.

The 18th century was an exciting time for science. By 1700, the influence of the Church was not as great as it had been. Many people no longer believed that God was responsible for disease. Instead, they focused on developing scientific explanations. New influences, such as the Enlightenment* caused people to seek answers to disease and illness.

This fashion for rational* explanations led to a Scientific Revolution. From c1700, new ideas began to replace the old ones that had been shown to be wrong.

Society itself was also changing. Cities began to grow. The new cities were not well planned and quickly became dirty and disease-ridden. Diseases like tuberculosis, typhus and smallpox were a big threat to the new working population. Therefore, understanding the causes of disease and illness became even more important.

Continuity and change

Although medical ideas by 1900 were very different, not many of these changes happened during the 1700s. Most people no longer believed in the Theory of the Four Humours. People did still believe in miasma*, although this theory was also becoming less popular.

Key terms

The Enlightenment*

A change in thinking in Europe during the 18th century. It encouraged people to think for themselves and challenge traditional views.

Rational*

Logical ideas based on observation or scientific thinking.

Miasma*

Bad air.

Scientists in the early 18th century developed the new theory of **spontaneous generation*** as an alternative to theories like the Four Humours. Improvements in the quality of the glass lenses in microscopes meant that scientists could see microbes* present on decaying matter*. Most people believed that the decay was producing these microbes, rather than the microbes causing the decay.

In the 18th century, this was just a theory, and scientists were unable to prove that spontaneous generation was correct.

Key terms

Spontaneous generation*

An early theory that when things rotted they created living creatures. For example, if rotting meat had maggots and flies on it, people thought the rotting flesh had produced microbes that had grown into these flies and maggots. We now know that microbes cause the rotting, not the other way round.

Microbe*

A microbe is any living organism that is too small to see without a microscope. Microbes include bacteria.

Decaying matter*

Material, such as vegetables or animals, that has died and is rotting.

Medical breakthrough: Germ Theory

Louis Pasteur and the development of Germ Theory

By the middle of the 19th century, microscopes had improved. It was now possible to magnify substances to a much higher level.

Louis Pasteur, a French scientist, was able to observe microbes in wine and vinegar, which he believed turned both liquids 'bad'.

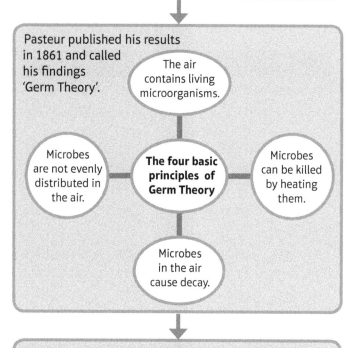

Pasteur published his results in 1861 and called his findings 'Germ Theory'.

The air contains living microorganisms.

Microbes are not evenly distributed in the air.

The four basic principles of Germ Theory

Microbes can be killed by heating them.

Microbes in the air cause decay.

To prove his theory, Pasteur put a liquid into separate containers. One was left open to the air and the other was sealed. The one that was sealed did not go 'bad', proving that microbes from the air caused decay. Decay did not cause microbes to appear.

Pasteur believed that microbes could also cause disease in humans, but he did not publish these ideas until 1878. This meant it took a while for other scientists to start to make the link between germs and disease.

Figure: Germ theory

Pasteur's influence in Britain

To begin with, Pasteur's work had almost no impact on British ideas about the causes of illness and disease. He was a scientist, not a doctor, and his work focused on decay and spoiled food, not disease.

In Britain, the theory of spontaneous generation continued to be important until the 1870s.

A few scientists did start to look for a link between microbes and disease. One of these was **Joseph Lister**, who read Pasteur's germ theory and linked it to the infection problems his surgical patients had experienced (see page 82).

Another scientist was **John Tyndall**. He had discovered that there were small organic* particles in the air. In January 1870, he gave a lecture, linking his discovery with Pasteur's Germ Theory and Lister's work on wound infection.

Key term
Organic*
Something that is living or that has once been alive.

Lister and Tyndall's ideas were also doubted. Tyndall could not prove his theory. Although microscopes meant that microbes were visible, there were lots of them in the blood, doctors could not yet identify what they were and what role they played. For example, microbes were also found in healthy people (especially in the gut). As a result many people doubted the link between germs and disease (see Source A). Now we know it is correct.

Source A

In this extract from an article published in the *British Medical Journal* in 1875, Dr Henry Bastian explains why he does not believe microbes (bacteria) cause disease.

Bacteria... habitually exist in so many parts of the body in every human being... as to make it almost inconceivable [impossible] that these organisms can be causes of disease. In support of this statement I have only to say, that even in a healthy person they may be found in myriads [large numbers]... the whole alimentary tract [digestive system] from mouth to anus; they exist throughout the air-passages, and may be found in mucus coming from the nasal cavities... They exist... within the skin, not only in the face, but in other parts of the body. Fresh legions... [more] of them are being introduced... with almost every meal that is taken.

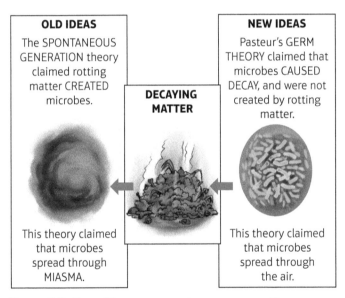

OLD IDEAS	NEW IDEAS
The SPONTANEOUS GENERATION theory claimed rotting matter CREATED microbes.	Pasteur's GERM THEORY claimed that microbes CAUSED DECAY, and were not created by rotting matter.
This theory claimed that microbes spread through MIASMA.	This theory claimed that microbes spread through the air.

Figure 3.2 Germ Theory vs. spontaneous generation.

Key terms

Anthrax*

A disease common in sheep and humans.

Tuberculosis*

A disease of the lungs.

Petri dish*

A round glass or plastic dish used in scientific study.

Agar jelly*

Jelly-like substance that comes from algae. Microbes grow very well in it.

Robert Koch's work on microbes

Pasteur had been the first scientist to identify microbes. However, it was German scientist Robert Koch who identified that germs caused disease in humans.

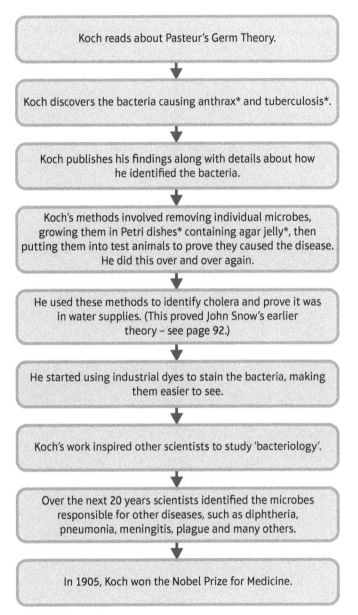

Koch reads about Pasteur's Germ Theory.

Koch discovers the bacteria causing anthrax* and tuberculosis*.

Koch publishes his findings along with details about how he identified the bacteria.

Koch's methods involved removing individual microbes, growing them in Petri dishes* containing agar jelly*, then putting them into test animals to prove they caused the disease. He did this over and over again.

He used these methods to identify cholera and prove it was in water supplies. (This proved John Snow's earlier theory – see page 92.)

He started using industrial dyes to stain the bacteria, making them easier to see.

Koch's work inspired other scientists to study 'bacteriology'.

Over the next 20 years scientists identified the microbes responsible for other diseases, such as diphtheria, pneumonia, meningitis, plague and many others.

In 1905, Koch won the Nobel Prize for Medicine.

Figure: The career of Robert Koch.

Source B

In this cartoon from 1880, Robert Koch is likened to St George. The saddle is labelled 'Investigation' and he is using a microscope as a weapon to slay tuberculosis, the snake.

KOCH AS THE NEW ST. GEORGE.

Koch's influence in Britain

The identification of microbes that caused particular diseases had a huge impact on the way doctors diagnosed* diseases. The medical profession had begun to recognise that to treat the disease, the microbes that caused it had to be removed.

For example, in 1883, the microbe that caused diphtheria was found. Diphtheria was a horrible disease that caused a painful cough and a fever. By studying the microbe, scientists saw that it produced a poison which stayed in the throat and caused the painful symptoms. Once the microbe had been identified, scientists were able to seek ways of killing it, rather than just treating the symptoms.

Summary: the impact of Germ Theory in Britain

Progress in treatment and prevention using Germ Theory was slow. Pasteur, Koch and other scientists had to find the specific microbe that caused each disease, before cures and vaccines could be tested.

Even the British government rejected the Germ Theory of disease at first. In 1884, Koch was able to prove that cholera was caused by a microbe in the drinking water supply. However, this was ignored by the British government. Instead, it kept to the idea that the disease was in the soil.

Though people were slow to accept Germ Theory in the 19th century, it would have an enormous impact on how diseases were identified and treated after 1900.

By the end of the 19th century, the mystery around what caused illness and disease had been solved. Now it was time to start looking for new treatments based on this new science.

Key term

Diagnose*
To identify what illness a person has.

Interpretation 1

In *Disease, Class and Social Change* (2012), Marc Arnold explains that Germ Theory only had a limited impact in Britain during the 19th century.

Many historians have attributed the growing concern with public health from the 1880s as being solely due to the advent of bacteriology*, and particularly to Robert Koch's discovery of the tuberculosis bacteria in 1882. However, the impact of germ theory in England during the 19th and early 20th centuries has probably been overstated. In 1897 the physician James Lindsay, reviewing the impact of Koch's discovery in Britain, noted that most of the respondents to an investigation by the British Medical Association did not view tuberculosis as an infectious* disease.

Before Koch's discoveries, symptoms were studied. Afterwards, diseases themselves were being studied by British scientists.

Koch's new methods of growing microbes made it easier for other scientists to study specific diseases.

The British government did not listen to Koch's discoveries in the short term.

By developing the dye to stain microbes, Koch made it easy to see microbes.

Koch inspired others to look for microbes responsible for other diseases.

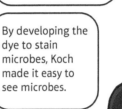

Figure 3.3 Koch's influence in Britain.

Key term

Infectious*

A person with a disease that could spread from person to person.

Key term

Bacteriology*

The study of bacteria.

THINKING HISTORICALLY Change and continuity (3a)

Significant change

Things change all the time. Every second, something in the world is changing. If historians treated every change as equal, they would never be able to write anything about the past that was useful. The decisions that historians make about what is historically significant and what is not is a very important part of their work.

The development of the Germ Theory of Disease

In 1861, Pasteur identified that microbes were causing decay in wine.	In 1854, John Snow used observation to show that cholera was water-borne.	In 1882, Koch identified the microbe that caused tuberculosis.
Koch developed a new method for growing and observing bacteria.	Joseph Lister read Pasteur's work and linked it with infection problems in surgery.	Leeuwenhoek observed microbes and wrote to the Royal Society about them (see Chapter 2).

Imagine you are investigating how scientists' understanding of the causes of disease developed over time.

1   With a partner, select three changes above which you think were most historically significant and discuss why. What criteria are you using to explain your choices? For example: how long the change lasted, or the wider consequences of the change, could affect how significant you think a change was. Write down your criteria.

2   Discuss your choice of criteria as a class, writing down all the suggestions. Assess your own criteria again and decide if you want to change any of them.

3   Using your criteria for deciding significance, put the six changes above into order of significance, with the most significant change at the top.

4   Compare your list with that of another pair in your class. Is the order similar?

5   Compare your list of criteria affecting significance with the other pair. Does this explain why you put the changes into different orders?

Activities ?

1 Create a timeline to show the development of Germ Theory. Include events from the work of both Pasteur and Koch.

2 Create flashcards to help you revise the new theories. Create one card each for Pasteur and Koch, showing the impact they had in Britain. Remember to include nationality, job, their big idea and their impact on medicine.

3 Did Pasteur or Koch do more to improve understanding of disease? Have a debate with a partner to help you better understand the role of each scientist.

Key terms

Enlightenment*

A change in thinking in Europe during the 18th century. It encouraged people to think for themselves and challenge traditional views.

Epidemic*

A very large outbreak of a particular disease.

Factors affecting the understanding of the causes of illness and disease

Individuals
- Pasteur – developed the original Germ Theory.
- Koch – proved link between bacteria and disease.
- John Tyndall – made links between Germ Theory and wound infection.

Attitudes in society
- The Enlightenment* meant that people were now more interested in finding the reasons behind disease.
- Overcrowded cities and poor living conditions led to dangerous outbreaks of disease. An unhealthy population could not work, so people wanted something to be done about epidemics*.
- However, it took a long time to prove that specific microbes caused particular diseases. People did not accept it as fact until it was proven.

Institutions: the British government

The British government **did not** help improve the understanding of disease because:
- it was not interested in getting involved with people's everyday lives until the late 19th century when more poor people could vote.
- Germ Theory did not immediately lead to any practical solutions that the government could use to solve problems like cholera.

Main factors affecting understanding of the causes of illness and disease

Technology
- Better microscopes made it easier to study microbes.
- The petri dish allowed Koch to grow bacteria outside the body that he could then study.
- Industrial dyes made it easier to see bacteria.

Science
- There was a strong desire to find scientific solutions to problems.
- Improved communication helped scientists share their work with each other.
- Ideas were shared across different branches of science. For example, Pasteur's work in chemistry and animal disease inspired Koch's work in biology and human disease.

Figure 3.4 Main factors affecting understanding of the causes of illness and disease c1700–c1900.

For the Germ Theory to be accepted people had to change what they had always believed. People are generally reluctant to change their minds and this slowed the spread of Germ Theory. Until proof that specific microbes caused specific diseases was provided in the 1880s, Germ Theory did not become an accepted fact.

Exam-style question, Section B

'There was rapid change in ideas about the causes of illness and disease in the period c1700–c1900.'

How far do you agree with this statement? You may use the following information in your answer:

- spontaneous generation
- Louis Pasteur.

You **must** also use information of your own. **16 marks**

Exam tip

Two hundred years is a long time. It is unlikely that rapid change would ever go on for so long. In your answer, try to pinpoint when exactly the rapid change occurred.

Summary

- In the 18th and 19th centuries, scientists thought that germs were produced by decaying matter, a theory named spontaneous generation.
- In 1861, Louis Pasteur, a French chemist, published Germ Theory. This proved that microbes in the air caused decay in substances such as wine and vinegar.
- Pasteur's work was picked up by some doctors and scientists quite quickly, particularly in Britain where Joseph Lister began attempting to remove microbes from his operating theatre. However, many doctors resisted the ideas.
- Robert Koch, a German scientist, began to look for specific microbes that caused disease. He identified lots of these, including the microbe that caused cholera.
- By c1900, the mystery of what caused many illnesses and diseases had been solved – it was just that not everybody believed the solution yet.

Checkpoint

Strengthen

S1 Describe in detail the roles of Pasteur and Koch in developing the Germ Theory of Disease.

S2 List the four basic principles of Germ Theory.

S3 Why didn't scientists always believe Koch's ideas about microbes?

S4 How much impact did the Germ Theory have on Britain by c1900?

Challenge

C1 Which factor do you think had the biggest impact on the development of understanding about the causes of disease and illness (see Figure 3.4)? Explain why you think this.

If you are struggling with these questions, ask your teacher for some hints.

3.2 Approaches to prevention and treatment

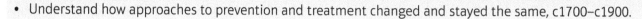

- Understand how approaches to prevention and treatment changed and stayed the same, c1700–c1900.

The extent of change in care and treatment

By 1900, the way that sick people were treated and cared for had changed almost completely since 1700. However, there was some continuity in treatment because it took a while for medical science to catch up with new ideas about the causes of illness and disease.

Change	Continuity
Most people accepted that germs caused disease and that treatment needed to focus on removing the germ.	Scientists were still not sure how to remove germs without harming the patient.
Scientists were working hard to use this knowledge to come up with new treatments.	Because there were no new treatments, people continued to use herbal remedies.
People began to realise that germs were everywhere, such as on dirty clothes and on unwashed hands.	Old beliefs about preventing illness by keeping people and things clean suddenly made sense. These practices continued.
The government was far more willing to take steps to prevent the spread of disease.	

Activities ?

1 Create a spider diagram to show changes and continuities in treatments by c1900.

2 Next to each label on your spider diagram, write a sentence to explain why this change/continuity occurred. Consider whether it is a change in attitudes, knowledge or how people live. Is it influenced by an individual or a new piece of technology?

Improvements in hospitals and the influence of Florence Nightingale

Hospitals in the 18th century

As we discovered in Chapter 2, most of England's hospitals closed down when Henry VIII dissolved the monasteries in the 1530s. By 1700, there were only five hospitals left in the country – and they were all in London.

However, new hospitals did begin to appear in other cities in the 18th century, founded using donations from wealthy people. Attitudes towards the role of hospitals were changing, too. Hospitals increasingly became places where sick people were treated, rather than places where they could rest and pray. Doctors visited patients regularly and there was a surgeon or apothecary on site for daily treatments. A small staff of untrained nurses cared for the patients.

However, the rich continued to receive medical treatment, and even surgery, in their own homes, which was much safer.

Hospitals would not treat everyone. Often only respectable working-class people would be treated – not the homeless or unemployed. Still, this was the first time poor people had access to trained doctors.

Unfortunately, as more people started to attend, hospitals became less sanitary. They became less strict about turning away infectious patients who could pass diseases on to other patients.

Doctors went from patient to patient and ward to ward without washing their hands or changing their clothes. Diseases spread quickly. People did not understand that germs caused disease until later in the 19th century, so they did not take steps to avoid spreading the germs.

By the middle of the 19th century, there were a lot more hospitals. However, hospital conditions were very poor.

Florence Nightingale

Source A

A photograph of Florence Nightingale, taken in 1855.

Florence Nightingale played an important role in improving the dirty conditions that were common in hospitals in the mid-19th century.

Name: Florence Nightingale

Job: Nurse
Nationality: English (from a wealthy family)
Period of work: 1840s–60s
Work:
- At age 17 she decided it was her mission to serve mankind and she trained as a nurse in Germany and Paris.
- In 1854 Britain went to war with Russia and Nightingale convinced the government to send her to improve the hospitals in the Crimea, along with 38 other nurses.
- She made several changes to the care of wounded soldiers and by the time she returned to Britain she was viewed as a national hero, which helped her to apply her improvements to British hospital care.

Big idea: Before Nightingale's changes, a wounded soldier's chance of dying was 40%. She organised nurses to:
- use scrubbing brushes to ensure there was no dirt near any patients
- provide clean bedding and good meals to patients.

Six months later a wounded soldier's chances of dying were just 2%.

Source B

A copy of a ballad that was written about Nightingale in 1855. Ballads like this, set to popular tunes from the time, would sell for a penny on street corners.

The Nightingale In the East.

TUNE,—"THE COTTAGE AND WATER MILL."

Ryle & Co., Printers, 2 & 3, Monmouth Court, Seven Dials. London.

ON a dark lonely night on the Crimea's dread
    shore,
There had been bloodshed and strife on the morn-
    ing before,
The dead and the dying lay bleeding around,
Some crying for help—there was none to be found
Now God in his mercy he pity'd their cries,
And the soldier so cheerful in the morning doth rise
So forward my lads, may your heart never fail,
You are cheer'd by the presence of a sweet
    Nightingale.

Now God sent this woman to succour the brave,
Some thousands she's sav'd from an untimely grave
Her eyes beam with pleasure, she's bounteous
    and good,
The wants of the wounded are by her understood
With fever some brought in, with life almost gone
Some with dismantled limbs, some to fragments
    is torn,
But they keep up their spirits, their hearts never fail
Now they're cheer'd by the presence of a sweet
    Nightingale.

Her heart it means good—for no bounty she'll take
She'd lay down her life for the poor soldier's sake
She prays for the dying, she gives peace to the
    brave,
She feels that a soldier has a soul to be saved.
The wounded they love her, as it has been seen,
She's the soldier's preserver, they call her their
    queen,
May God give her strength, & her heart never fail,
One of Heaven's best gifts is Miss Nightingale.

The wives of the wounded how thankful are they,
Their husbands are car'd for, how happy are they.
Whate'er her country, this gift God has given.
The soldiers they say she's an angel from Heaven
Sing praise to this woman, and deny it who can !
And all women was sent for the comfort of man,
Let's hope no more against them you'll rail,
Treat them well, and they'll prove like Miss
    Nightingale.

Source C

In this extract from *Notes on Hospitals*, published in 1859, Nightingale explains how important it is for hospitals to be well-ventilated.

To build a hospital with one closed court with high walls, or what is worse, with two closed courts, is to stagnate [make stuffy] the air even before it reaches the wards.

This defect [mistake] is one of the most serious that can be committed in hospital architecture; and it exists, nevertheless, in some form or other in nearly all the older hospitals, and in many even of recent constructions.

The air outside the hospital cannot be maintained in a state sufficiently pure to be used for internal ventilation, unless there be entire freedom of movement. Anything which interferes with this is injurious [bad]. Neighbouring high walls, smoking chimneys, trees, high ground, are all more or less hurtful; but worse than all is bad construction of the hospital itself.

The impact of Florence Nightingale in British hospitals

Following her return from the Crimea, Nightingale's experience and popularity meant that she was able to have a big impact on hospital care in Britain in two different ways:

- the way hospitals were designed
- the way nurses were trained.

Nightingale preferred hospitals to follow the 'pavilion plan'. This meant they were built with more windows, larger rooms and separate isolation wards to stop diseases spreading (see Source D).

Also, Nightingale established a nursing school at St Thomas' Hospital in London called the Nightingale School for Nurses in 1860. Figure 3.5 gives more detail on the impact of Nightingale's work.

I wrote *Notes on Nursing* in 1859, setting out the key role of a nurse and the importance of training.

In 1860, I set up the Nightingale School for Nurses at St Thomas' Hospital, London. Here, nurses were trained mainly on cleanliness.

On my recommendations, new hospitals were built that were easier to clean. I believe dirt spreads disease. Tiles on the floors and painted walls and ceilings made it possible to wash all surfaces properly.

I made nursing seem like a respectable job. 'Nightingale nurses' were often middle-class women. Previously, nurses had been from working-class backgrounds, and had a reputation for being drunk and uncaring.

I promoted 'pavilion style' hospitals, where separate wards were built to ensure that infectious patients could be kept separate.

Proper training turned nursing into a profession, rather than a simple, unskilled job. This encouraged more women to sign up, so the number of nurses grew rapidly.

Figure 3.5 The impact of Florence Nightingale's work.

Hospitals by 1900

Design

- Many different wards to separate infectious* and non-infectious patients.
- Separate operating theatres with specialist equipment.

Cleanliness

- Hospitals tried to remove germs using antiseptics*.
- Efforts were also made to stop germs getting into hospitals to begin with.

Function

- Instead of being a place to rest, hospitals had become a place to get treatment.
- There were more doctors, especially junior doctors.

New ideas about hospitals were adopted quickly. Everybody wanted to have the most modern hospital, to help them attract donations and new doctors.

Key terms

Infectious*

A person with a disease that could spread from person to person.

Antiseptics*

Substances that kill or stop the growth of bacteria (germs).

Source D

This picture and plan show the Birmingham hospital that was opened in 1888. It was built on open ground with separate isolation wards, modelled on the pavilion plan favoured by Florence Nightingale.

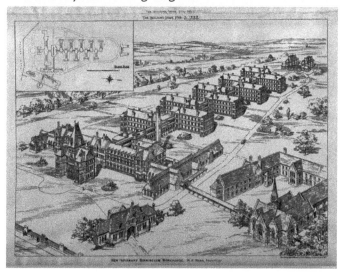

Activities ?

1 List the changes that had occurred in hospitals by c1900.

2 Explain the impact of more people attending hospitals.

3 Write an obituary for Florence Nightingale. Explain the impact she had on nursing and hospital design.

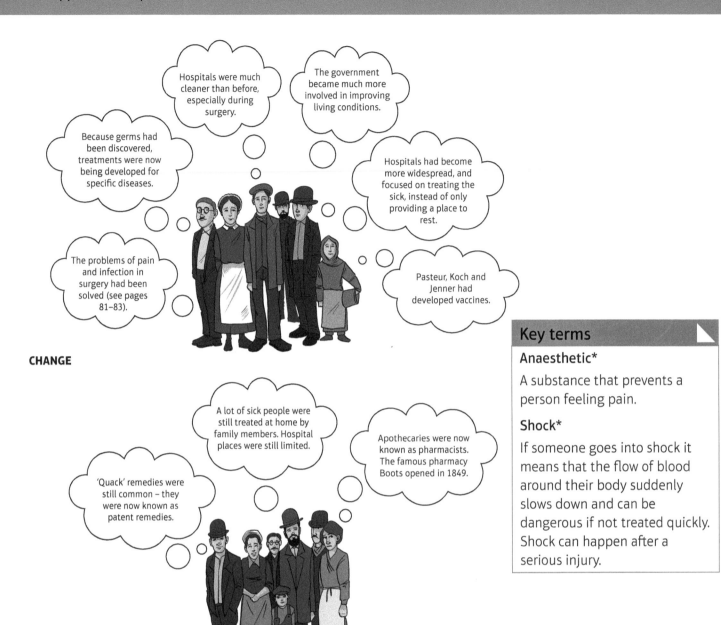

Hospitals were much cleaner than before, especially during surgery.

The government became much more involved in improving living conditions.

Because germs had been discovered, treatments were now being developed for specific diseases.

Hospitals had become more widespread, and focused on treating the sick, instead of only providing a place to rest.

The problems of pain and infection in surgery had been solved (see pages 81–83).

Pasteur, Koch and Jenner had developed vaccines.

CHANGE

A lot of sick people were still treated at home by family members. Hospital places were still limited.

Apothecaries were now known as pharmacists. The famous pharmacy Boots opened in 1849.

'Quack' remedies were still common – they were now known as patent remedies.

CONTINUITY

Figure 3.6 Extent of change in care and treatment.

> **Key terms**
>
> **Anaesthetic***
> A substance that prevents a person feeling pain.
>
> **Shock***
> If someone goes into shock it means that the flow of blood around their body suddenly slows down and can be dangerous if not treated quickly. Shock can happen after a serious injury.

Improvements in surgical treatment

In the 1700s, surgery was dangerous and usually fatal. Surgeons were faced with three big problems.

Bleeding
The skill of a surgeon was partly judged on speed because being quick was the only way to prevent too much blood loss.

The three big problems of surgery

Pain
There were no anaesthetics* to put the patient to sleep during the surgery. This meant they were able to feel the pain. Patients had to be held down, and sometimes went into shock*.

Infection
Surgery was not performed in a germ-free environment as people didn't know about germs. Most surgery still happened in the person's home, with the surgeon wearing the clothes he arrived in. Infection was common.

For these reasons, only simple surgeries were possible. The most common type of surgery was amputation*. Other types of surgeries were rare because the danger of death was so great. However, surgeons were becoming more respected.

In the 19th century, progress was made in tackling two of the three problems of surgery. Firstly, anaesthetics were developed so surgeons could put patients to sleep before operating on them – which helped with the **pain**. Secondly, Germ Theory meant people understood the importance of cleanliness in the operating room, and antiseptic surgery* was developed – this helped to stop **infection**.

Key terms

Amputation*

The surgical removal of part of the body, for example an arm or leg.

Antiseptic surgery*

Using substances that kill germs (antiseptics) to dress wounds after surgery or kill germs during surgery.

Tackling pain: the development of the anaesthetic

Doctors had been trying for a long time to find things that would relieve pain and keep patients still during operations.

- Early experiments with **laughing gas** proved successful for some small operations.
- A chemical called **ether** was discovered – but it made patients vomit, the gas irritated the lungs, and it could easily catch fire, so it was dangerous to use.

James Simpson and chloroform

James Simpson, a young surgeon from Edinburgh, and a group of friends inhaled* the vapours* of different chemicals to see what might work. After sniffing chloroform, all of them passed out. Clearly, chloroform was an effective anaesthetic.

Timeline

The development of the anaesthetic

1795 Humphry Davy, a dentist's assistant, tried inhaling nitrous oxide, or 'laughing gas'. He discovered that it numbed pain.

1842 William E. Clarke, an American chemist and doctor, successfully used ether to put to sleep a patient to remove a tooth.

1846 Robert Liston, a famous London surgeon, successfully used ether when amputating a leg.

1847 James Simpson, a surgeon in Edinburgh, discovered chloroform.

1853 Queen Victoria used chloroform during the birth of Prince Leopold and approved of it.

Key terms

Inhale*

To breathe in.

Vapour*

The gas resulting from heating a liquid.

Source E

An artist's impression of the night when James Simpson and his friends discovered the power of chloroform, c1860.

However, chloroform did have some negative side effects*.

- The dose had to be carefully controlled, as it was easy to overdose a patient and harm or even kill them.
- The chemical sometimes affected the heart, which caused some healthy and fit young people to die soon after inhaling it.

In spite of this, however, chloroform began to be used during operations to reduce pain. After it was administered to Queen Victoria during the birth of her son in 1853, chloroform became more popular in Britain. As a result, more surgeries took place and more complex surgeries became possible. However, because anaesthetics allowed for deeper surgery to be attempted, infection and bleeding became even bigger problems.

Tackling infection: the development of antiseptic surgery

Due to a lack of understanding about germs, surgeons did not make an effort to keep their surroundings, or even themselves, clean when they operated on patients. In fact, many wore their most stained doctor's coat to show how much experience they had. Instruments were not washed, and many people would be present during operations. As a result of this, many patients died after operations from infections such as gangrene* or sepsis*.

Key terms

Side effects*

Unintended symptoms that appear as a result of taking a medication.

Gangrene*

When the skin, muscle and soft tissue of the body die.

Sepsis*

When infection gets into the blood and travels all around the body attacking vital organs.

Joseph Lister and carbolic acid

Joseph Lister was an English surgeon. By studying infected wounds, he realised that the flesh was rotting. Lister compared his results with the recently-published work of Pasteur, who had identified germs as being responsible for rotting. If microbes in the air caused wine and vinegar to go bad, perhaps microbes also caused flesh to rot.

Lister started to look for a chemical that would clear bacteria from wounds. He knew about the use of **carbolic acid** in sewage treatments. So, in 1865, he operated on a patient with a broken leg and added a bandage soaked in carbolic acid. The wound healed cleanly.

From this, Lister developed a series of steps to ensure that wounds did not become infected. These included spraying carbolic acid in the air during operations.

Source F

This famous picture is taken from William Watson Cheyne's book *Antiseptic Surgery* which was published in 1882.

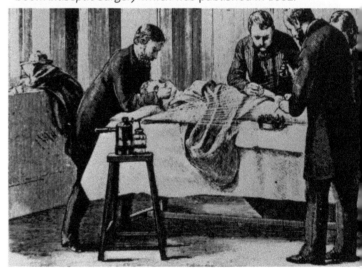

Lister published his results in *The Lancet*, a medical journal.

In spite of its success, antiseptic surgery did not catch on quickly.

- News of Lister's success spread more quickly than Germ Theory. Many surgeons refused to use the carbolic spray, as they still did not believe that the air was full of germs.
- Carbolic spray dried out the skin, making it sore, and left behind an odd smell.
- Lister focused on encouraging his colleagues to use the carbolic spray instead of scientifically proving his theory.

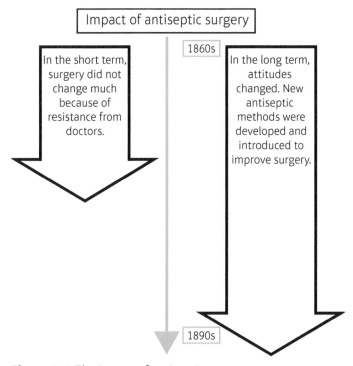

Impact of antiseptic surgery

1860s

In the short term, surgery did not change much because of resistance from doctors.

In the long term, attitudes changed. New antiseptic methods were developed and introduced to improve surgery.

1890s

Figure 3.7 The impact of antiseptic surgery.

In time, the attitude of surgeons towards antiseptic and aseptic surgery* changed. Surgeons finally understood that performing safe surgery was not only possible – it was their duty.

Key term

Aseptic surgery*
Surgery where microbes are prevented from getting into a wound in the first place, rather than being killed off with an antiseptic.

Other surgeons began to look for different methods of preventing infection. By 1900, instruments were steam cleaned, operating theatres were scrubbed spotless, rubber gloves and surgical gowns were introduced and surgeons used face masks during operations.

Opposition to change

Developments in anaesthetics and antiseptics helped to improve surgery, but not everybody welcomed the changes.

- Anaesthetics allowed for deeper surgeries, so infection and bleeding became even bigger problems. The death rate actually increased.
- Some Victorians believed that pain relief was interfering with God's plan, particularly in childbirth, which was meant to be painful.
- Some doctors believed that patients were more likely to die if they were put to sleep during the operation. They wanted them to be awake and screaming to be sure they were still alive.
- It took a long time for doctors to accept that germs caused infection, and that they had been infecting their patients.

Activities ?

1 Create an annotated timeline to show changes in the field of surgery during the 19th century.

2 Make flashcards for Simpson and Lister, explaining what they did and what impact this had on surgical techniques. Remember to include: nationality, job, their big idea and their impact on medicine.

Exam-style question, Section B

Explain why there was rapid change in surgical treatments in the period c1700–c1900.

You may use the following in your answer:

- chloroform
- Joseph Lister.

You **must** also use information of your own. **12 marks**

Exam tip

Make sure that you focus on the reasons why development of surgical treatment was rapid – don't just describe the use of anaesthetics and antiseptics.

Case study – Jenner and the development of the vaccination*

Smallpox in 18th-century Britain

At the start of this period, smallpox* was a a common disease in Britain. The problem was particularly bad in London, where there were 11 epidemics in the 18th century. The worst of these was in 1796, when 3,548 people died.

At this time, people still did not know what caused the disease, but they did have some ideas about how to avoid catching it. It had been noticed that people who caught a mild form of smallpox and then recovered from it did not catch it again. However, people did not understand why.

Some people attempted to inoculate* themselves against smallpox by catching a mild dose of the disease. Pus from a smallpox scab would be rubbed into a cut on the patient by a doctor. Unfortunately, this did not always work: some patients died of the smallpox they were given, as the disease did not affect everyone in the same way.

In spite of this, inoculation was seen by many as the best chance of surviving smallpox. However, the procedure was very expensive and so only the very rich could afford it. Many doctors made a fortune carrying out inoculations for wealthy people.

Key terms

Vaccination*

A different or weakened form of a disease is put into a healthy person. This makes them immune to the full version of the disease.

Smallpox*

A disease causing fever, vomiting and blisters on the skin. 30% of infected people die. Those who survive are left with scarred skin.

Inoculate*

Deliberately infecting oneself with a disease, in order to avoid a more severe case of it later on.

Cowpox*

A disease causing red blisters on the skin, similar to smallpox, but less deadly. It can be transmitted from cows to humans.

Jenner discovers the vaccination for smallpox

In the 1790s, an English doctor called Edward Jenner came up with a better way of preventing smallpox – he called it **vaccination**.

Name: Edward Jenner

Job: Country doctor

Nationality: English

Period of work: Late 18th century (1780s/90s)

Big idea: There were a lot of dairy farms in the area where Jenner worked. He regularly treated dairy maids for cowpox*. He noticed that when there was a smallpox epidemic those who had previously suffered from cowpox did not catch smallpox. He decided the two must be somehow connected.

Work: In 1796, he set about testing his theory by infecting a local boy, James Phipps, with cowpox. Six weeks later he attempted to infect James with smallpox, but James did not catch it.

In 1798, he wrote up his findings. He named the technique 'vaccination' after the Latin word for cow, *vacca*.

Limitations:
- Although Jenner knew that the system worked, he was not able to explain how or why it worked – and this made people suspicious.
- People thought infecting a person with an animal disease was very strange.

Figure 3.8 Differing opinions about vaccinations in the 19th century.

Reactions to the new vaccination

Although some people were against vaccination, parliament was in favour of it. As you can see from the timeline below, the British government favoured the new method of vaccination from the first half of the 19th century. This was because it was a safer alternative to inoculation. It was also cheaper.

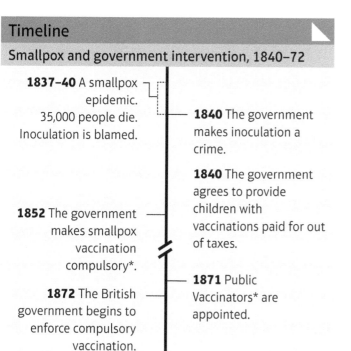

Timeline

Smallpox and government intervention, 1840–72

1837–40 A smallpox epidemic. 35,000 people die. Inoculation is blamed.

1840 The government makes inoculation a crime.

1840 The government agrees to provide children with vaccinations paid for out of taxes.

1852 The government makes smallpox vaccination compulsory*.

1871 Public Vaccinators* are appointed.

1872 The British government begins to enforce compulsory vaccination.

Key terms

Compulsory*

Something that has to be done and cannot be avoided.

Public Vaccinators*

Doctors paid by the government to vaccinate people against smallpox.

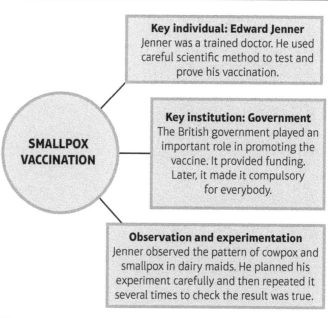

Key individual: Edward Jenner
Jenner was a trained doctor. He used careful scientific method to test and prove his vaccination.

Key institution: Government
The British government played an important role in promoting the vaccine. It provided funding. Later, it made it compulsory for everybody.

SMALLPOX VACCINATION

Observation and experimentation
Jenner observed the pattern of cowpox and smallpox in dairy maids. He planned his experiment carefully and then repeated it several times to check the result was true.

Figure 3.9 Factors helping Jenner to develop the smallpox vaccine.

Activity ?

Create a six-picture storyboard to show how Edward Jenner developed the smallpox vaccine.

The impact of the smallpox vaccine

Extend your knowledge

Smallpox today

In 1979, The World Health Organisation announced that smallpox had been completely wiped out. This would not have been possible without Jenner's early work.

Short-term impact
- Saved many lives – 100,000 people had been vaccinated by 1800.
- Very popular in other countries.
- Slightly less popular in Britain due to campaigns against Jenner and vaccination (see Source G).

Long-term impact
- Vaccination against smallpox became a normal part of life.
- In 1872 the British government made it compulsory to be vaccinated. As a result, the number of cases of smallpox fell dramatically.
- Jenner's work inspired other scientists, like Pasteur and Koch, to search for vaccines to other diseases.
- However, there were no other vaccinations discovered that worked in the same way as the smallpox vaccine – most diseases do not have a similar, less deadly version like cowpox. Scientists were unable to develop other vaccines based on Jenner's method.

Source G

This cartoon was drawn by Cruikshank in 1812. It is titled, *'The cowpox tragedy: scene the last.'* The year before, people vaccinated with cowpox had developed smallpox, because of an error with the samples used.

THE COW POX TRAGEDY
— Scene the Last. —

Exam-style question, Section B

Explain why there was rapid change in the prevention of smallpox after 1798.

You may use the following information in your answer:

- inoculation
- the government.

You **must** also use information of your own.

12 marks

Exam tip

In order to show what changed you should compare the situation before Jenner's research with the situation after it. Then explain why the change you have identified happened.

New approaches to prevention: the development and use of vaccinations

People still generally believed that the best way to avoid dying from a disease was not catching it at all. Although ideas about medicine were changing, few diseases could be cured yet. Therefore, scientists continued to focus on prevention and developed the idea of the vaccination.

Activities ?

1 Write a sentence for each of these individuals explaining how they helped to develop vaccines: Edward Jenner, Louis Pasteur, Robert Koch.

2 What factors made the development of new vaccinations possible? Remember to consider common factors that influence change, for example individuals, science and technology, money, governments and attitudes.

Pasteur's Germ Theory is published in 1861. Pasteur admired Jenner's work on the smallpox vaccination but quickly realised that other vaccines could only be produced if the germs causing specific diseases were identified.

In 1878, Pasteur identified the germ causing cholera in chickens. He found that by creating a weakened form of the disease and injecting it into the chickens, he could successfully vaccinate them. He did the same for anthrax and rabies.

Koch's work on identifying bacteria in humans, combined with Pasteur's work, inspired scientists like Emil von Behring to develop vaccinations for humans against tetanus and diphtheria.

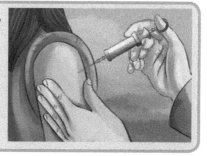

By 1900, scientists all over the world were busy isolating microbes and developing vaccines to prevent diseases.

Figure: How vaccinations were developed in the 19th century.

The Public Health Act, 1875

Besides vaccination, a great deal was also being done to improve living conditions in Britain, particularly in the larger cities. In c1700, the government had little interest in improving conditions in cities. It had a *laissez-faire** attitude and believed that it was not the government's responsibility to interfere in the way that people lived.

Key word

Laissez-faire*

This French term means 'leave be'. It is used to describe governments that do not get involved in the day-to-day lives of the people who live in that country.

During the 1800s, this *laissez-faire* attitude began to change. More men were given the right to vote, so the government began passing laws that helped ordinary people.

The arrival of cholera in Britain also led to change. The work of John Snow (see page 92) led people to understand that cholera was spread in dirty water.

From the 1860s, the government began to take more action to improve living conditions for people in cities.

- In London, 1,300 miles of sewers were built by 1865.
- In Birmingham, slums* were demolished.
- In Leeds, a local business stopped sewage from being drained into the river from which the city took its water.

There had been a change in the way people felt about public health. More people began to recognise that it was now everybody's responsibility.

Key term

Slums*

Poor-quality houses that were unhealthy to live in.

Extend your knowledge

Name: Edwin Chadwick

Job: Politician

Nationality: English

Period of work: 1830s and 1840s

Work: Research into the living conditions of the working classes and the poor, especially those living in Britain's cities. In 1842 he published a report of his findings.

Big idea: That the filthy living conditions he observed caused poor people in the inner-cities to die young. Campaigned to get the government to take some responsibility for disposing of waste and providing clean water.

Limitations: This was before the Germ Theory, so his suggested link between living conditions and health could not be proven.

Developments in understanding...	Factors, c1700–c1900	Factor
CAUSE	• Germ Theory • Work on **identifying microbes**.	• Role of technology (microscopes). • Role of science of chemistry. • Role of individuals.
TREATMENT	• Better **hospitals** and **nursing** thanks to the work of Florence Nightingale. • Improvements in surgical treatment, because of **anaesthetics** and **antiseptic surgery**.	• Role of individuals. • Role of science of chemistry.
PREVENTION	• Development of **vaccinations** begun by Edward Jenner. • **Improved water supply and drainage**, with 1875 Public Health Act.	• Role of individuals. • Role of government.

In response to this change in attitude, the government passed the **Public Health Act** in 1875.

City authorities had to follow the rules it set out. The responsibilities included:

- providing clean water to stop diseases that were spread in dirty water
- getting rid of sewage to prevent drinking and washing water from becoming polluted
- building public toilets to avoid pollution
- employing a public officer of health to record outbreaks of diseases

- making sure new houses were of better quality, to stop damp and overcrowding
- providing public parks for exercise
- creating street lighting to prevent accidents
- checking the quality of the food in shops. For example, some bakers mixed chalk into flour to make bread whiter.

These measures worked. The last cholera epidemic in Britain was in 1866–67.

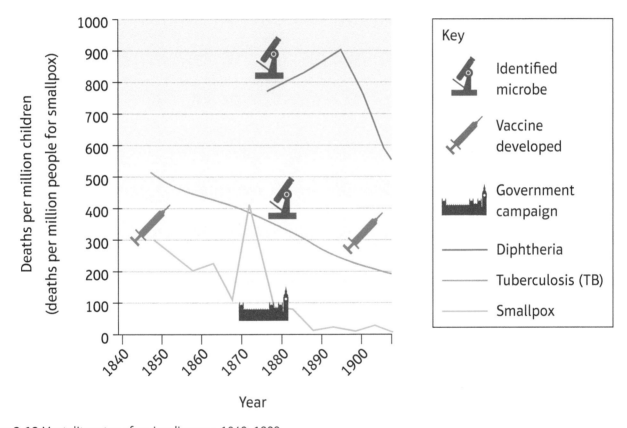

Figure 3.10 Mortality rates of major diseases, 1840–1900.

Summary

- By c1900, the treatment and prevention of disease had changed. This was due to an improved understanding of the cause of disease.
- More hospitals were built, making treatments more widely available.
- Hospitals were cleaner thanks to the work of Florence Nightingale. Nursing had become a respectable profession.
- Herbal and patent remedies were still popular for common illnesses, because few new treatments had been developed.
- Surgical procedures had become a more effective method of treatment as a result of the development of anaesthetics and antiseptics. However, blood loss was still a problem, so surgeons still had to work quickly.
- Scientists had developed a method for vaccinating people against diseases and had begun to develop vaccines for particular illnesses.
- One of these illnesses was smallpox – Edward Jenner proved that catching cowpox prevented people from catching smallpox.
- In the 19th century, the government began to take action to improve public health in cities. This was a result of a better understanding of the link between dirty conditions and disease, and it led to a healthier population.

Checkpoint

Strengthen

S1 What changes and continuities had there been in the treatment of disease by c1900?

S2 Describe the actions that Florence Nightingale took to improve hospital conditions in Britain.

S3 Identify the steps that led to improvements in surgical treatment during the 19th century.

S4 What were the short-term and long-term impacts of Jenner's new method of preventing smallpox?

Challenge

C1 As in the previous period (c1500–c1700), attitudes in society had a big impact on change in treatment. Can you list two ways that people's attitudes encouraged developments in treatment and prevention, and two ways that they held them back? Consider what ideas people accepted and what opposition there was to new ideas (especially in surgery).

If you are not confident about any of these questions, form a group with other students, discuss the answers and then record your conclusions. Your teacher can give you some hints.

Learning outcomes

- Understand how the government tackled the cholera epidemics of the 19th century.

Source A

This cartoon was drawn in 1852, for the magazine *Punch*.

A COURT FOR KING CHOLERA.

Fighting cholera

Cholera was a terrible disease. It caused diarrhoea and sickness that became so bad, the victim became dehydrated*. Sufferers usually died within two to six days. The disease often turned the skin blue, so cholera was nicknamed 'the blue death'. It was spread through person-to-person contact, or water contaminated* with the faeces* of a sufferer.

Cholera did not arrive in Britain until 1831. It spread quickly across the country. Cholera mainly affected the poorest people. There were lots of cases in slums and in workhouses*, prisons and asylums*. However, it still affected wealthier areas. As with the plague 200 years earlier, doctors found it impossible to treat.

Key terms

Dehydrated*
When the body does not have enough water to keep the organs working properly.

Contaminated*
When something is added to a clean substance making it dirty.

Faeces*
Poo

Workhouse*
A place where very poor people could get food and a bed in exchange for work.

Asylum*
A building for the care of people believed to be mentally ill.

Activity ?

Look carefully at the cartoon. List all the threats to health you can see in the picture.

Year of epidemic	Total cholera-related deaths in England and Wales
1831–32	21,882
1848–49	53,293
1853–54	20,097
1865–66	14,378

Source B

This letter was printed in *The Times* in 1849, during the second cholera outbreak. It was written by a group of residents of Soho, London.

Sir, May we be and beseech [ask for] your protection and power. We are Sir, as it may be, living in a wilderness, so far as the rest of London knows anything of us, or as the rich and great people care about. We live in muck and filth. We ain't got no privies [toilets], no dust bins, no drains, no water-supplies, and no drain or sewer in the whole place. The Sewer Company, in Greek Street, Soho Square, all great, rich powerful men take no notice whatsoever of our complaints. The stench of a gully-hole is disgusting. We all of us suffer, and numbers are ill, and if the cholera comes Lord help us all.

Key terms

Miasma*

Bad air.

Board of health*

A committee in charge of public health locally.

Anaesthetist*

Doctor specialising in pain relief (giving anaesthetics).

Attempts to prevent the spread of cholera

Some steps were taken to try to clean up the filthiest areas of the cities to prevent the spread of cholera. The belief that miasma* and rotting material caused disease was still widespread, so attempts were made to remove rubbish. The government encouraged cities to set up boards of health* and provide clean water supplies, but this led to little improvement.

John Snow

John Snow was a surgeon who moved to Soho in 1836 and became London's leading anaesthetist*. He gave Queen Victoria chloroform during the birth of Prince Leopold in 1851. He was popular and well-respected.

Source C

This cartoon was published in *Punch* in 1858. In it, the River Thames is offering his 'children' to London – the diseases diphtheria, scrofula (a type of tuberculosis) and cholera.

Snow observed cholera during the epidemic of 1848–49. He wrote up his theories in *On the Mode of Communication of Cholera*. In it, he suggested that:

- cholera could not be transmitted by a miasma because it affected the gut, not the lungs
- drinking water was being contaminated by the cholera-ridden faeces.

Snow concluded that cholera was transmitted by dirty drinking water.

The 1854 epidemic

In August 1854, cholera broke out in Soho. Snow investigated the 93 deaths in his local area.

Source D

A section of John Snow's cholera spot map, 1854. The instances of cholera are marked as black bars.

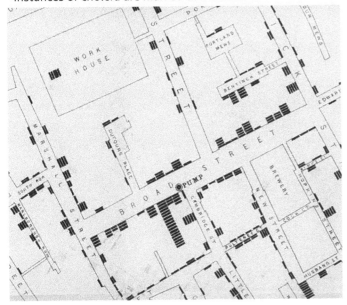

Snow took a street map and marked on where the deaths had occurred in the area around Golden Square and Broad Street (see Source D).

After looking at the map, John Snow realised that there was a pattern: deaths seemed to be centred around the water pump on Broad Street.

To Snow, it was clear that the water pump was the source of the infection. He removed the handle from the pump, preventing locals from using it. Deaths from cholera stopped.

Later inspections of the well underneath the water pump revealed that it was extremely close to a cesspit*. Waste from the cesspit was getting into the well and spreading cholera.

Key term

Cesspit*

A pit for storing sewage or waste.

Figure 3.11 How John Snow proved that the Broad Street pump was spreading cholera.

The impact and significance of John Snow and the Broad Street pump

In 1855, Snow presented his evidence to politicians. He recommended that the government start making massive improvements in the sewer systems of London to prevent cholera.

The government did eventually agree to invest in a new sewer system, which was planned by Joseph Bazalgette and completed in 1875. However, this was not just due to John Snow. An unusually hot summer in 1858 had caused 'The Great Stink'. The Thames river was low and the stench of the exposed sewage on the riverbanks next to parliament became terrible. This nudged the government into action and the work on the new sewers was begun in 1860.

Many people rejected Snow's work (see Source E). Other scientists pointed out that cases would still occur among people who lived further away from the pump, even if they were drinking less of the water. The General Board of Health continued to support the theory of miasma. Admitting that cholera was present in the water would mean having to provide clean water, which was going to be very costly – and there was no scientific proof that it would work.

Source E

These two drawings accompanied the General Board of Health's report on the cholera epidemic, which was published in 1855. The Board had rejected Snow's theory that cholera was spread through water. Here, they attempt to prove their theory by offering two drawings of water magnified 200 times. On the left, a drawing of water taken from the Broad Street pump. On the right, a drawing of water from the New River Company, elsewhere in London, which contained more microbes.

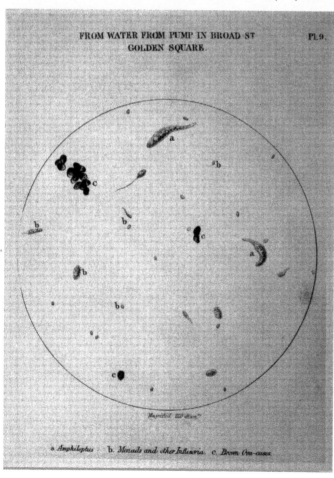

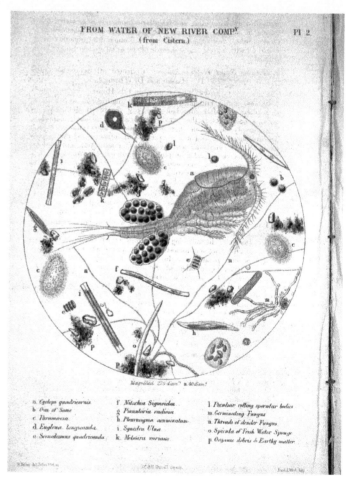

Snow had no scientific evidence of what caused the disease. It would be another seven years before Pasteur published his Germ Theory, and another 30 years before Koch finally identified the microbe that caused cholera.

In the short term, Snow's work had an immediate impact on the residents of Soho Square, who avoided cholera. However, his impact outside of this area was very limited. It was not until much later that the importance of clean water was accepted.

Preventing cholera: the role of individuals and institutions

Role of the government	Role of the individual: John Snow
Encouraged local councils to clean up their cities and provide clean water.	Observed the pattern of cholera cases.
Listened to John Snow's evidence about cholera.	Designed an experiment to prove that cholera was caused by dirty water.
Arranged for a new sewer system to be built in London.	Prevented residents from drinking the water.
Eventually passed the 1875 Public Health Act to force other cities to clean up.	Presented his findings to the government.

THINKING HISTORICALLY Change and continuity (3b)

Significant to whom?

Different historians are interested in different aspects of the past, and therefore ask different questions. What a historian is interested in is a very important factor in their decision about what is significant and what is not.

Historian's focus	Social historian	British historian	Scientific historian
Title of investigation	How did medical developments change **living standards** in Britain during the 19th century?	How did **British** scientists change our understanding of the causes of disease?	What role did **science and technology** play in the development of medicine?

Changes and events during the 19th century

In 1861, Pasteur identified that germs caused decay.	The British government passed laws to make cities cleaner and protect people's health.	In 1865, Lister developed a carbolic spray to make surgery safer.
In 1854, John Snow made a link between cholera and dirty water.	Better microscopes enabled scientists to see microbes and link them with diseases.	In 1797, Edward Jenner developed a vaccination against smallpox.
Robert Koch developed methods to allow bacteria to be grown and observed more easily.		

For each historian, make a diagram to show which changes and events would interest them. Write the historian in the middle of the page and then add the events and changes around them.

1 Which change or event is of most interest to the social historian? How important is it to the other historians?
2 Why would the work of Joseph Lister be of interest to the social historian and the scientific historian?
3 Why would the British historian ignore Pasteur's work? Why might they include or be interested in Pasteur's work?

Summary

- Cholera first appeared in Britain in 1831.
- There were four major epidemics in the 19th century and they particularly affected poor people living in cities.
- John Snow thought that cholera was spread by water, not by a miasma.
- During the 1854 epidemic, he mapped the cholera fatalities in Soho. The evidence suggested that the outbreak was connected to the Broad Street pump.
- Snow presented his findings to the government. However, they did not take action straight away.
- By 1858, the government were ready to take action to provide clean water for the population. The final outbreak of cholera was much less severe as a result of this action.

Checkpoint

Strengthen

S1 When were the four cholera epidemics in Britain?

S2 Describe the actions that John Snow took to prove that cholera was spread by dirty water.

S3 What event finally forced the British government to take action on cholera?

Challenge

C1 Explain why Snow's theory was not widely accepted when he published it. Consider what previous beliefs people held, and what people did and didn't know about in 1855.

If you are not confident about any of these questions, form a group with other students, discuss the answers and then record your conclusions. Your teacher can give you some hints.

Recap: c1700–c1900: Medicine in 18th- and 19th-century Britain

Activity ?

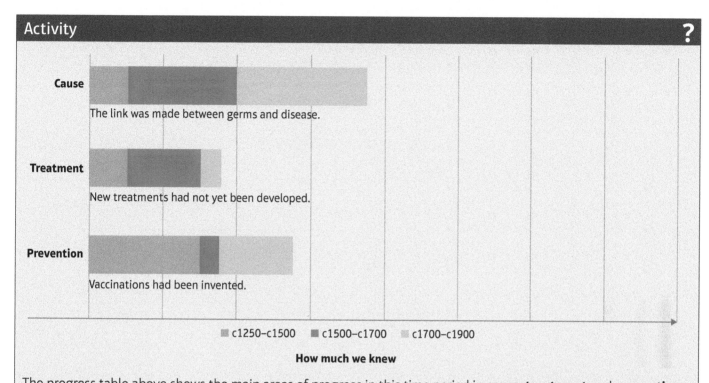

How much we knew

■ c1250–c1500 ■ c1500–c1700 ■ c1700–c1900

The progress table above shows the main areas of progress in this time period in **cause**, **treatment** and **prevention**. Using this table, make notes to explain why there was more knowledge in the causes of diseases, c1700–c1900.

Recall quiz

1 Why did the search for scientific explanations become more fashionable in the period c1700–c1900?

2 What incorrect theory had scientists come up with to explain decay in the early 18th century?

3 What was the impact of Pasteur's work?

4 Give two disease-causing germs identified by Robert Koch.

5 Why were herbal remedies still popular in the 19th century?

6 Where did Florence Nightingale first try out her theories about the importance of clean hospitals?

7 Name two anaesthetics that were developed during this period.

8 List three points from the 1875 Public Health Act.

9 When did Jenner develop his vaccination against smallpox?

10 Where did John Snow trace the 1854 Soho cholera epidemic to?

Exam-style questions, Section B

'Louis Pasteur's publication of the Germ Theory was the biggest turning point in medicine in the period c1700–c1900.'

How far do you agree with this statement?

You may use the following information in your answer:

• Edward Jenner
• Robert Koch.

You **must** also use information of your own. **16 marks**

Exam tip

To judge whether something is a 'turning point' think about its impact. Did it have an impact on diagnosis, treatment, prevention, public health? Was the impact rapid or did it take time?

Writing historically: using phrases to build detail

The best historical writing uses carefully structured phrases to incorporate facts.

Learning outcomes

By the end of this lesson, you will understand how to:

- add facts to your writing
- express your ideas in more detail.

Definitions

Adjective: a word that provides additional information about a noun, e.g. '<u>clear</u>, <u>precise</u> writing'.

Preposition: a word giving information about position or time, e.g. '**in** the 19th century', '**during** the war', '**after** several years'.

How can I add factual detail to my writing?

Prepositions show the connections between other words or phrases in a sentence. They include words like:

in	at	on	after	before	during	with	without	from	to	between

Prepositions can be used to add important information about the time and/or place that significant events took place in. For example:

During the Crimean War...	In the early 1800s...	Before Pasteur's discovery...
With Koch's work on microbes...	Without this knowledge...	From 1853 to 1856...

1. Look at the response to this exam-style question. Rewrite the response, adding more information using prepositions. The highlighted sections show where the answer needs more information – usually, **when** or **where** these events happened.

> 'The role of science and technology was the main reason why diagnosis improved in the 18th and 19th centuries.' How far do you agree? **(16 marks)**

The Scientific Revolution (when did this happen?) focused on finding answers to big questions in science. People wanted to prove new theories. Individuals helped improve diagnosis using science and technology. French chemist, Louis Pasteur, proved Germ Theory (in what year?/where was he working?). Once this was known, the search for specific causes and specific treatments began. The breakthrough came with Robert Koch's work on microbes, (when?) identifying the germs that cause tuberculosis, was developed. Others followed (what did they follow?), but all were dependent on Pasteur's theory and being able to identify the individual causes. The British government rejected Germ Theory at first (before or after what?).

How can I add detail to my writing?

One way in which you can add more information to your answer is by adding **adjectives** and **prepositions**.

Compare these two versions of a sentence:

> *Florence Nightingale brought people new ideas. Without her experience in the war, the development of hospitals and training would not have benefitted people.*

> *Florence Nightingale brought the people of the United Kingdom new ideas on medical practice. Without her experience in the Crimean war, the development of cleaner hospitals and improved training of nurses would not have benefitted such a large number of people.*

Look at the copy of the second version below. The adjectives and phrases using prepositions have been highlighted.

> *Florence Nightingale brought the people of the United Kingdom new ideas on medical practice. Without her experience in the Crimean war, the development of cleaner hospitals and improved training of nurses would not have benefited such a large number of people.*

2. What **kind** of information and detail can adjectives and prepositions add to historical writing?

    a. Why is it better to say the 'training of nurses' rather than 'training'?

    b. Why is it better to say 'the development of cleaner hospitals' rather than 'development of hospitals'?

Improving an answer

3. Now look at the next section of this response below. How could you use prepositions and adjectives to make the response more precise and detailed? Use your own ideas or look at the comments for help.

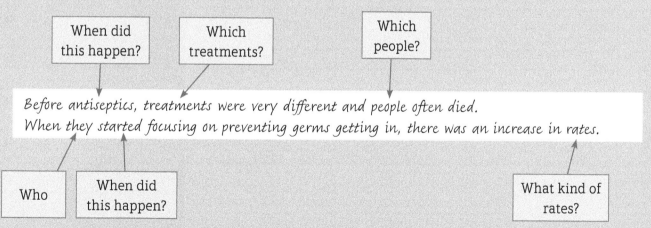

99

04 | c1900–present: Medicine in modern Britain

By 1900, people now understood that illness and disease could be caused by microbes, and scientists had begun to experiment with ways of treating and preventing diseases using what they knew.

Scientists began to investigate causes of disease that were not related to microbes.

More and more treatments used chemicals to cure diseases. Antibiotics were discovered that could treat many illnesses that previously might have been fatal. Improvements in surgery made it possible to carry out life-saving treatments, such as transplants.

The British government also increased its role in the nation's health. Free medical care was provided for everyone through the National Health Service (NHS).

However, diseases such as cancer continue to puzzle scientists, who struggle to understand their cause or develop treatments for them. Lifestyle factors such as obesity have created new challenges. The fight with disease is not yet over.

Learning outcomes

By the end of this chapter, you will:

- assess the changes in understanding the causes of illness and disease since 1900, including the impact of improved technology on diagnosis
- understand the changes in the treatment of disease
- assess the changes in medical treatment brought about by the introduction of the NHS and improvements in science and technology
- consider new approaches to the prevention of disease.
- understand how penicillin was discovered and developed.

4.1 Ideas about the cause of disease and illness

Learning outcomes

- Understand how advanced understanding of genetics and lifestyle choices affect health.
- Understand how improvements in technology have helped to improve diagnosis.

By 1900, Germ Theory had been around for nearly 40 years, and microbes* had been clearly identified as the causes of disease.

By the 20th century, doctors no longer referred to miasmata*, the Theory of the Four Humours or the supernatural when diagnosing illness. This is the first period in which doctors were working only with proven scientific discoveries.

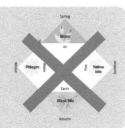

At the start of the 20th century, to diagnose a patient a doctor observed the patient and considered the symptoms. They would look in medical textbooks and diagnose* the disease based on this knowledge – but this was about to change.

During the 20th century, laboratories* were used to get a more accurate diagnosis, through medical testing:

- **Samples** of skin and blood were studied in the laboratory using microscopes.

- **Biopsies*** were used to gather samples of flesh and unusual tissue* in the body.

- **X-rays** were used to see what was going on inside the body.

Figure: Medicine at the start of the 20th century.

Advances in understanding: the influence of genetic and lifestyle factors on health

The science of genetics

In 1900, it was clear to scientists that microbes did not cause all illnesses and diseases. For example, some babies were born with conditions that appeared to have developed in the womb, where they had not been in contact with bacteria.

This fact continued to puzzle doctors for the first half of the 20th century. It was thought to be linked to the way that children inherited certain traits* from their parents and how that related to hereditary diseases*.

Key terms

Microbe*

A very small (micro) living thing (organism), e.g. bacteria or germ.

Miasmata*

Bad air. Plural form of miasma.

Diagnose*

To identify the illness or disease the patient is suffering from.

Laboratory*

A place where scientific tests are carried out.

Biopsy*

Taking a sample of human tissue.

Tissue*

Groups of specialised cells within the body.

Traits*

A person's physical and mental characteristics.

Hereditary diseases*

Diseases caused by genetic factors, meaning they can be passed on from parents to their children.

Early research into genetics

By 1900, a German scientist, called Gregor Mendel, had the idea that genes* are in pairs, and one part is inherited from each parent. These were known as the **fundamental laws of inheritance**. Unfortunately, Mendel could not prove that his laws were correct. Microscopes were not yet powerful enough to study genes.

Timeline

Early work on genetics

1902 Archibald Garrod, an English doctor, suggests that hereditary diseases are caused by missing information in the body's chemical pathways.

1941 US scientists George Beadle and Edward Tatum prove Garrod's theory.

1951 At King's College in London, Rosalind Franklin and Maurice Wilkins create images of DNA using x-rays (see Source A).

Source A

Rosalind Franklin took this x-ray photograph of DNA in 1951 whilst working alongside Maurice Wilkins.

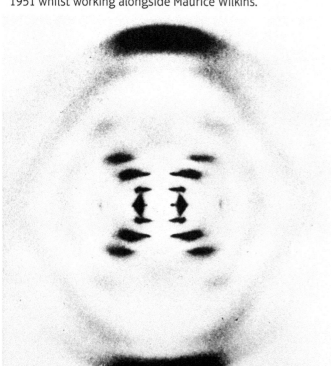

Scientists knew that children often look like their parents. By 1951, it was thought that something in human cells passed on this information (and possibly some diseases) from one person to the next. However, it was not until 1953 that technology allowed scientists to identify that this information was carried in DNA*.

Key terms

Gene*
A section of your DNA that holds information passed down from your parents.

DNA*
Short for deoxyribonucleic acid, DNA carries genetic information. DNA information decides characteristics like hair and eye colour.

Watson, Crick and the discovery of the human gene

James Watson was an American biologist. Francis Crick was an English physicist. In 1953, they were both working at Cambridge University.

Crick and Watson saw the x-rays provided by Franklin and Wilkins (see Source A). Based on these, they built their model of DNA. With further details and corrections from Franklin and Wilkins, Crick and Watson were able to solve the puzzle of the structure of DNA. They discovered that it was shaped as a double helix (see Figure 4.1).

Watson and Crick published their paper in April 1953. Now that scientists understood the shape of DNA they could begin to look at its structure and identify the parts that caused hereditary diseases.

The mapping of the human genome*

Once the structure of DNA was understood, teams of scientists began to break it apart to understand how it worked. All the information that builds a person is stored in their DNA.

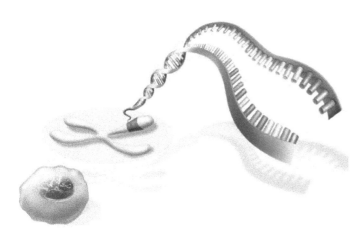

Figure 4.1 An image of the double helix structure of DNA. DNA is stored in every human cell.

Being able to create images of this information – mapping the DNA's code – helped scientists understand the cause of genetic diseases, such as haemophilia*.

The Human Genome Project was launched in 1990. For ten years, 18 teams of scientists all over the world worked together to map the human genome.

Once the human genome was mapped, scientists were able to use this map to look for mistakes in the DNA of people suffering from hereditary diseases.

For example, scientists have now identified a gene that is sometimes present in women who have breast cancer. They cannot use this knowledge to **treat** breast cancer, but women can now help to **prevent** this disease by finding out their risk of developing it, and then having a mastectomy*. A famous example of this is the actress Angelina Jolie, who had herself tested for the gene because her mother had died of breast cancer.

Key terms

Genome*

The complete set of DNA containing all the information needed to build a particular organism. In humans, this is more than three billion DNA pairs. It is unique for every human being, except identical twins.

Haemophilia*

A genetic disease passed from parent to child that stops blood clotting. People with haemophilia must be careful, as an open wound will not heal correctly.

Mastectomy*

Surgery where a person has one or both of their breasts removed.

Source B

In this 2013 news article, Angelina Jolie explains why she chose to have a mastectomy.

Angelina Jolie bravely reveals she has had a preventive double mastectomy after tests showed an 87% chance of contracting [getting] breast cancer.

The Hollywood actress is healthy and made the decision to undergo the procedure after discovering she carries the BRCA1 cancer gene.

Angelina said: 'My doctors estimated that I had an 87% risk of breast cancer and a 50% risk of ovarian cancer. I made a decision to have a preventive double mastectomy.'

The surgery was successful and doctors believe Angelina's chances of developing breast cancer have reduced to less than 5%.

Factors helping the development of genetics

Technology

Discovering the shape of DNA, understanding how it works and then mapping the individual genes has been made possible through improvements in technology.

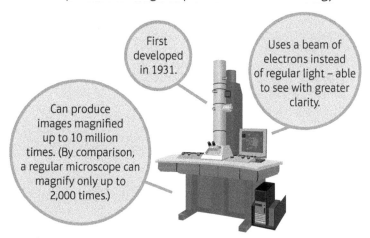

First developed in 1931.

Uses a beam of electrons instead of regular light – able to see with greater clarity.

Can produce images magnified up to 10 million times. (By comparison, a regular microscope can magnify only up to 2,000 times.)

Figure: An electron microscope

Science

Understanding DNA required scientists to work together. The Human Genome Project was an example of this, with thousands of scientists from all over the world working together to solve the same puzzle. All the data produced was made public, so that it could benefit as many people as possible.

The impact of the science of genetics

Understanding how each part of the genome affects the body has helped scientists to identify what causes genetic disorders*, such as Huntington's disease and Down's Syndrome. These disorders are caused by mistakes in the genome: if the mistakes can be corrected by scientists, this could possibly lead to a treatment.

A good understanding of genetics has helped doctors to know more about what causes diseases and illnesses, but this has **not yet led to treatments**.

Key term

Disorder*

A medical problem not necessarily caused by bacteria.

Diabetes*

When the body struggles to control the amount of sugar in the blood.

Activities ?

1 Create a chain of paper people. Each person should be a different figure who was important in the discovery of DNA. How many people can you make in your chain?

2 Two factors have influenced our understanding of genetics – science and technology. Describe how each has made a difference.

Lifestyle and health

During the 20th century, we gained a better understanding of the impact of lifestyle choices on the body and how these are linked with diseases and illnesses.

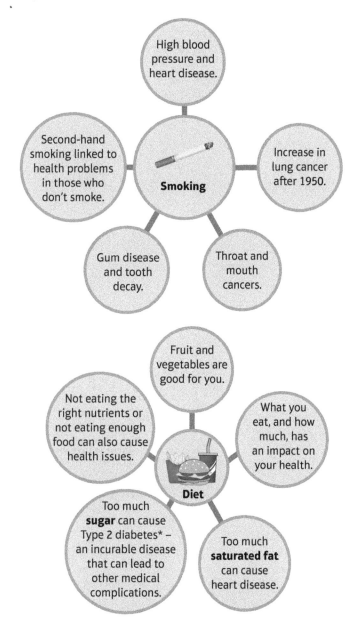

High blood pressure and heart disease.

Second-hand smoking linked to health problems in those who don't smoke.

Increase in lung cancer after 1950.

Smoking

Gum disease and tooth decay.

Throat and mouth cancers.

Fruit and vegetables are good for you.

Not eating the right nutrients or not eating enough food can also cause health issues.

What you eat, and how much, has an impact on your health.

Diet

Too much **sugar** can cause Type 2 diabetes* – an incurable disease that can lead to other medical complications.

Too much **saturated fat** can cause heart disease.

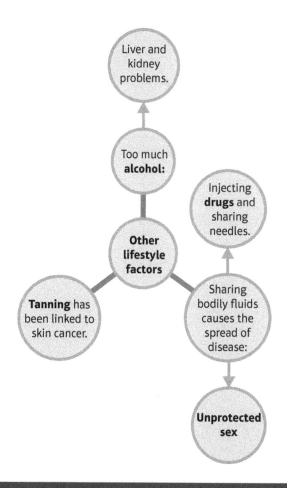

The impact of technology

The enormous leap forward in technology since 1900 has made diagnosing disease much more accurate. As a result, doctors are better able to treat patients as they know exactly what they are fighting.

New methods of diagnosing disease are being developed all the time.

Source C

This article was published on the *Medical News Today* website in November 2015. It describes the use of a special type of dressing to help diagnose infection in burn patients.

Infections are the primary cause of complications in burn injuries, especially in children. Even a relatively mild hot water scald can readily become infected. Many deaths from burn injuries are due to sepsis [blood poisoning].

... Researchers at the University of Bath, in conjunction [together] with the Healing Foundation Children's Burns Research Centre and the University of Brighton, have created a ground breaking solution to diagnosing wound infection. The team has developed a prototype dressing that changes colour when a wound becomes infected. The wound dressing on an uninfected area displays a discrete circular design. Within four hours of an infection, the colour and pattern change.

Activities ?

1 Create flashcards to show different lifestyle factors and the diseases that they may cause. Write the factor on one side and the associated illnesses on the other.

2 Select one lifestyle choice and write an advice leaflet to explain the threats to health.

3 Discuss with a partner how your leaflet is different from a leaflet that might have been made for people in the 15th century.

Exam-style question, Section B

Explain **one** way in which understanding of the causes of disease and illness was different in c1750 from the present day. **4 marks**

Exam tip

It is important to make sure you clearly identify the *change* in this question. Think about your knowledge of 'understanding about the cause of disease' in c1750 (from Chapter 3) and in the present day (from this chapter). Identify at least one difference to describe.

Improvements in diagnosis: the impact of the availability of blood tests, scans and monitors

New methods of diagnosis

The development of machines and computers allow doctors to understand a patient's symptoms better than in any previous time. For example, x-rays and CT scans (see Figure 4.2) allow doctors to see inside the body without opening it up.

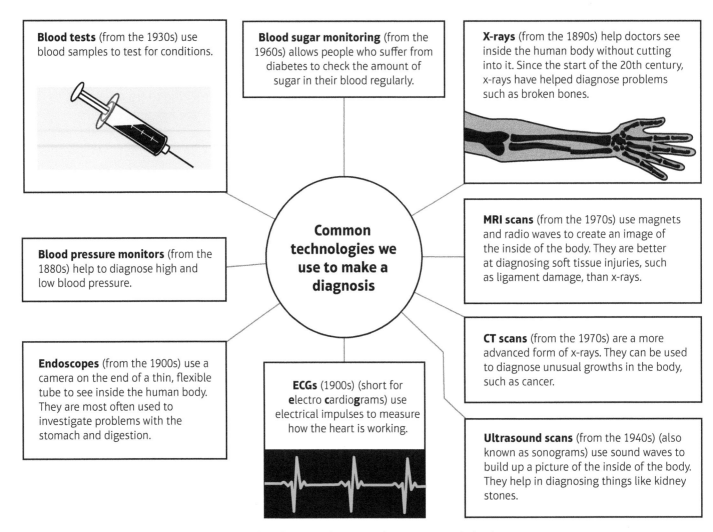

Blood tests (from the 1930s) use blood samples to test for conditions.

Blood sugar monitoring (from the 1960s) allows people who suffer from diabetes to check the amount of sugar in their blood regularly.

X-rays (from the 1890s) help doctors see inside the human body without cutting into it. Since the start of the 20th century, x-rays have helped diagnose problems such as broken bones.

Common technologies we use to make a diagnosis

Blood pressure monitors (from the 1880s) help to diagnose high and low blood pressure.

MRI scans (from the 1970s) use magnets and radio waves to create an image of the inside of the body. They are better at diagnosing soft tissue injuries, such as ligament damage, than x-rays.

Endoscopes (from the 1900s) use a camera on the end of a thin, flexible tube to see inside the human body. They are most often used to investigate problems with the stomach and digestion.

ECGs (1900s) (short for **e**lectro **c**ardio**g**rams) use electrical impulses to measure how the heart is working.

CT scans (from the 1970s) are a more advanced form of x-rays. They can be used to diagnose unusual growths in the body, such as cancer.

Ultrasound scans (from the 1940s) (also known as sonograms) use sound waves to build up a picture of the inside of the body. They help in diagnosing things like kidney stones.

Figure 4.2 Common technologies developed in the period 1900 to the present, to help diagnosis.

Summary

- After 1900, understanding about the causes of disease and illness progressed rapidly.
- By the end of the 20th century, doctors recognised that many factors caused disease.
- The structure of the gene was discovered by Watson and Crick in 1953 and the human genome was mapped by 2000.
- Lifestyle factors such as smoking, a poor diet and drinking alcohol can all contribute to illness and disease.
- New technology has enabled doctors to carry out more detailed diagnoses of their patients.

Checkpoint

Strengthen

S1 Give one example of how the mapping of the human genome helped doctors to better understand the causes of disease and illness.

S2 Describe two ways that technology has led to a better understanding of the causes of disease and illness.

Challenge

C1 Describe five pieces of technology that have had an impact on diagnosing the causes of illness and disease.

If you are struggling, discuss the answers to these questions in groups. Your teacher can give you some hints.

4.2 Approaches to prevention and treatment

- Understand the impact of the development of magic bullets, including antibiotics.
- Understand the impact of the NHS on public health.
- Understand how the government tried to prevent certain diseases.

Medical treatments

The first chemical cures: magic bullets

The term 'magic bullet' was used to describe a chemical cure that would **attack the microbes in the body causing disease**, whilst **leaving the body unharmed**.

In the late 19th century, more microbes responsible for specific diseases were being discovered. This meant that scientists could search for substances to attack and destroy these microbes.

Doctors now understood that the body produces antibodies* to fight diseases. The hunt was on for artificial or chemical treatments that would work in the same way, attacking the infection without harming the body.

The first big breakthrough was made in the treatment of syphilis*. There had been some success with arsenic compounds*. However, it was very difficult to find a form of arsenic that attacked the disease and not the body, as arsenic is poisonous.

Key terms

Antibodies*

Proteins created by your immune system to fight a specific bacteria.

Syphilis*

A sexually transmitted infection.

Compound*

A mixture of two or more different elements.

Immune system*

The body's built-in defence against infections.

 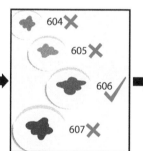 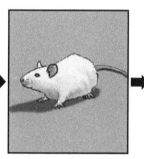  

In the early 20th century, a scientist named Paul Ehrlich tested as many arsenic compounds as he could, to find a cure for syphilis. By 1907, he had tested over 600 compounds, but had not found a cure.	In 1909, a Japanese scientist named Sahachiro Hata retested all of the compounds and found that compound number 606 cured syphilis. The drug, named **Salvarsan 606**, was the first 'magic bullet'.	In 1932, scientist Gerhard Domagk discovered that a bright red dye called **Prontosil** killed bacterial infections in mice. Domagk tested Prontosil on his own daughter, who had developed blood poisoning: it cured her.	Scientists at the Pasteur Institute in Paris discovered that Prontosil worked by preventing the bacteria from multiplying. This made it possible for the body's own immune system* to kill the bacteria. These drugs are called antibiotics.	Scientists began to look for other drugs that worked in the same way. In 1938, British scientists developed **M&B 693**. This was another antibiotic. It was successfully used to treat Winston Churchill for an infection during the Second World War.

Figure 4.3 The discovery of the first magic bullets: Salvarsan, Prontosil and M&B 693.

The development of antibiotics

The term **antibiotic** is used to describe any treatment that destroys or limits the growth of bacteria in the human body. The first true antibiotic was **penicillin**.

The creation of penicillin

In 1928, Alexander Fleming discovered a microorganism in a mould sample that killed bacteria. He named it penicillin (see pages 119–21). Penicillin was different to Salvarsan 606 and Prontosil as it was created using microorganisms, not chemicals.

↓

More moulds!

- Inspired by penicillin, other scientists started to study different moulds in the hope of finding more antibiotics.
- In 1943, an antibiotic was discovered that was so strong it could cure tuberculosis* (which was thought to be incurable).
- Through the 1950s and 60s many more antibiotics were discovered.

↓

And more…?

The search for new antibiotics has not stopped. One reason for this is that some bacteria have developed **resistance** to the antibiotics we already have. If new treatments are not developed, scientists fear that the old antibiotics will stop working on diseases we can currently cure.

The impact of science and technology on advances in medicines

As with diagnosis, the way that we treat diseases now is very different from the way that people treated them before 1900. This is mainly due to huge **advances in science and technology**.

Scientists have now developed medicines that treat specific diseases. Even if they are unable to cure some diseases, such as diabetes and lung cancer, treatments help patients live longer, more normal lives. Scientists are now able to identify the causes of disease

---

Key terms

Tuberculosis*

A disease that attacks the lungs. Also known as TB.

Source A

This article, entitled 'Too much of a good thing', was published in *The Telegraph* in 2013, by Joe Shute.

```
Antibiotics are no longer effective. The
drugs that have transformed life and
longevity [living longer] and saved countless
millions since penicillin was discovered by
Sir Alexander Fleming in 1928 now saturate
[fill] every corner of our environment. We
stuff them into ourselves and our animals;
we spray them on crops, dump them in rivers,
and even — as emerged at a meeting of science
ministers from the G8 last year - paint them
on the hulls of boats to keep off barnacles
[type of shellfish].

As a result, an invisible army of super-
resistant bacteria has evolved, one that is
increasingly claiming lives — currently more
than 25,000 a year in Europe alone...

Many leading scientists and doctors and
politicians are freely adopting the language
of global catastrophe. Infections such as
tuberculosis and septicaemia - the scourge of
earlier centuries - are once again killing
us at frightening rates. We have used, or are
using, our so-called drugs of last resort.
```

in most cases – for example, a microbe, a tumour* or an unusual gene. This information helps them to know what type of treatment to try.

Improved scientific understanding has also led to better testing of new treatments before they are given to patients. In the past, drugs were not thoroughly tested before being used to treat disease. This meant that mistakes were made.

Now, it takes several years for a new drug to be tested and approved. This slows down progress but makes sure drugs are safe for everybody.

Key term

Tumour*

A growth made up of abnormal cells.

THINKING HISTORICALLY — Change and continuity (4b&c)

The bird's eye view

Development	Example of immediate changes	Example of change in the medium term	Example of change in the long term
The development of antibiotics		Scientists developed a way of making antibiotics, which meant they could be modified to attack particular diseases.	Antibiotics are still used widely to treat diseases and infections. However, an increasing number of diseases are resistant to them.

Imagine you are looking at the whole of history using a zoomed-out interactive map like Google Maps™. The table above gives a general view of the long-term changes caused by antibiotics, but you cannot see much detail. If you zoom in to the time when antibiotics were first developed, you can see the event in detail but you can no longer see its consequences in the medium or long term.

Look at the table above:

1   Discuss with a partner what detail you might expect to see in the 'immediate changes' column.

2   Look at the medium-term changes and the long-term changes. How are they similar? How are they different?

3   Write a brief explanation of how the time scale you are looking at affects how important a change might seem.

New technology has made it easier to create drugs to treat diseases.

- **Mass production* of pills** has made the distribution of drugs much easier.
- **The development of capsules***, which dissolve in the stomach to release the drug, means taking drugs to treat disease is easier.
- **Hypodermic needles*** allow the precise dose to be introduced directly into the bloodstream.
- **Insulin* pumps** for people suffering from diabetes: these pumps deliver insulin to the blood without the need for injections.

Key terms

Mass production*

To make a lot of something in a short time.

Capsule*

A small container for a drug that can be swallowed.

Hypodermic needle*

A needle that can inject a medicine under the skin.

Insulin*

A substance that helps control the level of sugar in the blood.

Activities

1   Draw a timeline to show when the different drugs described in this section were developed. Try to select at least four different drugs. Label each one with details, such as who was responsible for its development and which diseases the drug fights.

2   Describe two ways that science and three ways that technology assisted in the development of new treatments.

Medical care: impact of the NHS

Phase one: Improved access to care

The National Health Service (NHS) was launched in 1948 by the British government. Its aim was to provide medical care for everybody in Britain. It was paid for by National Insurance contributions, which are like a tax.

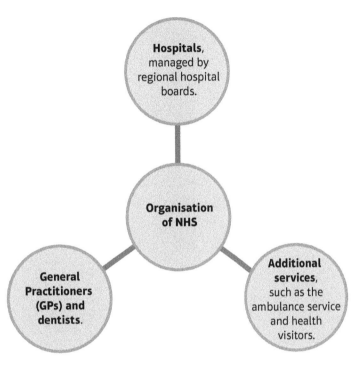

Figure 4.4 The three parts of the NHS in 1948.

The government aimed to provide the same level of service for everybody in the country, no matter how rich or poor they were.

Poor working men had already been entitled to free medical care since 1911. The NHS ensured that women, children and the unemployed also had access to medical care.

To begin with, hospitals changed little due to the NHS. Having just fought the Second World War, Britain did not have much money to spend on medical care. Many hospitals had been built in the 19th century and needed updating.

Many GP* surgeries were in need of updating, and GPs also needed training in new methods. GPs had even less time for training due to the NHS, because more and more people began visiting GPs.

Therefore, **access had improved** because the NHS was available to all. However, the **standard of care had not improved** in the short term. During the 1960s, the government made changes to improve the NHS. This led to improvements in the standard of care.

Phase two: High-tech medical and surgical treatments in hospitals

Hospital treatments have changed a lot since 1900. Treatments that we think of as routine today, like hip replacements and blood transfusions*, did not exist before 1900. Once the three major problems of surgery – **pain, infection** and **blood loss** – had been solved, doctors were able to carry out longer, more complicated surgeries. The development of new machinery to treat the body and even to replace body parts, also improved treatment in hospitals.

There are hundreds of examples of new high-tech medical and surgical treatments being carried out. The table opposite shows a few of the most famous examples.

Key terms

GP*

This stands for General Practitioner. A GP doctor provides care for people locally rather than in a hospital.

Blood transfusions*

Where donated blood is passed into a person.

	New technology	Treatment made possible
Medical treatments	Advanced x-rays	Doctors can now use x-rays to target and shrink tumours growing inside the body, using a treatment known as **radiotherapy**. This helps to treat cancers.
	Smaller, cheaper machines	Processes like **dialysis**, where the blood of patients with kidney failure is 'washed' by a machine, have become more widely available as machines have become smaller and more portable.
	Robotics	Better **prosthetic limbs*** are now produced. This is partly in response to the number of soldiers surviving bomb attacks in recent wars.
Surgical treatments	Microsurgery	The first successful kidney transplant was performed in the USA in 1956. This led to transplants of other organs, including lungs (from 1963), and livers and hearts (from 1967). These were made possible by improved surgical techniques, such as microsurgery which can reattach tiny nerve endings and blood vessels.
	Keyhole surgery	Surgeons use tiny cameras and narrow surgical instruments to operate inside the body through tiny holes made in the patient. This allows for quicker healing and less trauma* to the body.
	Robotic surgery	Surgeons use computers to control instruments inside the body, allowing for more exact surgery with smaller cuts.

Key terms

Prosthetic limbs*

Artificial arms, legs, hands or feet.

Trauma*

Serious damage.

Extend your knowledge

3D printers

At the cutting edge of medical research, scientists are trying to develop a way of creating new body parts using 3D printers. However, this is still years away from being a usable treatment.

Interpretation 1

In this interpretation, taken from *Health and Medicine in Britain since 1860* by Anne Hardy (2001), the author challenges the short-term impact of the NHS.

The implementation of the NHS by no means resolved the problem of delivering adequate health care to Britain's people, although it did offer a considerable improvement over the combination of private and insurance medicine that had preceded it. The medical services offered under the 1948 Act were pre-eminently [mainly] providers of treatment for existing illness rather than agents [helpers] for preventing its development.

Interpretation 2

Former Labour Prime Minister Tony Blair wrote this at the start of a document about the modernisation of the NHS. It was published in 1997.

Creating the NHS was the greatest act of modernisation ever achieved by a Labour Government. It banished the fear of becoming ill that had for years blighted [made worse] the lives of millions of people.

The extent of change in care and treatment

Treatment

In 1900, 25% of deaths were caused by infectious diseases. By 1990, that number had fallen to less than 1%.

In c1900, most people were still taking herbal remedies bought from the chemist to treat their illnesses. Now, due to advances in science after 1900, there are a wide variety of specific, effective medicines which treat particular diseases.

However, scientists continue to face problems when developing treatments.

New diseases keep appearing that do not respond to any chemical treatments we currently know.

Microbes are living organisms. They have evolved* to resist some of the cures doctors have been using. These are sometimes called 'super bugs' e.g., MRSA*.

It is very difficult to develop a vaccine against some viruses*. For example, scientists have to find a new vaccine for the flu virus every year.

Lifestyle factors have caused an increase in illnesses such as heart disease and cancer. There are no certain cures for these illnesses.

We may not be facing the same problems as our ancestors when researching treatments for illness and disease, but we face many new ones. Therefore, remedies such as herbal medicines, acupuncture and homeopathy are still popular treatments for disease.

Key terms

Evolved*

Changed over time in order to be able to survive.

MRSA*

A drug-resistant bacteria that is particularly hardy and resistant to antibiotics.

Virus*

A very small microbe that gets inside cells and causes disease.

Improved access to care

In c1900, most sick people were still cared for in the home by women. Doctors had to be paid and so were only used for serious illnesses.

The situation improved slowly during the first half of the 20th century. In 1919, the government set up the Ministry of Health to oversee health care across the country.

There was rapid improvement in the availability of care outside the home from 1948 onwards. The NHS made medical care and treatment free and available to all.

However, the NHS made it clear that hospitals were just for treating the sick. Previously, hospitals had been places for the elderly to rest, and sometimes spend their last months or even years. This was no longer possible.

Exam-style question, Section B

'Treatment of diseases and care of the sick completely changed after c1800.'

How far do you agree with this statement?

You may use the following information in your answer:

- magic bullets
- the NHS.

You **must** also use information of your own.   **16 marks**

Exam tip

Focus on the word 'completely' in this question. Nobody would argue that treatment and care has stayed the same since c1800, so in your answer you should focus on whether it is very different or whether there are some things that are similar to previous centuries.

Activity

Copy and complete the table below to show the change and continuity in care and treatment from earlier periods to the end of the 20th century. Try to include at least one thing in each box.

	Continuity	Change
Treatment		
Care		

Preventing disease

By c1900, many different measures to prevent disease were in place. The government now took responsibility for providing clean water and removing waste.

There are two reasons for the government taking action to improve public health in the 20th and 21st century.

1 Increased understanding of cause

Now that we understand what causes disease, the government recognises that its involvement can make a difference.

2 Proven methods of prevention

Once the causes of disease were understood, proven methods of prevention could be introduced. These have included:

- **compulsory vaccinations:** inspired by the positive impact of the smallpox vaccination, other campaigns* were launched in the 20th century.
- **passing laws to provide a healthy environment:** these include the Clean Air Acts (see page 114).
- **communicating health risks:** lifestyle campaigns encourage people to tackle health risks for themselves.

Charities also contribute to healthy lifestyle campaigns. For example, the British Heart Foundation creates adverts encouraging people to protect their heart by giving up smoking, eating less fat and exercising.

New approaches to prevention: mass vaccinations

Source B

This poster advertising diphtheria immunisation was published in 1943, one year after the national campaign was launched.

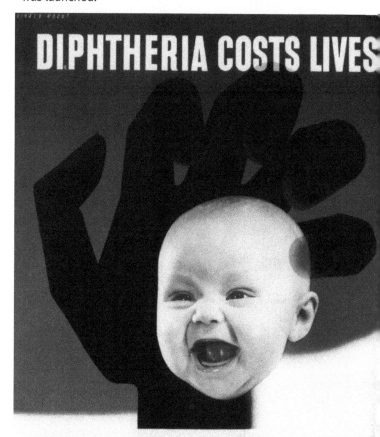

DIPHTHERIA COSTS LIVES

IMMUNISATION COSTS NOTHING

Timeline

Government introduction of vaccinations

1942 Diphtheria

1950 Poliomyelitis and whooping cough

1961 Tetanus

1968 Measles

1970 Rubella

Key term

Campaign*

Organised activities with a specific purpose.

The national vaccination campaign against diphtheria was launched in 1942 – the first of its kind. Before this, around 3,000 children were still dying each year of diphtheria.

The national campaign vaccinated all children, so the number of cases of diphtheria declined rapidly. By the middle of the century, diphtheria was seen as a disease of the past.

Another significant vaccination campaign was against poliomyelitis (polio). Polio is a very contagious* disease that causes paralysis*. In the early 1950s, there were 8,000 cases every year in Britain. The vaccination was introduced to the UK in 1956, followed by a more effective vaccination in 1962. The number of infections dropped rapidly. The last case of a person contracting polio in the UK was in 1984.

Other vaccines target diseases that can lead to other diseases. The HPV vaccine, for example, protects women against an infection that has been linked to cervical cancer.

However, some people fear that vaccines are unsafe. While vaccination prevents the spread of dangerous diseases, individuals can still choose not to get vaccinated.

New approaches to prevention: government legislation

The government has passed laws to provide a healthy environment. Examples of these are the Clean Air Acts of 1956 and 1968. These were passed in response to terrible smog* in London in 1952. At a time when everybody burned coal to heat their homes, there was a great deal of smoke and soot in the air, particularly in London.

Smog is no longer a significant problem in the UK. However, the government continues to pass laws to protect people from air pollution, for example by limiting car emissions*.

The government also passed a law making it illegal to smoke in all indoor workplaces, as part of the Health Act of 2006.

Key terms

Contagious*
A disease that can be passed from one person to another easily.

Paralysis*
Not being able to move.

Smog*
Very heavy fog caused by air pollution.

Emissions*
The gases that come out of a car exhaust.

Source C

Lavinia Hand was born in London in 1924. During the Great Smog she lived with her husband, George, and their two-year-old son Peter. Here she remembers what conditions were like.

It was really a very terrible fog. Everybody had coal or wood fires at that time so there was a lot of soot in the air, but it was traffic pollution as well. The air was so dangerous that thousands of people died. We lived in Wood Green and George worked in Finchley. He wore a mask but the smog made our eyes sting as well and the mask didn't help with that. I wouldn't take Peter out in it.

Source D

A picture of a London policeman wearing a facemask in the last London smog, in 1962. Masks were sold to help people avoid the effects of breathing in the pollution.

New approaches to prevention: government lifestyle campaigns

The government also aims to help people prevent disease themselves, by promoting healthier lifestyles. Some examples of their work include:

- advertising campaigns warning against dangers to health, such as smoking, drinking, recreational* drug use and unprotected sex
- events such as Stoptober, which encourage people to stop smoking for a month
- encouraging people to eat more healthily and get more exercise, such as the Change4Life campaign (see Source E).

Source E

A poster published by Change4Life in 2015. Change4Life is a Public Health England campaign designed to help families eat well and move more.

Key term
Recreational*
Done for enjoyment.

Exam-style question, Section B

Explain why there was rapid progress in disease prevention after c1900.

You may use the following in your answer:

- government intervention
- vaccinations.

You **must** also use information of your own. **12 marks**

Exam tip

Remember that your knowledge needs to **support** your arguments – avoid simply describing disease prevention. For example, show how vaccinations led to progress in disease prevention by explaining how many people died of particular illnesses before and after the vaccinations were introduced.

THINKING HISTORICALLY — Cause and Consequence (2a)

The web of multiple causes

Why were doctors able to treat more diseases in the 20th century?

Study these causes that would help historians to explain why doctors were able to treat diseases successfully in the 20th century.

Fleming and other scientists developed penicillin, which led to the discovery of other antibiotics.	Technology such as x-rays made it easier for doctors to identify the specific causes of disease.	Everybody now understood and accepted that many diseases were caused by microbes.
Scientists identified the microbes that caused different diseases.	Chemical cures, such as 'magic bullets', had been developed.	The NHS provided medical care that was free and available to all.

Work in pairs. Take an A3 sheet of paper. You will need to use all of this.

1   Write the six causes on the paper, placed as shown here.

2   How did the fact that scientists were able to identify different microbes lead to the development of chemical cures? Draw a line between these two causes and complete the sentence 'Once scientists had identified a microbe that causes a disease they could start to develop a cure because…'

3   Select another two causes (different from those you have just connected). Draw an arrow between them. Try to describe a way they could be connected. Use your knowledge from this chapter to make as many links on the diagram as possible.

```
1          2          3



4          5          6
```

Summary

- Penicillin was discovered and then developed into a usable treatment for a wide variety of diseases.
- New technology helped to improve the way that medicines were given to patients.
- The government established the NHS in 1948. This made free medical care available to everybody.
- High-tech treatments, such as organ transplants and radiotherapy, helped doctors tackle diseases.
- Government sponsored campaigns encouraged people to lead healthier lives in order to prevent disease.

Checkpoint

Strengthen

S1 Choose one piece of new technology and explain how it has helped to treat disease.

S2 Give one positive and one negative impact of the NHS on the health of the nation.

S3 List three methods of preventing disease that have appeared since c1900.

Challenge

C1 Which factor do you think has had the biggest impact on treatment and prevention since 1900: government, science or technology? Select one example from this chapter to support your answer.

Before writing your answer to question C1, you might find it useful to create a mind map listing your examples.

4.3 Fleming, Florey and Chain's development of penicillin

The development of penicillin into a usable drug has dramatically changed the way we treat infections. It has saved many lives.

Timeline
The development of penicillin

1928 Fleming identifies penicillin in his lab.

1929 Fleming publishes his findings.

1939 Florey and Chain study Fleming's research.

1940 Florey and Chain successfully treat mice with penicillin.

1941 Florey and Chain trial penicillin on a human, with some success.

1942 US pharmaceutical companies begin mass producing penicillin.

1945 Dorothy Crowfoot Hodgkin, a scientist at Oxford University, identifies the chemical structure of penicillin.

1957 Chemist John C. Sheehan creates a chemical copy of penicillin. This allows the drug to be changed in order to target different diseases.

Alexander Fleming and the discovery of penicillin

Name: Alexander Fleming

Job: Doctor with a specific interest in bacteriology*

Nationality: British

Period of work: 1910s and 1920s

Work:

- One of the first doctors to use 'magic bullets'.
- During the First World War he had treated wounded soldiers.
- In the 1920s he decided to research the bacteria that caused infections in wounds – staphylococcus infection.

Big idea: After returning from a trip during his studies he noticed that a mould had grown on his dirty petri dishes. They still had the bacteria he had been studying on them, but on closer inspection he noticed there was a ring around the mould with no bacteria. Fleming believed the mould had produced a substance that had killed off the harmful bacteria and tested this further. He called his discovery 'penicillin'.

Limitations: Fleming did not believe the mould would kill bacteria in living humans, so he did not bother with any further testing.

Key term

Bacteriology*

The study of bacteria.

Source A

A photograph of a plaque on the wall of St Mary's Hospital in Paddington, London, commemorating Fleming's achievement.

Source B

A photograph of Alexander Fleming studying mould in his laboratory at the Wright Fleming Institute in London.

Source C

In 1945, Alexander Fleming was awarded the Nobel Prize in Medicine for his discovery of penicillin. He shared this with Howard Florey and Ernst Chain. In this extract from his acceptance speech, Alexander Fleming describes the process of discovering the antibiotic.

In 1928 an accidental contamination [making impure] of a culture plate [a dish in which bacteria are grown] by a mould set me off on another track. I was working on a subject having no relation to moulds or antiseptics [substances that kill germs] and if I had been a member of a team engaged on this subject it is likely that I would have had to neglect the accidental happening and work for the team with the result that penicillin would not then have been described and I would not be here today as a Nobel Laureate [someone who wins a Nobel Prize]...

... I isolated the contaminating mould. It made an antibacterial substance which I christened penicillin. I studied it as far as I could as a bacteriologist. I had a clue that here was something good but I could not possibly know how good it was and I had not the team, especially the chemical team, necessary to concentrate and stabilise the penicillin.

Florey and Chain and the development of penicillin

Howard Florey was an Australian pathologist working at Oxford medical school. His colleague, Ernst Chain, had escaped Nazi Germany, where he had been a biochemist*.

1 Scientists Florey and Chain were researching antibiotics when they came across Fleming's work. They decided to test the mould further.

2 In 1940 they tested their penicillin on infected mice. It seemed to work but they didn't have enough of the drug to completely cure them.

3 They would need a lot more mould for human tests. They started to experiment with different growing containers – milk churns, bed pans and even a bath tub!

4 In 1941 they had the opportunity to try their penicillin on a human – a policeman who had developed blood poisoning from a scratch.

5 When given penicillin, the policeman started to get better. But the drug ran out. He became worse, and eventually died.

6 Despite this first failure, Florey and Chain had proved that penicillin could be used to treat and possibly cure infections in humans.

Interpretation 1

There is some controversy over who should get the credit for the development of penicillin. In this study of the role of science in science education, published in 1996, Patricia Harding sets out an alternative point of view.

Fleming did not develop penicillin. He found it in 1928, extracted it from a culture of [the mould] *Penicillium*, and worked on it for a short time. By 1931 he had abandoned it as an antiseptic for medical use and used it only as an ingredient in culture medium to selectively grow certain organisms. Penicillin was developed therapeutically* in 1940 by a group of scientists at Oxford under the leadership of Howard Florey. However, when penicillin made such an impact on the world, Fleming managed to get the credit, and the group at Oxford were ignored by the public. Early accounts propagated [spread] the 'myth' of the development of penicillin, but several scientists who knew what had happened later told the real story.

THINKING HISTORICALLY Change and continuity (4a)

Significance

Look at Source C on page 118 and Interpretation 1 above.

1 Identify one reason why Fleming thinks he was significant in the discovery of penicillin.

2 Historian Patricia Harding thinks Fleming's role was much less significant. Identify one reason she gives to support the idea he was not that significant.

3 Think about whose opinion is being shown in each of these sources. Why do you think these views are so different?

Key terms

Biochemist*
A scientist who specialises in chemistry, which has a role in the study of living things.

Therapeutically*
Treating someone with a drug.

Mass production of penicillin

Florey and Chain proved that penicillin could treat infections, but they were still struggling to make large amounts of it. They needed a large-scale factory where the penicillin could be grown and extracted on a large scale.

Florey first approached British pharmaceutical companies* for help, but they were too busy making other chemicals for fighting the Second World War.

However, the USA had not yet joined the war. In July 1941, Florey visited the USA and convinced pharmaceutical companies to begin penicillin production. The companies started growing the mould in beer vats. It was a very slow process – after a year, they only had enough penicillin to treat ten people.

However, the effectiveness of penicillin could now be shown. The US government funded 21 pharmaceutical companies to begin mass production. British pharmaceutical companies also started to mass produce the drug in 1943. By D-Day*, in June 1944, there was enough penicillin available to treat all Allied casualties.

Key terms

Pharmaceutical companies*

Companies which produce and sell medicines.

Staphylococcus*

A bacteria that causes infections in wounds.

D-Day*

The invasion of northern France by British, American and other Allied troops in order to defeat Nazi Germany.

Factors enabling the development of penicillin

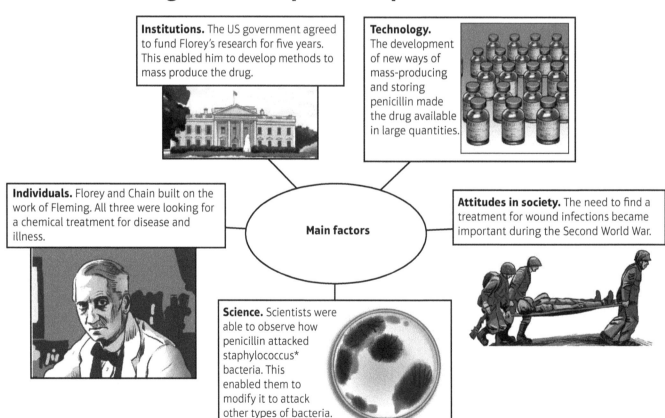

Institutions. The US government agreed to fund Florey's research for five years. This enabled him to develop methods to mass produce the drug.

Technology. The development of new ways of mass-producing and storing penicillin made the drug available in large quantities.

Individuals. Florey and Chain built on the work of Fleming. All three were looking for a chemical treatment for disease and illness.

Main factors

Attitudes in society. The need to find a treatment for wound infections became important during the Second World War.

Science. Scientists were able to observe how penicillin attacked staphylococcus* bacteria. This enabled them to modify it to attack other types of bacteria.

Figure 4.5 The main factors that enabled the development of penicillin.

Use of penicillin

Penicillin is effective in treating diseases caused by one family of bacteria. It is also used to **prevent** infection, particularly with patients who have had teeth taken out.

The development of penicillin encouraged scientists to look for other moulds that could be used to fight infections. An example is streptomycin, which was the first drug found to be effective against tuberculosis (see page 108). Once Dorothy Hodgkin had mapped the chemical structure of penicillin (see the timeline on page 117), scientists were able to work on other versions to treat other diseases.

Now that doctors could offer treatments that worked against a wide range of illnesses, confidence in medical treatments began to rise. Patients were more willing to seek out medical treatments from doctors.

Unfortunately, as explained on page 112, some bacteria are now resistant to penicillin. Bacteria can mutate, or change, to resist attack from penicillin. The first penicillin-resistant strain of bacteria appeared in 1942.

Pharmaceutical companies continue to work hard to develop new antibiotics.

Summary

- Alexander Fleming discovered penicillin by accident in 1928. His research went unnoticed until 1938, when it was developed by Howard Florey and Ernst Chain.
- Florey and Chain were able to create a usable drug from the mould, which they tested on mice and then a human being. However, it was very difficult to mass produce.
- When the Second World War broke out, Florey was able to get money from the US government to mass produce the drug.
- Penicillin is effective against a wide range of illnesses.

Checkpoint

Strengthen

S1 Describe how Fleming discovered penicillin.

S2 How did Florey and Chain test penicillin when they isolated it?

S3 Describe how penicillin has been used since the Second World War.

Challenge

C1 With a partner, discuss the roles played by Fleming, Florey and Chain in the discovery and development of penicillin. Was it the right decision to award them the Nobel Prize jointly?

You could also discuss the answer to C1 in groups. Your teacher can give you some hints.

4.4 The fight against lung cancer in the 21st century

Lung cancer is the second most common cancer in the UK. It mainly affects people over the age of 40.

Most lung cancers are caused by external* factors. Around 85% of people with lung cancer smoke, or have smoked. However, some people develop lung cancer for no clear reason.

There were very few cases of lung cancer discovered in the 19th century. However, by 1918, that had increased to 10% of all cancers, and by 1927 it was more than 14%. There had been a large rise in the number of smokers after the First World War.

A study in 1950 proved the link between lung cancer and smoking. In spite of the results of the study, deaths from lung cancer continued to rise until the 1970s.

The use of science and technology in diagnosis

Lung cancer is hard to treat because usually, by the time the cancer is found, it is already very advanced*. Patients often mistake their symptoms for other diseases. People are not routinely tested for lung cancer because the tests are not accurate, and have some negative effects (for example, exposure to radiation* during an x-ray scan can be harmful). Diagnosis is difficult, but technology has led to improvements in this area.

Key terms

External*
Things happening outside the body.

Advanced*
When a disease has been developing in the body for a long time or has developed very quickly.

Radiation*
A type of energy that can damage the body's cells if a person is exposed to it too much.

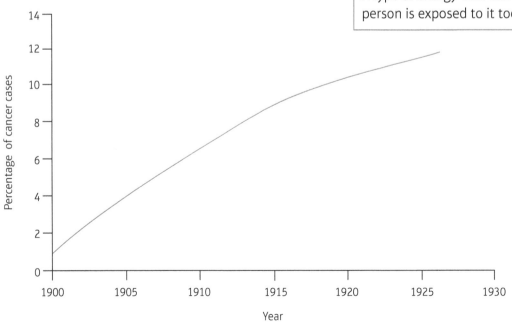

Figure 4.6 A graph showing the increase in lung cancer cases between 1900 and 1926.

Diagnosing lung cancer

Before more advanced technology had been discovered, lung cancer was diagnosed using an x-ray machine. A doctor would examine the x-ray to look for a tumour*.

This way of diagnosing was not ideal. Often other things, like lung abscesses*, might be mistaken for cancer – or, worse, cancer could be mistaken for something less serious. X-rays were not detailed enough to accurately diagnose cancer.

Figure 4.7 shows how lung cancer is diagnosed today.

Key terms

Tumour*
A lump made up of abnormal cells.

Abscess*
A collection of pus in the body, often caused by bacteria.

Radioactive*
Something that gives off radiation.

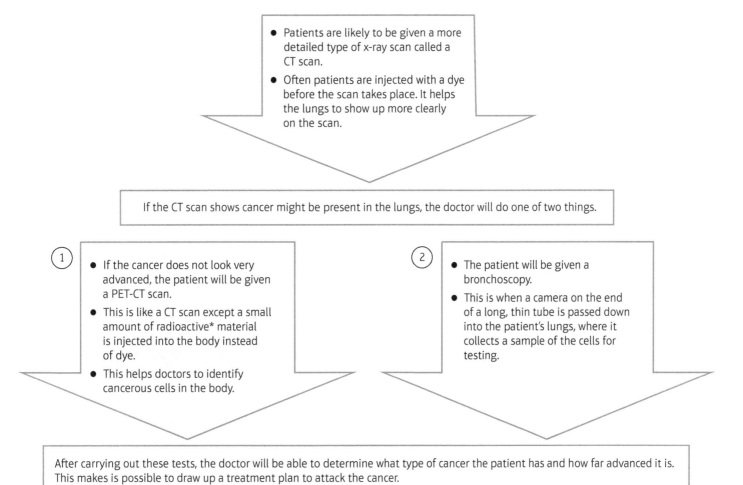

Figure 4.7 The stages of diagnosing lung cancer.

Activities

1 Identify and describe the most common cause of lung cancer.

2 Explain one reason why lung cancer is difficult to treat.

3 Give one example of how science and technology have helped in the diagnosis of lung cancer.

The use of science and technology in lung cancer treatment

If lung cancer is diagnosed early, doctors can perform an operation to remove the tumour and the affected part of the lung. This can range from the removal of just a small piece, to the removal of the entire lung. It is possible to breathe normally with only one lung. There are also other treatments, as shown in the diagram below.

Lung cancer patients are now likely to be treated using a mixture of surgery, radiotherapy and chemotherapy. For example, they might have surgery to remove the tumour and then have radiotherapy and chemotherapy to tackle any remaining cancerous cells.

Prevention: the British government take action

The government was slow to respond to the evidence that cigarette smoking was linked to lung cancer. Smoking-related deaths cost the NHS a huge amount, but the government made even more money from the tax it charged tobacco companies. Also, many UK jobs depended on the tobacco industry. There was also a question about whether a government should be able to take away a person's freedom to smoke.

However, as time passed, it became clear that the government needed to intervene. The death rate was too high.

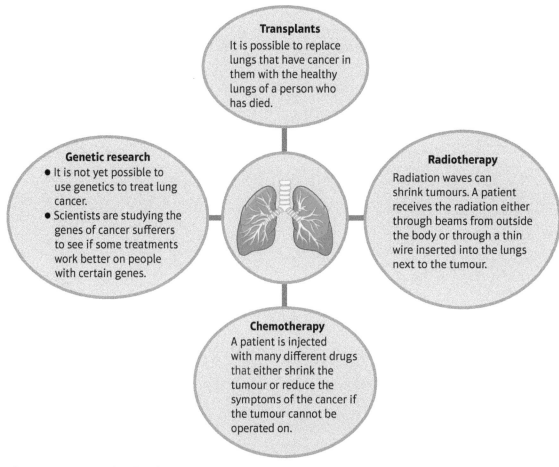

Figure: Science and technology in lung cancer treatment.

This table shows some of the actions that the government took.

Changing behaviour	Influencing behaviour
When the government passes laws to **force** people to change behaviour that damages their health.	When the government uses communication to **persuade** people to change behaviour that damages health.

Changing behaviour	Influencing behaviour
In 2007, the government **banned smoking in all workplaces**. In 2015, the **ban was extended to cars** carrying children under the age of 18. There is significant evidence to suggest that other people's smoke has a negative impact on health, particularly among children.	**Limits on tobacco advertising** began with a ban on cigarette television advertising in 1965. Over time, the government banned cigarette advertising in more and more places, until it banned cigarette advertising entirely in 2005.
In 2007, the government **raised the legal age for buying tobacco** from 16 to 18. It did this to try to reduce the number of teenagers who start to smoke.	The government has produced many **campaigns* to advertise the dangers of smoking** over the past decades. Education to discourage young people from smoking is now included in schools.
Tax on tobacco products was increased.	Now, all cigarette products in shops must be **removed from display**.

Source A

A 2012 Department of Health consultation (when a group of people meets to discuss an idea or issue) on smoking, which sets out the reasons why the government has taken action to limit visibility of cigarettes.

```
Evidence shows that cigarette displays in shops can encourage young people to start smoking.
The figures for England show that:
```

- ```5% of children aged 11-15 are regular smokers```

- ```more than 300,000 children under 16 try smoking each year```

- ```39% of smokers say that they were smoking regularly before the age of 16.```

```
Covering tobacco displays will protect children and young people from the promotion
[advertisement] of tobacco products in shops, helping them to resist the temptation to start
smoking. It will also help and support adults who are trying to quit.
```

```
More than 8 million people in England still smoke - it is one of the biggest preventable
killers causing more than 80,000 deaths each year. Nearly two-thirds of current and ex-smokers
say they started smoking before they were 18.
```

Government campaigns and laws have led to a change in attitude among the public. The number of smokers is falling.

Key term

Campaigns*
Organised activities for a specific purpose.

125

Case study comparison: government action against cholera vs government action against lung cancer

Government action	
Cholera	**Lung cancer**
Slow response initially. John Snow presented his findings about the link between dirty water and cholera in 1855, but a new sewer system took 20 years to be completed (and was not a direct response to Snow's findings).	**Slow response initially.** The first evidence linking smoking to lung cancer was published in 1950, but government did not directly intervene until death rates became too high to ignore.
More direct response in late 19th century. The 1875 Public Health Act forced cities to be cleaner to stop the spread of cholera. This was after more proof that Snow's findings were true.	**More direct response in early 21st century.** Government tried to both force and persuade people to change smoking behaviour. Smoking bans were introduced in 2007 and changes were made on how tobacco could be advertised.

Activities   ?

1   Create a timeline to show the rise in lung cancer cases since c1900.
2   Describe two examples of how technology has changed the way lung cancer is diagnosed and treated.
3   Government action to combat lung cancer can be divided into three categories:
    a   encouraging current smokers to quit
    b   preventing people from becoming smokers
    c   protecting non-smokers from the dangers of second-hand smoke.
Using the information above, give one example to support each category.

Summary

- Lung cancer became a much more common disease after 1900.
- In 1950, scientists proved that smoking was linked to lung cancer.
- Lung cancer patients are diagnosed using a combination of scans and analysis of cells from the lung.
- Treatments including surgery, radiotherapy and chemotherapy have been developed. However, there is not yet a conclusive cure for lung cancer.
- Since the 1950s, the government has taken more action to combat smoking.

Checkpoint

Strengthen

S1 Which organisation published the 1950 study linking smoking with lung cancer?
S2 Name one method by which lung cancer is diagnosed.
S3 Describe three government actions aimed at preventing lung cancer.

Activity ?

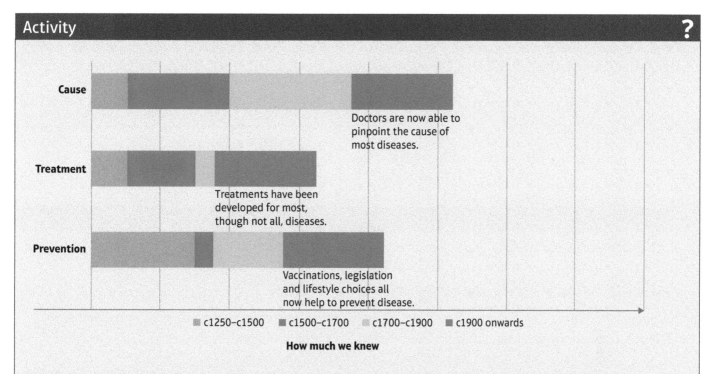

Doctors are now able to pinpoint the cause of most diseases.

Treatments have been developed for most, though not all, diseases.

Vaccinations, legislation and lifestyle choices all now help to prevent disease.

■ c1250–c1500   ■ c1500–c1700   ■ c1700–c1900   ■ c1900 onwards

How much we knew

The progress table above shows the main areas of progress in this time period in **cause**, **treatment** and **prevention**. Using this table, make notes to explain why knowledge about cause, treatment and prevention of diseases all progressed rapidly, c1900–present.

Recall quiz

1 Name the scientists who discovered the structure of DNA.

2 In what year was the human genome mapped?

3 What key piece of technology enabled the discovery of DNA?

4 When did the government pass the Clean Air Acts?

5 List three new methods of diagnosing patients since c1900.

6 Who developed the first 'magic bullet' and what was it called?

7 What are the three strands of care available from the NHS?

8 Name two diseases that can now be prevented by immunisation.

9 Which key individuals were responsible for the discovery and development of penicillin?

10 Name three different treatments for lung cancer.

Activities ?

You've now completed your thematic study of medicine. It is a good time to look back over the whole time period and recap some of the things you have learned.

1 Draw a timeline from 1250 to 2000. Add onto it at least five pieces of information for each of the following (present each in a different colour):

- ideas about what causes disease
- treatments
- preventions.

You can use the timeline on pages 10–11 to help you.

2 In a group, discuss what factors influenced change during this final time period. Consider the impact of the key factors: individuals, institutions, science and technology, and attitudes in society.

WRITING HISTORICALLY

Writing historically: a well-structured response

Every response you write needs to be clearly written and structured. To help you achieve this, you need to give clear signs about how you are answering the question.

Learning outcomes

By the end of this lesson, you will understand how to:

- use your writing to show chronological order
- use your writing to show how you are structuring your answer.

Definition

Chronological: sequenced in order of time; the order in which a series of events took place.

How can I signal the order of chronological events?

When you explain or describe a process, such as the development of antibiotics, you can use words to signal the **chronological** order of events.

Look at this sequence of events describing the development of penicillin:

> The antibiotic, penicillin, was accidentally discovered by Alexander Fleming in 1928.
>
> Florey and Chain recognised its potential and began to refine the drug in 1939.
>
> The first human was treated with penicillin in 1941.
>
> Because of the Second World War, the drug was produced on an industrial scale from 1944.
>
> Fleming, Florey and Chain were awarded the Nobel Prize in 1945.

1. Write a paragraph about the development of penicillin, using the points above and as many of the words below as possible, to signal clearly the order of these events.

> Firstly... Secondly... Then... Soon... Next... During... Eventually... From 1939 to 1945...

How can I signal the structure of my argument?

You can use words like those below to link your ideas and guide the reader through your argument. For example:

> Similarly... For example... Such as... However... Therefore... Consequently...
>
> For the most part... Nonetheless... Furthermore... On the other hand... In addition...
>
> Above all... Significantly... In conclusion...

2. Now look at the two extracts below from a response to the following exam-style question. Make a note of all the words from the box at the bottom of page 128 the writer used to link their ideas and structure their argument.

'The greatest factor on the advancement of the treatment of disease between 1700 and 1900 was science and technology.' How far do you agree? **(20 marks)**

For most of the 19th century, doctors could do little to treat specific diseases. Consequently, traditional approaches such as bleeding remained common. However, the science of chemistry improved in the second half of the 19th century and the French chemist, Louis Pasteur, proved Germ Theory — that specific bacteria caused specific diseases, such as anthrax.

Science and technology were, therefore, a key factor in the improvements in medical treatment. There are, on the other hand, other factors to consider.

Did you notice?

These signal words can be positioned at a number of different points in a sentence.

3. At what point in the sentences above are most of the signal words positioned – at the start of the sentence, the middle of the sentence, or the end of the sentence?

Improving an answer

Now look at the final paragraph below, which is a response to the exam-style question above.

Both of these factors are important. The scientific and technological breakthroughs of the 19th and 20th centuries (x-rays, antibiotics, radiotherapy) were the more important. The funding of the NHS by government had a huge impact on people's access to healthcare. Without the breakthroughs in technology, this would have had considerably less impact.

4. Rewrite this conclusion using some of the words from the box at the bottom of page 128 to signal the structure of the argument clearly.

Preparing for your GCSE Paper 1 exam

Paper 1 overview

Paper 1 is in two sections that examine the Historic Environment and the Thematic Study. Together they count for 30% of your History assessment. The questions on the Thematic Study: 'Medicine in Britain' are in Section B and are worth 20% of your History assessment. Allow two-thirds of the examination time (50 minutes) for Section B. There are an extra 4 marks for spelling, punctuation and grammar in the last question.

History Paper 1	Historic Environment and Thematic Study			Time 1 hour 15 mins
Section A	Historic Environment	Answer 3 questions	16 marks	25 mins
Section B	Thematic Study	Answer 3 questions	32 marks + 4 SPaG marks	50 mins

Section B: Medicine in Britain, c1250–present

You need to answer Questions 3 and 4, and then **either** Question 5 or Question 6.

Q3 Explain one way... (4 marks)

You are given about half a page of lines to write about a **similarity** or a **difference**. Allow 5 minutes to write your answer. This question is only worth 4 marks and you should keep the answer brief. Once you have identified whether the question is asking for a similarity or a difference, you only need one comparison. You should **compare** by referring to both periods given in the question.

Q4 Explain why... (12 marks)

This question asks you to explain the **reasons why something happened**. Allow about 15 minutes to write your answer. You are given two information points as starting ideas to help you. You do not have to use them and you will not lose marks by leaving them out. You will be given at least two pages of lines in the answer booklet for your answer. This does not mean you should try to fill all the space. The front page of the exam paper states 'there may be more space than you need'. Aim to write an answer giving at least two explained reasons.

EITHER Q5 OR Q6 How far do you agree? (16 marks + 4 for SPaG)

This question is worth 20 marks, including SPaG (spelling, punctuation and grammar) – more than half your marks for the whole of the Thematic Study. Make sure to keep 30 minutes of the exam time to answer it and to check your spelling, punctuation and grammar. You will be given ideas to help, like in Question 4. You have a **choice** of questions: Q5 or Q6. Before you decide, think about what topic information you will need to answer it. The statement may be about one of the following concepts: significance, cause, consequence, change, continuity, similarity, difference. It is a good idea during revision to practise identifying the concept focus of statements. You could do this with everyday examples and test one another:

- 'The bus was late because it broke down' = statement about cause;
- 'The bus broke down as a result of poor maintenance' = statement about consequence;
- 'The bus service has improved recently' = statement about change.

You should think about both sides of the argument. Plan your answer before you begin to write, putting your points under two headings: **For** and **Against**. Think of each point as making one side of the argument or the other stronger. Make sure that you write in full paragraphs. Make your point and then support it with details from your own knowledge. Try to explain how your supported point answers the question. In this question, four extra marks will be gained for good spelling, punctuation and grammar and the use of specific words from the history of medicine. Use sentences, paragraphs, capital letters, commas and full stops, etc.

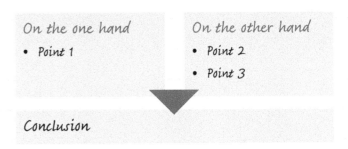

On the one hand
- Point 1

On the other hand
- Point 2
- Point 3

Conclusion

Paper 1, Question 3

Explain **one** way in which ideas about the treatment of disease were different in the 17th century from ideas in the 13th century.　　(4 marks)

Basic answer

Herbal remedies such as mint and camomile were very common. Then there were more chemical treatments, although they still used herbal remedies as well.

This answer identifies different treatments but it does not specify periods, so is vague. It lacks supporting examples of what specific treatments 'chemical treatments' might include.

Verdict

This is a basic answer because the student has provided general comments about the difference in treatment between the two periods.

Use the feedback to rewrite this answer, making as many improvements as you can.

- Consider where you would add the names of the relevant time periods.
- What example would you give of a chemical treatment?

Good answer

In the 13th century, many people were treated with herbal remedies. These were usually made with local plants and herbs such as mint and camomile. Recipes for these included theriaca, a popular remedy.

Although herbal remedies were still used in the 17th century, more materials were available. New ingredients included nutmeg and cinnamon. There were also experiments with chemical treatments, for example, the use of mercury to treat syphilis.

This answer describes treatments in both centuries. It gives specific examples of treatments used. It is very clear about what happened in the different centuries.

Verdict

This is a good answer because it features specific information about the topic and identifies both time periods by name.

Paper 1, Question 4

Explain why there was rapid change in the prevention of smallpox in the period c1750–c1900.

You may use the following information in your answer:

- inoculation
- Edward Jenner.

You **must** also use information of your own.   (12 marks)

Exam tip

Look at the question to identify the topic (prevention of smallpox) and the concept (change). Use this to make sure that your answer answers the question. Make sure you bring in your own knowledge.

Basic answer

People used to be inoculated against smallpox. They did this by making a cut in their arm and rubbing in pus from a person with smallpox. This sometimes worked.

Edward Jenner observed that people who had had cowpox didn't catch smallpox. He thought that if he gave someone cowpox they would be immune to smallpox.

There is some knowledge of the different techniques used to prevent smallpox.

This answer could be more detailed by stating what Edward Jenner's technique was called.

It needs to be more clear about what has **changed** and **why**.

Verdict

This is a basic answer because:

- by identifying different preventions the student has shown they know the question is about change, but they need to answer the question more directly to explain **why** there was change
- there is some accurate and relevant information.

Use the feedback to rewrite this answer, making as many improvements as you can.

Paper 1, Question 4

Explain why there was rapid change in the prevention of smallpox in the period c1750–c1900.

(12 marks)

Good answer

At the start of the period 1750–1900, people were inoculated against smallpox. This was done by making a cut in their arm and rubbing in pus from a person with a mild case of smallpox. This sometimes worked, but there was risk of this becoming a serious case of smallpox. Some people even died as a result of inoculation.

In 1798, Edward Jenner saw that people who had had cowpox didn't catch smallpox. Cowpox was a much less serious disease than smallpox, so there would be less risk if someone was given cowpox. To test his theory, he carried out an experiment where he rubbed the pus from a cowpox sufferer into a cut on the arm of a boy. The boy became immune to smallpox. Jenner called this a vaccination, after the Latin word for cow.

Gradually people stopped using smallpox inoculations and started using the less risky vaccination to prevent smallpox.

Information about the different methods of prevention are supported with some specific details from the student's own knowledge.

The answer still does not include any details not related to the starter ideas. It should include information about small pox prevention in the 1800s.

The final sentence makes more direct reference to the change that has happened and gives a more direct answer to the question. It could be developed by explaining the role of government in making vaccinations compulsory.

Verdict

This is a good answer because:

- it has included relevant information
- it shows a more direct focus on the reasons for change.

It could be improved further by going beyond the two points in the question, for example, by mentioning the role of the government in making vaccination widespread. There could also be a stronger focus on explaining why change was 'rapid'.

Paper 1, Question 5/6

'The Theory of the Four Humours was the main idea about the cause of disease in the Middle Ages.'

How far do you agree? Explain your answer. You may use the following information in your answer:

- university training
- Galen's ideas.

You **must** also use some information of your own.

(16 marks + 4 for SPaG)

Exam tip

As well as 16 marks available for answering the question, this response also offers up to 4 marks for good spelling, grammar and punctuation, and the use of specialist terms. Take extra care over things like capital letters and make sure you spell key words correctly. As with Question 4, make sure you identify the topic and the concept, to ensure your whole answer is relevant.

Basic answer

During the Middle Ages, people believed in the Theory of the Four Humours as the explanation for what caused disease. The theory said that people got ill because their humours were unbalanced. The four humours were blood, phlegm, black bile and yellow bile. Too much or too little of one meant that a person would become ill. For example, a person suffering from a fever had too much blood. The treatment for this was eating something cool, like cucumber, and being bled, either by cutting into the body and draining blood or using a more gentle method, like leeches.

Some people believed that God sent disease as a punishment for sin, particularly after the Black Death arrived in Britain and people became desperate to explain what was causing disease. People thought that if they avoided sin or prayed for forgiveness, then they would not get sick.

Some relevant information is given, for example the explanation of the Theory of the Four Humours.

Some details are not relevant to the question. For example, the section about treatments is not relevant to a question about what people thought caused disease.

By including a second idea about what people believed caused disease, the answer shows understanding that the question is asking about significance but it does not directly answer the question.

There is no judgement about which was the 'main idea'.

Verdict

This is a basic answer because:

- it includes some specific information, although some of this is not relevant to the question
- there is an understanding that this question requires a comparison of ideas about what caused disease, but there is no judgement about to what extent the Theory of the Four Humours was the main idea.

Use the feedback to rewrite this answer, making as many improvements as you can.

Paper 1, Question 5/6

'The Theory of the Four Humours was the main idea about the cause of disease in the Middle Ages'.
How far do you agree? Explain your answer. **(16 marks + 4 for SPaG)**

Good answer

During the Middle Ages, the Theory of the Four Humours was the main idea about the cause of disease. This theory had been created in ancient Greece by Hippocrates and developed by Galen in the Roman Empire. It was preferred by the medieval Church because the theory suggested that the body was perfectly designed and this fitted with their ideas about man being made by God. The theory said that people got ill because their humours were unbalanced. The four humours were blood, phlegm, black bile and yellow bile. An imbalance in one meant that a person would become ill. For example, a person suffering from a fever had too much blood.

The Theory of the Four Humours was mainly used by physicians when diagnosing illnesses. This was because the Church was responsible for training doctors and it taught the works of Galen.

There were some other, different ideas about the causes of disease in the Middle Ages. For example, some people believed that God sent disease as a punishment for sin, particularly after the Black Death arrived in Britain in 1348. However, before 1348 most people believed in the Theory of the Four Humours because that's what doctors used.

Although people continued to believe that God could send disease as a punishment, the fact that the Church supported the Theory of the Four Humours and used it to train doctors meant that the Four Humours was the main idea about what caused disease in the Middle Ages.

Detailed knowledge is given and is relevant to a question about ideas about the cause of disease though the information about the origin of the Theory is not needed.

There is some attempt to answer the question by explaining the significance of each idea.

There is a brief judgement about which was the most significant idea. The answer could be improved by explaining the criteria for making this judgement more fully.

Verdict

This is a good answer because:
- it includes mostly relevant knowledge about ideas about the cause of disease
- it starts to explain how these ideas were significant during the Middle Ages
- there is an overall judgement that attempts to answer the question directly.

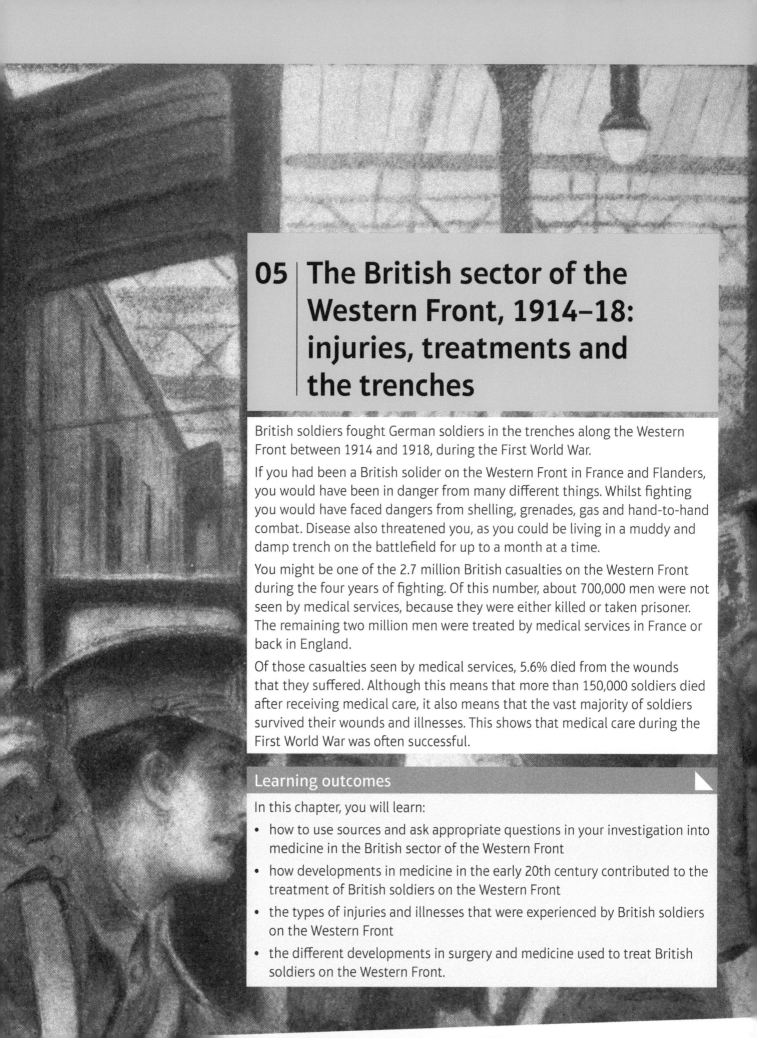

05 | The British sector of the Western Front, 1914–18: injuries, treatments and the trenches

British soldiers fought German soldiers in the trenches along the Western Front between 1914 and 1918, during the First World War.

If you had been a British solider on the Western Front in France and Flanders, you would have been in danger from many different things. Whilst fighting you would have faced dangers from shelling, grenades, gas and hand-to-hand combat. Disease also threatened you, as you could be living in a muddy and damp trench on the battlefield for up to a month at a time.

You might be one of the 2.7 million British casualties on the Western Front during the four years of fighting. Of this number, about 700,000 men were not seen by medical services, because they were either killed or taken prisoner. The remaining two million men were treated by medical services in France or back in England.

Of those casualties seen by medical services, 5.6% died from the wounds that they suffered. Although this means that more than 150,000 soldiers died after receiving medical care, it also means that the vast majority of soldiers survived their wounds and illnesses. This shows that medical care during the First World War was often successful.

Learning outcomes

In this chapter, you will learn:

- how to use sources and ask appropriate questions in your investigation into medicine in the British sector of the Western Front
- how developments in medicine in the early 20th century contributed to the treatment of British soldiers on the Western Front
- the types of injuries and illnesses that were experienced by British soldiers on the Western Front
- the different developments in surgery and medicine used to treat British soldiers on the Western Front.

Sources and the examination

Source A

From an interview with Gunner William Towers in 1989. Here, he is remembering his treatment following a wound to his leg at Ypres (Belguim) in October 1917.

They took us to a hospital at Étaples and fitted me with a Thomas splint, a round wooden ring with iron bands and a footrest. The pain from my knee was getting terrible so when I saw an officer coming up with his arm around two sisters and laughing, I said, 'Excuse me, Sir, could you have a look at my knee?' He came over and he stank of whisky. When the nurses took the bandages off he said, 'Oh there's fluid above the knee. We'll tap that tonight.' So they came for me to go to the theatre and I thought, 'Thank God for that.' But when I woke up in the early hours of the morning I thought, 'Oh my God. My leg's gone.' They'd guillotined [chopped] it off without saying a word. There had been no hint at all that I was going to lose my leg. They hadn't even looked at it until I asked the doctor.

After that they put me on a boat and I was taken to England. A civilian doctor came to look at me and when he took the bandages off the smell was terrible. He thought I was going to die.

In the examination you will be given **two** sources. You will be asked to do **two** things with these sources:

- comment on the **usefulness of both** sources for an enquiry
- write about **a detail in one source** that you would **follow up**.
  You will need to:
    - consider the question you would ask about that detail
    - consider what type of source might provide an answer to that
    - explain why that type of source might answer the question.

Because most of the marks in this section of the examination are for your work with sources, there are more sources in this chapter than the rest of the book. Sources A and B are both examples of records of medical work on the Western Front. They are included to help you understand how the examination works.

Source B

From Pat Beauchamp's autobiography*, *Fanny Goes to War*, published in 1919. Beauchamp first worked as a nurse, bringing in the wounded from the trenches, and from 1916 as an ambulance driver. Here she is describing driving casualties* to the Base Hospitals.

The battle of the Somme was in progress. Besides barges [canal and river boats] and day trains, three ambulance trains arrived each week. The whole convoy [vehicles travelling together as a group] turned out for this; and one by one the twenty-five odd cars would set off, keeping an equal distance apart, forming an imposing looking column down from the camp, across the bridge and through the town to the railway siding... Arrived at the big railway siding, we all formed up into a straight line to await the train... The ambulances were then reversed right up to the doors, and the stretcher bearers soon filled them up with four lying cases [wounded who could not walk]... Those journeys back were perfect nightmares. Try as one would, it was impossible not to bump a certain amount over those appalling roads full of holes and cobbles. It was pathetic when a voice from the interior could be heard asking, "Is it much farther, Sister?" and knowing how far it was, my heart ached for them. After all they had been through, one felt they should be spared every extra bit of pain that was possible. When I in my turn was in an ambulance, I knew just what it felt like. Sometimes the cases were so bad we feared they would not even last the journey, and there we were all alone, and not able to hurry to hospital owing to the other three on board.

Usefulness (utility) of a source

No source is useful (or useless) until you have an enquiry*. Our enquiry is:

How useful are Sources A and B for an enquiry into the problems that faced the medical services during battles on the Western Front? To answer this question you will need to use criteria* to make a judgement.

You might base your judgement on the following:

Criteria	Questions you might ask about the source	How useful is it?
Content	What does the source tell you?	How does this make it useful/less useful?
Nature	What was the original purpose of the source?	How does this make it useful/less useful?
Context	How does the source fit in with what you already know about the Western Front?	How does this make it useful/less useful?

How does this work in practice?

- Source A is a person remembering events that happened about 70 years previously. William Towers provides us with a description of traumatic events that he personally experienced. Although he is talking a long time after the event, the trauma is likely to have stuck in his mind. This would support the source being useful because it is **likely** to be true. The comment shows you have thought about the actual source, rather than just saying it is 70 years later so he may have misremembered. You could say that about any source that relies on memory.

- Source B tells us that the wounded were transported by ambulance from the ambulance trains to the Base Hospitals. More interestingly, it tells us about the personal reaction of one ambulance driver to the job she was doing. This makes the source useful because it tells us something unusual and relevant.

Key terms

Enquiry*
Question you plan to answer.

Criteria*
The measure by which you judge something. It is vital in History that you know your criteria, or criterion (singular), before judging a source.

Oral*
Spoken.

Archaeology*
The study of objects found under the ground.

Artefact*
A historical object.

You will use the criteria to build your answer. The best answers will use criteria drawn from all the three possible areas:

- content
- nature/origin/purpose (provenance)
- context (how it fits into what you already know).

Following up on sources

Where possible, historians try to use as many different types of source as they can. This is because each different type of source has different strengths and weaknesses. Figure 5.1 shows the range of different types of source a historian can use.

The second question about sources asks you to pick a detail from one of the sources, and explain how you would follow that detail up using a different type of source.

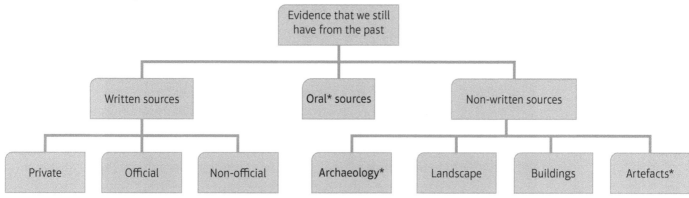

Figure 5.1 Types of historical sources.

Activities ?

1   In small groups, study Source C and complete a table, like the one on the previous page, to consider the criteria you could use to judge usefulness.

2   Using Figure 5.1 to help you, make a list of sources that could be used to study your own life.

    a   Give at least one example source in each category.

    b   Explain why each example would be useful to find out more about your life.

Source C

Photograph of a wounded British soldier being carried on a stretcher by German prisoners of war, 15 September 1916. This followed a battle that was part of the Somme campaign.

Provenance (nature, origin and purpose)

Historians think very carefully about their sources. They test them to check whether they are really appropriate for the way they want to use them. The tests are:

*   what is its purpose?
*   what is the opinion of the author or artist?
*   is it part of the action or reflecting on the action?

What is its purpose?

When, where and why was the source created, and who by? If a source is written by someone who was there, it is helpful to know if they wrote it at the time or many years later. Just because it was written at the time does not mean it is true as it may not be why the source was created. For example, a nurse writing to her parents back home would likely not tell them in detail about deaths that she saw. In this case, the purpose of the source might be to keep in contact with her parents, rather than to tell the whole truth about what she was doing.

What is the opinion of the author or artist?

Does the person have a particular point of view? If you are reading a description of medical treatment during the Battle of the Somme (Northern France), it might be useful to know whether the author supported what the government was doing. For example, propaganda was deliberately created to encourage people to support the government. It might be exaggerated, it might leave things out or it might just not be true. This doesn't mean historians don't use propaganda – it might be useful in finding out what the government wanted people to believe.

Is it part of the action or reflecting on the action?

What is the difference between a live radio commentary on a football match, and the account of that same game written years later in a player's autobiography? Both have their strengths, but they are very different.

Turning a source into evidence

A source is only useful, and it can only be turned into evidence, when you have a question or enquiry. For example, Source B: If we ask 'What is the role of ambulance drivers in driving the wounded to Base Hospitals?' It is useful as it provides evidence to help us answer this question. However, if we ask 'What were the conditions like in the Casualty Clearing Stations?' It is not useful.

Judging sources

Start with the provenance (the nature, origin and purpose of the source)
Does this suggest strengths or weaknesses when using this source for this particular enquiry?

↓

Move on to content usefulness
What does the source tell you?
What does it suggest?

↓

Consider what you already know about the enquiry
Does the source give a typical picture of medicine in the trenches, or something unexpected?
This is particularly useful for thinking about photos, as we often don't know exactly **why** a particular photo was taken.

THINKING HISTORICALLY Evidence (2a)

Information and evidence

Information only becomes evidence when we use it **to work out** something about an issue in the past. Information needs to be questioned before we can use it as **evidence** to draw conclusions. Without a question, information doesn't tell us very much.

Study the following questions about the Western Front:

1 How was medical treatment at the frontline carried out?	2 Why did trench warfare begin?	3 What were the main battles?
4 What sort of injuries did the soldiers receive?	5 What did people in Britain think about the Western Front?	6 Where were the medical facilities located?

Study Sources A, B, and C.

1   Which of the six questions could we **not** answer with any of the sources?

2   Which question is Source A most useful in providing evidence for?

Look at Source C. Draw up a table with three columns labelled 'Question', 'Answer' and 'Evidence'.

3   Write out Question 1 in the first column. Then use Source C to fill in the other two columns with ideas that answer the question, and evidence from the source that backs up the answer.

4   Write out Question 5 in a new row, and add answer ideas and evidence for this question from Source C.

5   Look at the inferences you've made from Source C. Are they the same for both questions?

6   In your own words, explain how the question you ask affects what evidence you find in a source.

5.1 The historical context of medicine in the early 20th century

In the years before the outbreak of the First World War, many medical breakthroughs had occurred. These allowed medical improvements in the British sector* of the Western Front to take place. These included aseptic surgery*, x-rays and blood transfusions.

Understanding infection and the move towards aseptic surgery

Joseph Lister first used carbolic acid to prevent infection in surgery in 1865, based on Louis Pasteur's Germ Theory.

By the late 1890s, Lister's methods had been developed into aseptic surgery. By 1900, most operations were carried out using aseptic methods.

All medical staff had to wash their hands, faces and arms before entering the operating theatre.

Rubber gloves and gowns were worn, decreasing the rate of infection in wounds.

The use of steam sterilisation. A machine called an autoclave was invented in 1881. It sterilised* surgical instruments in boiling steam.

The air was sterilised by being pumped over the heating system to kill germs.

Figure 5.2 The key features of early 20th-century aseptic surgery.

Exam-style question, Section A

Describe **two** features of aseptic surgery in the early 20th century. **4 marks**

Exam tip

Make sure that you develop each feature you identify with some supporting information. For example, surgical instruments were sterilised. This was done using an autoclave.

Key terms

British sector*
Section of the battlefield where the British troops were fighting.

Aseptic surgery*
Surgery where microbes are prevented from getting into a wound in the first place, rather than being killed off with an antiseptic.

Sterilise*
To kill the bacteria on an object.

The development of x-rays

X-rays were discovered by accident in 1895. **Wilhelm Roentgen**, a German physicist, was studying the effects of passing an electrical current through a glass tube covered in black paper.

He noticed that a nearby screen started to glow slightly. Further experimentation proved that the glow was caused by rays that were able to pass through objects.

Roentgen placed some photographic paper between the tube and his hand and created the first x-ray image of a person's bones.

As early as 1896, radiology departments* were opening in a number of British hospitals.

At Birmingham General Hospital, Dr John Hall-Edwards was one of the first doctors to make a diagnosis* based on information from an x-ray, when he located a needle in a woman's hand. Being able to see more clearly what was wrong with someone before an operation would be a big help for medical treatments on the Western Front.

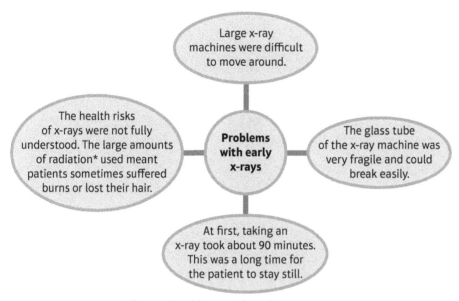

Figure: Problems with early x-rays.

However, these dangers and problems did not stop x-rays being used.

Source A

A 19th-century x-ray machine in a hospital.

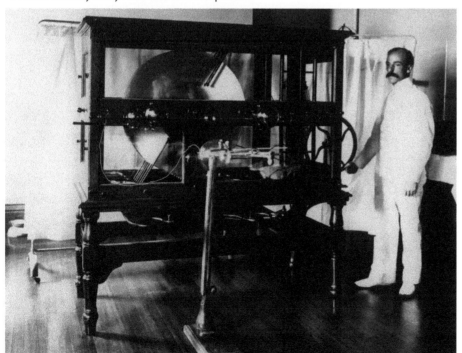

Key terms

Radiology department*
The hospital department where x-rays are carried out.

Diagnosis*
Working out what is making a person unwell.

Radiation*
Energy that passes from one place to another, e.g. x-rays.

Activities ?

Look at Source A.

1 Describe the main features of the x-ray machine shown.

2 Describe two problems which might arise from the use of this machine? If you are not able to identify two problems from the picture, look again at the spider diagram above for ideas.

3 What other types of sources might help you to understand the problems linked to the use of x-rays?

143

Key terms

Blood transfusion*

Blood taken from a healthy person and given to another person.

Rejection*

When the body does not accept the donor blood. This can make the patient's condition worse.

Activities ?

1 Describe two main features of aseptic surgery.

2 List two benefits of x-rays and two dangers. Why did the benefits outweigh the dangers?

3 With a partner, discuss how successfully the problems associated with blood transfusions had been solved by the early 20th century.

The development of blood transfusions and the storage of blood

If somebody loses too much blood, then they are likely to go into **shock** and die. In the 19th and early 20th centuries, blood loss in surgery was common.

With the development of aseptic surgery and x-rays in the late 19th century, it was possible to carry out more complex operations safely. However, people could still die from blood loss during these complex operations.

James Blundell did the first experiments in human blood transfusion* in 1818 to help women who lost blood when they gave birth. Between 1818 and 1829, Blundell carried out ten transfusions, with up to half of the patients surviving. As blood could not be stored, the donor (the person giving the blood) was directly connected to the recipient (the person receiving the blood) by a tube.

The table below shows the main problems with blood transfusions, and the attempts that had been made to solve them by the early 20th century.

Problem with transfusion		Attempted solution to the problem
Blood coagulates (clots) as soon as it leaves the body. This meant that the tubes which transfused blood from one person to another could become blocked up.	→	There were attempts to find chemicals to prevent clotting. In 1894, Professor Almroth Wright, a British scientist, created a solution of acids to put in the blood, but these could cause the patient additional medical problems (such as fits).
Rejection* of the transfused blood because the donor and recipient had different blood types.	→	In 1901–1902, the four blood types – A, B, O and AB were discovered. This information was used in 1907 by Reuben Ottenberg, an American doctor, who was the first person to match a donor and a recipient's blood type before a transfusion.
Danger of infection from unsterilised equipment.	→	The introduction of aseptic methods of surgery had largely solved this problem in hospital conditions by the early 20th century.

Summary

- By 1900, most surgery was carried out using aseptic methods.
- X-rays were discovered in 1895. They were used almost immediately for diagnosing patients.
- Blood transfusions had to take place person-to-person because there was no way to store blood.
- The discovery of different blood groups enabled blood transfusions to become more effective.

Checkpoint

Strengthen

S1 Explain the impact that the following had on developments in medicine.
- Aseptic surgery
- X-rays
- Blood transfusions

Challenge

C1 Although there had been many advances in medicine (as mentioned above), there were still many problems remaining. Identify one problem for each of the developments in Question S1.

If you are not confident about any of these questions, form a group with other students, discuss the answers and then record your conclusions. Your teacher can give you some hints.

5.2 The context of the British sector of the Western Front

Flanders and northern France

Britain declared war on Germany on 4 August 1914. Germany invaded France through Belgium. The British government sent the British Expeditionary Force (BEF) to northern France and Belgium to try to stop the German advance. The BEF faced a German army that was more than double their size. Although they stopped the German advance briefly, they were ordered to retreat to the River Marne in order to protect Paris. After the **Battle of the Marne**, the German forces pulled back and trench warfare began.

The trench system

By the end of 1914, much of Belgium and northern France had been occupied by the Germans. Both sides dug trench systems to defend their positions. The war moved very little, though both sides launched attacks against the other's trenches. A line of trenches was eventually established all the way from the English Channel in the north, to Switzerland in the south.

Construction and organisation

The trenches were generally dug to a depth of about 2.5 m. The main elements in the trench system are shown in Figure 5.3.

Trenches were easier to defend than attack. Machine guns in the trenches could fire rapidly, and barbed wire was placed in **no-man's-land** (the area between two opposing lines of trenches) to slow down any attack.

New tactics were developed to make trenches harder to defend. These included the use of gas.

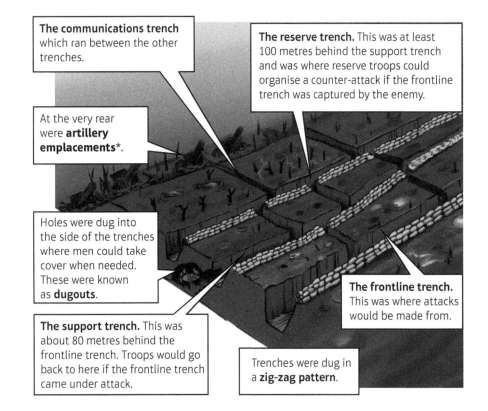

The communications trench which ran between the other trenches.

At the very rear were **artillery emplacements***.

Holes were dug into the side of the trenches where men could take cover when needed. These were known as **dugouts**.

The support trench. This was about 80 metres behind the frontline trench. Troops would go back to here if the frontline trench came under attack.

The reserve trench. This was at least 100 metres behind the support trench and was where reserve troops could organise a counter-attack if the frontline trench was captured by the enemy.

Trenches were dug in a **zig-zag pattern**.

The frontline trench. This was where attacks would be made from.

Figure 5.3 The trench system during the First World War.

Source A

A typical trench system, sketched during the war. The exact date and artist is not known. It was probably sketched after 1915.

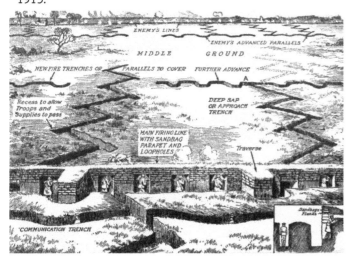

Source B

A trench during the Battle of the Somme, July 1916.

Activities ?

Study Sources A and B.

1 Give two differences between the sketch diagram of a trench system and the photo of a trench.

2 What are the benefits and problems of each of these types of sources for the historian? Copy and complete the table below:

	sketch	photo
benefit		
problem		

Figure 5.4 Cross section of a trench.

The Ypres Salient*, the Somme, Arras and Cambrai

This section outlines the key battles in the British sector of the Western Front. It is important to refer back to this section when looking at specific medical advancements on the Western Front.

Key term

Salient*

An area of a battlefield that extends into enemy territory, so that it is surrounded on three sides by the enemy and is therefore in a vulnerable position.

Figure 5.5 Map of the Western Front.

1914: the First Battle of Ypres

During the first months of the war, the British had moved to the town of Ypres in western Belgium, in order to prevent the Germans taking the coast. In the autumn of 1914, the Germans launched an attack on the British positions. Although the British lost over 50,000 troops in this battle, they held on to Ypres. This meant they controlled the English Channel ports, so that supplies and reinforcements could reach them from Britain.

The use of mines at Hill 60

Hill 60 was a man-made hill to the south-east of Ypres. The Germans had captured it in December 1914 and its height gave them an advantage, as they could see the enemy approaching. The British used mining to take it back in April 1915. This involved tunnelling under the hill and placing explosives in the tunnel. The explosion blew the top off Hill 60 and the British were able to take back the high ground.

Extend your knowledge

Digging tunnels on the Western Front

The men who joined the Tunnelling Companies had all worked underground before the war. They included coal miners from Northumberland, sewage drain diggers from Manchester and tube tunnel diggers from London. The job was dangerous and many died whilst working.

1915: the Second Battle of Ypres

As soon as the battle for Hill 60 was finished, the Second Battle of Ypres began. It is significant in the history of the First World War as it was the first time that the Germans used chlorine gas on the Western Front (see pages 154–155). By the end of the battle, the British had lost 59,000 men and the Germans had moved about two miles closer to the town of Ypres.

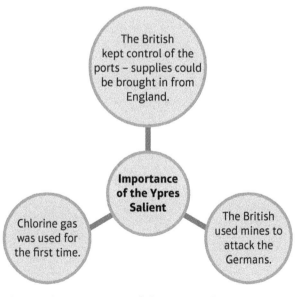

Figure: The importance of the Ypres Salient.

1916: the Battle of the Somme

Source C

A still from the 1916 British film, *The Battle of the Somme*.

Activity ?

This photograph claimed to show British soldiers advancing at the start of the Battle of the Somme. It is now thought this sequence was acted out away from the frontline. Give one reason why this might still be useful to a historian.

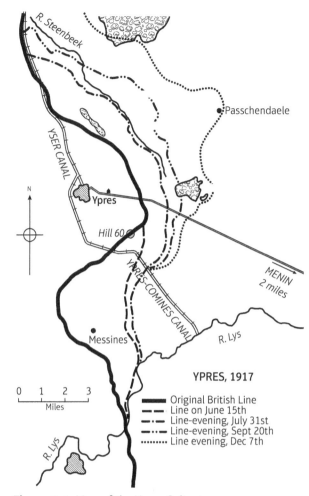

Figure 5.6 Map of the Ypres Salient.

The British attack on the Somme was launched on 1 July 1916. The casualties on both sides were enormous: on the first day alone, British casualties were over 57,000, with deaths totalling around 20,000 men. The British tried two new strategies:

- **the use of the creeping barrage** – artillery fired on the Germans just ahead of the British soldiers as they moved forward towards the German lines.
- **the first use of tanks in warfare** – however, the tanks had many technical problems and they were not very successful.

By the end of the Battle of the Somme in November 1916, the British had suffered an estimated 400,000 casualties.

Tunnels, caves and quarries at Arras

The ground around Arras is chalky and easy to tunnel through. Many quarries and tunnels had been dug in the area. In 1916, the British decided to link the existing tunnels, caves and quarries around Arras to act as shelters against German attacks. Up to 25,000 men could be stationed in the tunnels, which contained electric lights, running water, a light railway system and a fully functioning hospital (see page 162).

1917: the Battle of Arras

In April 1917, 24,000 British soldiers who had been hiding in tunnels attacked the nearby German trenches. In the first few days, the British advanced about eight miles. However, the advance slowed, virtually no further progress was made, and by the end of the attack there were a large number of casualties (nearly 160,000 British and Canadians).

Source D

From 'The General', a poem written by Siegfried Sassoon in 1918. Sassoon served as an officer on the Western Front from 1914. He was treated for shell shock (a psychological* condition caused by prolonged exposure to bombing) in 1917, after which he returned to fight on the Western Front.

> "Good morning, good morning," the General said,
> When we met him last week on our way to the line.
> Now the soldiers he smiled at are most of 'em dead,
> And we're cursing his staff for incompetent* swine.
> "He's a cheery old card," muttered Harry to Jack
> As they slogged up to Arras with rifle and pack.
> But he did for them both by his plan of attack.

Activities ?

Study Source D.

1   Select a detail in the poem that matches the events at the Battle of Arras.
2   What questions should you ask before using a poem as a piece of historical evidence?

1917: the Third Battle of Ypres

The aim of the Third Battle of Ypres in 1917 was for the British army to break out of Ypres and take the higher ground from the Germans. The British launched their main attack on 31 July, east towards **Passchendaele**. The army advanced about two miles on the first day. Soon though, the weather turned to rain and the ground became waterlogged – so much so that men fell in the mud and drowned. This campaign lasted until November. The Germans were pushed back seven miles at the cost of an estimated 245,000 British casualties.

1917: the Battle of Cambrai

The Battle of Cambrai was launched on 20 October 1917. It was the first large-scale use of tanks – nearly five hundred were used in this battle. This time, they were able to move easily across the barbed wire and their machine guns were very effective.

Problems of transport and communications

The constant shelling*, and the type of ground, left the landscape full of craters and holes and destroyed many roads. This led to major problems in transporting injured men away from the frontline. Before the war, this region had been used as farmland, and the farmers had put lots of fertiliser* on the land. This meant there was a lot of bacteria in the soil that could lead to infected wounds.

Stretcher bearers, like Edward Munro (see Source E), carried away the large numbers of wounded from the frontline, both during the day and at night. This meant they were often at risk from shelling and gunfire. Further away from the frontline, it was possible to carry out more advanced medical procedures. The faster an injury could be treated, the more likely a person was to survive.

Key terms

Psychological*
Something that has an impact on the way the brain works.

Incompetent*
Not having the ability to do something successfully.

Shelling*
Firing shells through the air towards the enemy. A shell is a large metal container filled with explosive.

Fertiliser*
Something spread on land to make plants grow better, for example animal dung.

Source E

From Edward Munro's *Diaries of a Stretcher Bearer*. This entry comes from 7 November 1916, when Munro was in the Somme.

> We commenced [started] to carry down the wounded of whom there were a considerable number. The 7th Brigade had made an attack on the German line the previous night and had suffered many casualties. The country over which we have to carry is most difficult to traverse [walk across], being pitted with shell holes, mostly waterlogged. Fritz [the Germans] keeps up a fairly constant shelling. Yesterday he caught some of the 6th Ambulance bearers, killing two. In this area was started the system of carrying the stretchers shoulder high — four to a stretcher, this being much less fatiguing than the old method of two carrying with slings... The carrying at night is very trying as there are no clearly defined tracks. The landmarks that serve to guide one in the daytime are not visible at night.

Source F

Stretcher bearers carrying a wounded man to safety at the Third Battle of Ypres in August 1917. This photograph was taken by Lieutenant John Brooke, an official photographer for the British army on the Western Front.

Horse-drawn and motor ambulances

At first, the British only used horse-drawn ambulances. The first motor-powered ambulances arrived in October 1914.

Problems		Benefits
• Could not cope with the number of casualties, leaving some injured men to die or be captured. • Injured men were shaken about, making injuries worse.	**Horse-drawn ambulance**	• They did not break down. • They coped better than motorised ambulances on rough ground.
• Broke down in the muddy conditions. (Due to the nature of the conditions, horse-drawn ambulances continued to be used during the war.)	**Motorised ambulance**	• A smoother journey meant injuries were not made worse. • A faster way to transport injured soldiers.

Activities ?

Study Source F.

1 What is happening in the photo?
2 What does this source tell us about the problems that faced stretcher bearers? Describe one problem shown in the source.
3 Give two other types of source that would be helpful in investigating the problems faced by stretcher bearers on the Western Front.

Train, barge and ship ambulances

Wounded men might also be transported by train or by canal barge* in the final stage of their evacuation to the Base Hospitals on the French coast (see page 162). At first, ordinary trains were used. The first ambulance train designed for carrying wounded soldiers arrived in France in November 1914. It had spaces for stretchers fitted down both sides of the carriage.

Later, some ambulance trains even contained operating theatres. To relieve pressure on the railways, barges were also used to transport the wounded to Base Hospitals. Although the journey was slow, it was more comfortable. Some of the wounded bypassed the Base Hospitals and were transferred directly onto the ships back to Britain.

Key term

Barge*
A long, flat boat designed to travel on canals.

Source G

From a speech made by Walter Roch in Parliament, 23 June 1915. Roch was a Liberal MP and was taking part in a debate on how the government should spend its money.

I want to bring to the notice of the House information in connection with the treatment of the wounded in Flanders. The information is not my own personal knowledge, but from several very close personal friends who have been connected with this, although I cannot give their names. I am told that it is of the utmost importance that the men who are wounded should be treated as quickly as possible, and that their wounds should have the best possible attention as soon as may be. The suggestion I have to make is that there should be many more of these evacuation hospitals than there are in France at the present moment, that they should be much better equipped with operating theatres and other appliances, and that they should be more sanitary and hygienic in their nature.

Evidence (1b&c)

There are many sources of information about the past. Historians use these sources to help them **draw conclusions**. When information is used to help you form a conclusion, it is used as **evidence**.

Read Source G. In this source, Walter Roch, a Liberal MP, says a number of things. Roch was making a public speech that he knew would be:

a heard in London by his audience

b reported in parliamentary records and possibly in the press.

The message

What **information** does the source contain? What was Roch **saying**? Answer the following questions to find out.

1 What does Roch say is important for wounded men?

2 What does he say the conditions in the hospitals should be like?

The messenger

Historians are not usually interested in content just for information. They want to be able to use it to **answer** questions about the past. **Use** the information you have just extracted from the source and the information about its **context** (who the audience was and who might hear about it) to try and work out answers to the following question about the way in which Parliament was helping the wounded in 1915.

3 What do you think Roch wanted Parliament to spend some of its money on?

Summary

- Trench warfare had begun on the Western Front by the end of 1914.
- As the trench system developed, a complex network of trenches was created in which men could live and fight.
- Tunnels and caves at Arras were used as part of the defensive system.
- Chlorine gas was first used by the Germans at the Second Battle of Ypres in 1915.
- The first motorised ambulances were sent to France in October 1914.
- Wounded men were also moved away from the frontline by trains and canal boats.

Checkpoint

Strengthen

S1 List three problems of transporting wounded men. Describe how these problems were dealt with.

Challenge

Think about the different types of source used in this section on the context of the British sector of the Western Front.

C1 Look at the types of sources in Figure 5.1 (page 139). List all the sources in this section and then try to identify the type of source for each one. For example, for 'Written and official' an example is Source G on page 151.

If you are not confident about any of these questions, your teacher can give you some hints.

5.3 Conditions requiring medical treatment on the Western Front

Learning outcomes

- Understand the main medical problems that were faced on the Western Front and how they were dealt with.
- Understand the main types of wounds and injuries that were experienced by soldiers fighting on the Western Front.

Main medical problems on the Western Front

Life in the trenches was very unpleasant. With so many people living there, it was difficult for them to keep clean. In summer, sewage and dead bodies made the smell dreadful, whilst in winter, bad weather brought flooding and frostbite. Rats were everywhere. A number of medical problems were caused by these conditions.

The nature of wounds

Rifles and explosives

A study of over 200,000 wounded men admitted to Casualty Clearing Stations (CCS) on the Western Front, found that high-explosive shells and shrapnel* were responsible for 58% of wounds. When a shell exploded, it killed anyone close by. A shell explosion also scattered **shrapnel** (fragments of metal in the casing), over a wide area. This meant that anyone who was in the way of the shrapnel was likely to be wounded. The study also found that bullets were responsible for 39% of wounds. Machine guns could fire 450 bullets a minute, and their bullets could fracture bones or hit organs*. Rifles could fire accurately at up to 500 m.

Key terms

Organs*

Parts of the body that keep your body working, e.g. heart, lungs, kidneys.

Amputate*

To cut off a body part.

Lice*

Small insects that live on the body and in clothes. They feed on blood, creating itchy bites.

Gangrene*

When body tissue starts to rot.

Shrapnel*

Bits of metal from explosions.

I have painful, swollen feet as a result of standing in cold mud and water. I'm worried it will turn to gangrene*.

You have **trench foot**. Prevention is best.
- Rub whale oil into your feet to protect them.
- Keep your feet dry and change your socks regularly.

If gangrene does set in, our only option will be to amputate* your leg.

You have **trench fever**. Since 1918 we believe this is caused by your contact with lice*. Go to one of the delousing stations that have been set up.

I have a high temperature, headache and aching muscles.

I am tired. I have headaches, nightmares, loss of speech, uncontrollable shaking and complete mental breakdown.

You have **shell shock**. There is not much understanding about your condition. You could be treated at a hospital in Britain. But you may be accused of cowardice – and possibly be shot!

Figure: Medical problems caused by life in the trenches.

Shrapnel, wound infection and head injuries

Problems	Solutions
When bullets or shrapnel entered the body, they often took with them fabric and dirt from the soldier's uniform. The soil on the Western Front contained the bacteria that cause gas gangrene* and tetanus.	An anti-tetanus injection was produced from the end of 1914. However, there was no cure for gas gangrene.
The soldiers' uniform cap was made of cloth. This did not protect the head from shrapnel and bullets.	In 1915 the metal **Brodie helmet** was introduced. It reduced fatal head wounds by 80%.

Key terms

Gas gangrene*

A serious bacterial infection that produces a gas which kills cells.

Haemorrhage*

Heavy, uncontrolled bleeding.

Septic*

Full of bacteria, and therefore dangerous.

Suffocation*

Not being able to breathe.

Odourless*

Has no smell.

Source A

From an interview with Captain Maberly Esler in 1974. He was a medical officer. Here he is recalling events at Hooge, in the Ypres Salient, in June 1915.

We'd never attempt any major surgery or anything like that in the trenches – one couldn't do it. The only thing you could do was to cover a wound to keep it from getting infected, or stop a haemorrhage* by compression if they were bleeding to death. Several people got tetanus afterwards from an infection in the ground which was carried in shelled areas. The ground had been shelled for such a long time it was in rather a septic* sort of condition.

The effects of gas attacks

Gas attacks caused great panic and fear, as is shown in Wilfred Owen's poem *Dulce et Decorum Est* in Source B. It was not, however, a major cause of death. The British army gave troops on the Western Front gas masks from 1915, and developed more effective ones over time. Still, gas attacks were greatly feared by soldiers on the Western Front.

Chlorine
First used by the Germans in 1915 at the Second Battle of Ypres. It led to death by **suffocation***.

The medical services had no experience in dealing with gas attacks, and so had to experiment with treatments.

Gas masks were given to all British troops in July 1915. Before this, soldiers soaked cotton pads with urine and pressed them to their faces to help stop the gas entering their lungs.

The British tried their own chlorine attack later in 1915 at the Battle of Loos, but the wind changed direction and the gas blew back over the British lines.

Phosgene
First used at the end of 1915 near Ypres. Its effects were similar to those of chlorine but it was faster acting, killing a person within two days.

Mustard gas
First used in 1917 by the Germans. It was an **odourless*** gas that worked within 12 hours, causing blisters inside and outside of the body. It could pass through clothing to burn the skin.

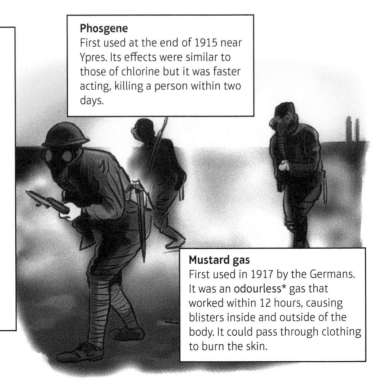

Figure 5.7 Three types of gas attacks on the Western Front.

Source B

From *Dulce et Decorum Est*, a poem written by Wilfred Owen in 1917 whilst he was being treated for shell shock. He served on the Western Front in 1916–17 and returned in 1918, where he was killed in action shortly before the end of the war. The text in the title and the end of the poem is in Latin and means 'it is sweet and fitting to die for one's country'.

```
Gas! Gas! Quick, boys! — An ecstasy of
   fumbling,
Fitting the clumsy helmets just in time;
But someone still was yelling out and
   stumbling,
And flound'ring like a man in fire or lime...
Dim, through the misty panes and thick green
   light,
As under a green sea, I saw him drowning.

In all my dreams, before my helpless sight,
He plunges at me, guttering, choking, drowning.
```

```
If in some smothering dreams you too could pace
Behind the wagon that we flung him in,
And watch the white eyes writhing in his face,
His hanging face, like a devil's sick of sin;
If you could hear, at every jolt, the blood
Come gargling from the froth-corrupted lungs,
Obscene [disgusting] as cancer, bitter as the cud
Of vile, incurable sores on innocent tongues, –
My friend, you would not tell with such high zest
To children ardent for [wanting] some
   desperate glory,
The old Lie; Dulce et Decorum est
Pro patria mori.
```

Source C

From the notebook of Lance Sergeant Elmer Cotton, who served in the 5th Northumberland Fusiliers in 1915. He is describing the effects of a chlorine gas attack.

```
It produces a flooding of the lungs. It is
the equivalent to drowning, only on dry
land. The effects are these - a splitting
headache and a terrific thirst (but to drink
water is instant death), a knife-edge pain in
the lungs and the coughing up of a greenish
froth off the stomach and the lungs, finally
resulting in death. It is a fiendish [cruel]
death to die.
```

Activities ?

1 Study Sources B, C and D.

2 Note down what each source suggests about the effects of a gas attack. Do you notice any similarities? Are there any differences?

3 What other types of source could you use to find out more about the effects of a gas attack?

Source D

From a 1919 painting by John Singer Sargent. Sargent was commissioned by the British War Memorials Committee to paint this in 1918 and researched the painting by visiting both Arras and Ypres before the end of the war. These soldiers have experienced a mustard gas attack.

Asking questions: dealing with gas attacks

Sources require historians to ask themselves three sorts of questions. Look at Source E.

Content questions

Question: What can you learn from the content?

Answer: *You can see that the source is a soldier wearing a mask.*

Provenance questions

How does provenance affect the usefulness of the source? Remember, for provenance, you need to break things down into nature, origin, and purpose.

1   Nature – *it is a photograph.*
2   Origin comes from the caption – *this was taken in the same month that the Second Battle of Ypres began.*
3   Purpose – *can be difficult to determine for a photograph. Might it have been for use as propaganda? In this case, it is hard to think of a propaganda purpose. Does it look like it was set up? Perhaps it was to inform soldiers about the best way that they could protect themselves against gas attacks.*

Context questions

What do you know that is relevant to Source E?

1   *The first use of chlorine gas by the Germans took place in April 1915 at the Second Battle of Ypres.*
2   *The British were not prepared for gas attacks and so they had to experiment to find the best way to protect soldiers.*

So, if you were asked how useful Source E is for an enquiry into British gas masks, you could say something like this [key: content, provenance, context]:

Source E is useful because it shows the first attempts to make a gas mask. The photo might have been set up so that soldiers could learn how best to protect themselves. We know that proper gas masks were not provided at the time because the gas attacks were unexpected.

By doing this you have explained why the source is useful, using criteria based on the three types of question.

Source E

Photograph of a man wearing a cotton wool pad respirator, April 1915. This was a simple form of gas mask. The Second Battle of Ypres also began in April 1915.

Source F

From the autobiography of Geoffrey Keynes, *The Gates of Memory* (1981). This account was originally published in 1968. Keynes was important in developing blood transfusions during the war.

On 6 February 1915 I was detailed for duty on an ambulance train. The numbers of patients carried on each journey varied between 100 and 400. During my turn of duty in the train we carried nearly 19,000 patients. Medical duties were usually restricted to ensuring that the wounded men, who had already been attended in a Dressing Station or Casualty Clearing Station travelled as comfortably as possible with the help of sedative and pain-killing drugs. Frequently they had to suffer violent jolts during shunting operations.

Usually the patients had been fully cared for before being sent on by train to the base hospitals, but on one occasion (12 March 1915), the train was ordered to go close to the frontline and take on casualties who had barely received first aid.

Now look at Sources F and G. Source F describes the work done by doctors on an ambulance train. Although it was written many years later, it includes details of dates and figures, suggesting the author wrote down the details at the time to help him to remember. Source G, on the other hand, is a historical photograph, preserving a moment in time. Its purpose was possibly to record the awful conditions on the Western Front. Both sources tell us something about the different types of transport used to carry the wounded to safety and treatment.

Source G

A photograph of a wagon belonging to the Field Ambulance service, in use in the Somme region, September 1916.

Activity ?

Pick a source type that could be used by a historian who was studying day-to-day life in your school now.

  a Describe the source.

  b Pick and complete an example of a question, from the list below, that could be asked about the content of the source:
What does the source say about…? What does the source show us about…? What does the source suggest…?

  c Pick an example of a provenance question (nature, origin, purpose), from the list below, that could be asked about the source, and answer it:
What type of source is it? Who created it? When was it created? Why was it created?

  d Pick an example of a context question, from the list below, that could be asked about the source, and answer it:
What do you know about the school at the time it was created? Do you have any knowledge that supports or challenges the content?

Summary

- Common medical problems that faced men fighting on the Western Front were trench foot, trench fever and shell shock.
- The introduction of the Brodie helmet saved many lives by protecting the head against shrapnel injuries.
- Gas attacks caused burning skin and suffocation.

Checkpoint

Strengthen

S1 Explain all the medical problems and possible injuries that soldiers faced in the trenches that are referred to in this section. Then note down all the solutions to the problems.

Challenge

C1 Select Source B, C or D. How useful is that source for investigating the effects of gas attacks on the Western Front? Remember to consider each of the criteria when making your judgement:

- content (what does it say)
- provenance (nature, origin and purpose)
- context (how it fits into what you already know).

If you are not confident about any of these questions, form a group with other students, discuss the answers and then record your conclusions. Your teacher can give you some hints.

5.4 The work of the RAMC and FANY

Learning outcomes

- Understand the main stages of the chain of evacuation and what happened to wounded soldiers at each stage.
- Know about the role played by the RAMC* and FANY* in dealing with wounded soldiers.

Key terms

RAMC*

Royal Army Medical Corps. This branch of the army was responsible for medical care.

FANY*

First Aid Nursing Yeomanry. This was the first women's organisation to send volunteers to the Western Front. It provided frontline support for the medical services, for example by driving ambulances and providing emergency first aid.

To deal with the large numbers of casualties in the First World War, the number of medical professionals needed to be increased dramatically.

The table below shows the number of medical professionals in 1914 and 1918.

	1914	1918
Medical officers	3,168	13,063
Other ranks (e.g. private)	16,331	131,099

More than half of Britain's doctors were serving with the armed forces.

The system of transport and the stages of treatment

Because of the large numbers of casualties, an efficient system was needed to get the wounded from the frontline to a safe area where they could be treated. This system became known as the **chain of evacuation.**

Source A

From F. S. Brereton, *The Great War and the RAMC*, published in 1919. Brereton served as a Lieutenant-Colonel in the RAMC on the Western Front. This is a diagram showing how the chain of evacuation might operate in theory.

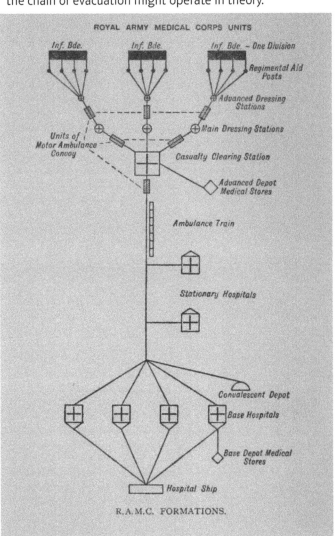

R.A.M.C. FORMATIONS.

The main stages in the chain of evacuation were **Regimental Aid Posts (RAP)**, **Dressing Stations (ADS and MDS)**, **Casualty Clearing Stations** and **Base Hospitals**. Remember – these were not always followed in the same order for every casualty.

Source B

From Ward Muir's *Observations of an Orderly**, published in 1917. Muir was a Lance Corporal in the RAMC and worked in a hospital in London that received patients from the Western Front at the end of the chain of evacuation.

We orderlies meet each convoy at the front door of the hospital. The walking-cases are the first to arrive — men who are either not ill enough, or not badly enough wounded, to need to be put on stretchers in ambulances. They come from the station in motor-cars supplied by the London Ambulance Column. The few minutes which the walking-case spends in the receiving hall are occupied in drinking a cup of cocoa, and in 'having his particulars taken'. Poor soul! — he is weary of giving his 'particulars' [details]. He has had to give them half-a-dozen times at least, perhaps more, since he left the front. At the field dressing-station they wanted his particulars, at the clearing-station, on the train, at the base hospital, on another train, on the steamer, on the next train, and now in this English hospital.

Activities ?

Study Source A and Source B. When Source B refers to 'particulars' it means personal details.

1 Why do you think the first thing that happened to the new arrivals was that they were given a cup of cocoa and had their 'particulars' taken?

2 How useful are these two sources in showing the key stages in the chain of evacuation?

3 Suggest one other source that would give you useful information on the chain of evacuation.

Regimental Aid Posts (RAP)

Where were they?
RAPs were generally located within 200 m of the frontline, in communication trenches or deserted buildings.

Who worked there?
RAPs were made up of a Regimental Medical Officer, with some help from stretcher bearers with first-aid knowledge.

Who did they care for?
Wounded men would either walk in themselves or be carried in by other soldiers.

What was their purpose?
The purpose of the RAP was to give immediate first aid and to get as many men back to the fighting as possible.

Limitation
It could not deal with serious injuries. These were passed to the next stage of the chain of evacuation.

Dressing Stations (ADS and MDS)

Where were they?
There should have been an Advanced Dressing Station (ADS) about 400 m from the RAP and a Main Dressing Station (MDS) a further half a mile back, but this was often not the case – there may only have been one Dressing Station. To offer protection from shelling, they were in dugouts or bunkers, but when this was not possible, tents were used.

Who worked there?
Each dressing station would be staffed by ten medical officers, plus medical orderlies and stretcher bearers of the RAMC. From 1915, there were also some nurses. Those working at the Dressing Stations belonged to part of the RAMC called the **Field Ambulance**. This should not be confused with the vehicles that carried the wounded, which were known as **ambulance wagons**.

Who did they care for?
Men too seriously injured to be cared for at the RAPs walked or were carried by stretcher to the dressing stations.

Source C

From the diary of E.S.B. Hamilton, 19 August 1916. Hamilton had been in France for over a year at this time, as part of the Field Ambulance. At the time of this diary entry, he was working at an Advanced Dressing Station on the Somme.

The dugout [of the ADS] is awfully overcrowded both night and day and it is impossible to get it cleaned or aired. [There were] something like 800 people through here in about thirty hours the day before yesterday. This is far too much work for the personnel [of] three officers and about 115 men. Result [is] a lot of the men are done up [exhausted] and the officers seedy and depressed.

Key term

Orderly*
Someone who works in a hospital to move patients and fetch supplies.

Source D

A photograph of an Advanced Dressing Station. This was taken in August 1916 at Pozieres Ridge, which was part of the Somme campaign.

What was their purpose?

Field Ambulance units at dressing stations would treat men so they could return to the front. More seriously wounded men would be passed to the next stage in the chain of evacuation.

Limitations

The Field Ambulance units did not have the facilities to tend to wounded men for more than a week, so the wounded did not stay there long. Each Field Ambulance unit could deal with 150 wounded men, but during major battles they were forced to deal with many more.

Casualty Clearing Station (CCS)

Where were they?

Casualty Clearing Stations were located far enough from the frontline to provide some safety against attack, but close enough to be reached by ambulance wagons. They were set up in buildings such as factories or schools and were often located near to a railway line to allow the next stage of the chain of evacuation to take place quickly.

Who did they care for?

Men sent there by the dressing stations. When wounded soldiers arrived here, they were divided into three groups, to help medical staff make decisions about treatment. This process was called **triage**.

Who worked there?

The CCSs were staffed by trained doctors and nurses.

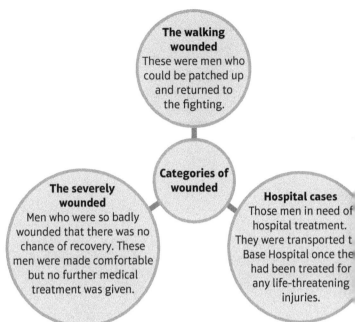

The walking wounded
These were men who could be patched up and returned to the fighting.

Categories of wounded

The severely wounded
Men who were so badly wounded that there was no chance of recovery. These men were made comfortable but no further medical treatment was given.

Hospital cases
Those men in need of hospital treatment. They were transported t Base Hospital once the had been treated for any life-threatening injuries.

Figure: The triage system

What was their purpose?

Triaging the patients was an important role. Life-saving operations were performed at the CCS. Often the CCS closest to the frontline would specialise in operating on the most critical injuries, such as those to the chest.

Limitations

Not everyone would survive their wounds. When the CCS was busy, medical resources had to be saved for those more likely to survive.

Exam-style question, Section A

How useful are Sources C and D for an enquiry into the treatment of the wounded at ADSs on the Western Front?

Explain your answer, using Sources C and D and your knowledge of the historical context. **8 marks**

Exam tip

Go through these steps when preparing your answer.

- Always concentrate on the enquiry – in this question, the **treatment of the wounded at ADSs**. Make a list of what each source says or shows about this.
- Think about the provenance (nature, origin, purpose) of both sources.
- Think about what you know about the context – the treatment of wounds at Advanced Dressing Stations. Does this match up with the content of the source?

Source E

Photograph of a ward in the Casualty Clearing Station at Hazebrouck in 1915. Hazebrouck was close to Ypres.

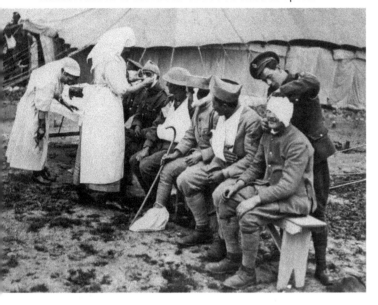

Activities

In pairs, study Source E.

1 Describe the main features of the Casualty Clearing Station in the photograph.

2 From Source E, can we tell if medical treatment in the Casualty Clearing Stations was effective? Complete the sentence below, selecting an option where necessary.

From Source E we (can/can't) tell that medical treatment in the Casualty Clearing Stations was effective because...

The role of FANY

FANY stands for First Aid Nurses Yeomanry. They were a group of female volunteers. At first the British army wouldn't work with them, but in January 1916, the British army decided to allow FANYs to drive ambulances. They became the first women to carry out this role, replacing British Red Cross male ambulance drivers. They were used to transport wounded troops by ambulance in the Calais region. Though there were never more than 450 of them, they opened the way for other women who were attached to other organisations, such as the Voluntary Aid Detachments (VADs), to participate at the frontline.

Extend your knowledge

What else did FANY do?

As well as driving ambulances:

- they drove supplies, such as food and clothes, to the frontline
- they had a mobile bath unit that provided baths for the soldiers in water heated by the power from the van's engine
- they set up cinemas to entertain soldiers.

Source F

From Pat Beauchamp's autobiography, *Fanny Goes to War*, published in 1919. Beauchamp first worked as a nurse, bringing in the wounded from the trenches, and from 1916 as an ambulance driver. Here she is writing about an account of FANYs from an English newspaper.

The following is an extract from an account by Mr. Beach Thomas in a leading daily: "Our Yeomanry nurses who, among other work, drive, clean, and manage their own ambulance cars... have done prodigies [wonders] along the Belgian front. One of their latest activities has been to devise and work a peripatetic [travelling] bath... Ten collapsible baths are packed into a motor car which circulates behind the lines. The water is heated by the engine in a cistern [water container] in the interior of the car and offers the luxury of a hot bath to several score men."

Base Hospitals (also known as Stationary Hospitals or General Hospitals)

Where were they?

Base Hospitals on the Western Front were located near the French and Belgian coast, so that men could be easily transported back to Britain for further treatment.

What was their purpose?

The Base Hospitals became increasingly responsible for continuing treatment that was begun in the CCSs, before men were either returned to frontline fighting or transported back to Britain. They also experimented with new techniques. For example, by dividing patients up into different wards according to their wounds, such as amputees, head wounds, chest wounds, and by allocating doctors to a specialised ward, doctors became expert in the treatment of particular wounds.

Limitations

As the war progressed, Casualty Clearing Stations did more of the operations instead of Base Hospitals. If contaminated wounds were not dealt with quickly, wounded men were more likely to develop gangrene, so it was better not to wait until the patient reached the Base Hospital to treat them.

The Casualty Clearing Stations did most of the operations until the spring of 1918. Trench warfare had meant that the CCSs had been relatively safe early on in the war, but in March 1918, the Germans launched the Spring Offensive and many CCSs came under attack. Operations had to be moved back to the safety of Base Hospitals.

Key term

Mortuary*

A place where the bodies of the dead were stored until they could be buried.

Source G

A photograph of a British Base Hospital in 1916. The nurses are preparing for a visit from King George V.

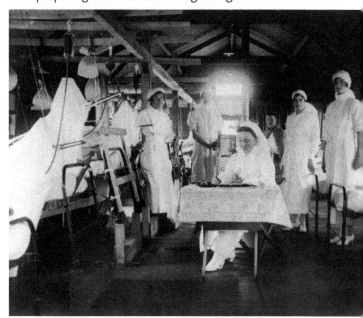

The underground hospital at Arras

In November 1916, tunnelling began under the town of Arras. In 800 m of tunnels, a fully working hospital was created. It was so close to the frontline that it was, in reality, a Dressing Station. It was sometimes called **Thompson's Cave** after the RAMC officer who set it up. There were waiting rooms for the wounded, 700 spaces for stretchers, an operating theatre, rest stations for stretcher bearers, and a mortuary* to lay out the dead. Electricity and piped water were supplied to the hospital.

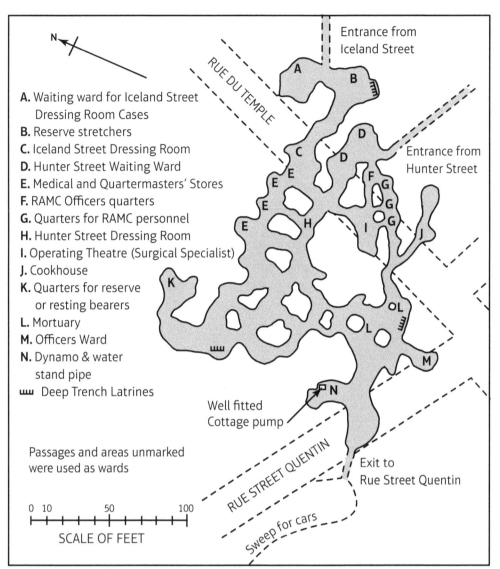

A. Waiting ward for Iceland Street Dressing Room Cases
B. Reserve stretchers
C. Iceland Street Dressing Room
D. Hunter Street Waiting Ward
E. Medical and Quartermasters' Stores
F. RAMC Officers quarters
G. Quarters for RAMC personnel
H. Hunter Street Dressing Room
I. Operating Theatre (Surgical Specialist)
J. Cookhouse
K. Quarters for reserve or resting bearers
L. Mortuary
M. Officers Ward
N. Dynamo & water stand pipe
ㅛ Deep Trench Latrines

Passages and areas unmarked were used as wards

0 10   50   100
SCALE OF FEET

Figure 5.8 Plan of the Arras Underground hospital, also known as Thompson's Cave, based on a drawing from April 1917.

Source H

From Major-General Sir W. G. Macpherson, *Medical Services General History*, published in 1924. Macpherson was on the Western Front from 1914. From 1916–18, he was in charge of the RAMC. He wrote this history based on official records to which he had access. Here he is writing about the underground hospital at Arras.

Dressing Stations were established in caves, cellars and basements of buildings, protected as strongly as possible with sandbags on the outskirts of the town. The chief of these was in a large subterranean [below ground] cave, from which stone had been excavated [dug out] for building the town in the 16th century. It was close to the 3rd Division trenches and only 800 yards from the frontline. Two entrances for stretchers were tunnelled into it from the communication trenches, and an exit tunnelled out from the back into Rue St Quentin, where an approach was constructed for ambulance cars. This cave was fitted with electric light and a piped water supply and was able to accommodate 700 wounded on stretchers in two tiers [levels].

Source I

From *The Daily Telegraph*, a British newspaper, 29 April 1915.

POISON BOMBS: CANADIAN'S HEROIC CONDUCT

There appears little doubt that the material used by the Germans in the "poison bombs" is chlorine. This is the only conclusion one can arrive at after hearing the graphic narration of a Canadian who was enveloped in the fumes near Ypres.

The Canadian said, "Directly we opened fire the Germans rained shrapnel over us. We kept the guns going, wounded as some of us were. That we could stand. We had no complaints, because it was honest warfare. Then came the surprise. We saw bombs burst in the air and throw off a greenish-yellow vapour [visible gas]..."

At yesterday's meeting of the London Education Committee, the chairman (Mr. Gilbert) called attention to the request of the Government for respirators [gas masks] for the troops.

Using the range of sources

Following up an enquiry

In the examination, you are asked to suggest a possible question and a type of source that you could use to follow up another source. This is the framework, and some possible answers.

Detail in Source I that I would follow up:
The request for respirators.

Question I would ask:
How many gas masks were given to Canadian troops after April 1915?

Type of source I could use:
Either private diaries, local newspapers or official records.

How this might answer my question:
I could follow up Source I with a private diary because gas attacks would be a common event that soldiers would write about in their diaries.

National newspapers

Source I shows you some of the strengths and weaknesses of national newspapers as sources. The report tells us about events that are going on both at the Western Front and at home. The chairman of the London Education Committee is named, but the soldier is not. He is only referred to as 'the Canadian'. The article appears to give valid information, but it is also a form of propaganda.

Activity ?

Read Source I in small groups.
- **a** What information can you find about the German attack at Ypres, and the types of weapon used?
- **b** How useful is this national newspaper for studying gas attacks?

CONTENT What does it tell you about gas attacks?

PROVENANCE Who wrote it, when and why?

CONTEXT How does Source I fit with what you already know about gas attacks?

Summary

- The Royal Army Medical Corps (RAMC) provided both doctors and other staff to support the medical services.
- The First Aid Nursing Yeomanry (FANY) provided additional support to the RAMC.
- Moving the wounded from the frontline to the appropriate medical facility was known as the chain of evacuation.
- The main stages for the most severely wounded were the Regimental Aid Post, the Dressing Station, Casualty Clearing Station and Base Hospital.

Checkpoint

Strengthen

S1 Create a flow diagram that shows the main stages in the chain of evacuation.

If you are not sure, go back to the text in this section to find the details you need.

5.5 The significance of the Western Front for experiments in surgery and medicine

Learning outcomes

- Understand how the experience of war on the Western Front gave rise to new techniques in medical treatment.
- Understand how new methods of surgery developed to treat the large number of head injuries that were a result of trench warfare.

New techniques in the treatment of wounds and infection

A major problem that faced the RAMC at the start of the war on the Western Front was dealing with infections caused by gas gangrene. It was not possible to perform aseptic surgery in Dressing Stations and many Casualty Clearing Stations, due to the dirty conditions and because of the large numbers of wounded men needing treatment.

Therefore other methods of treatment had to be found.

> **Key term**
>
> **Antiseptics***
> Substances that kill bacteria.

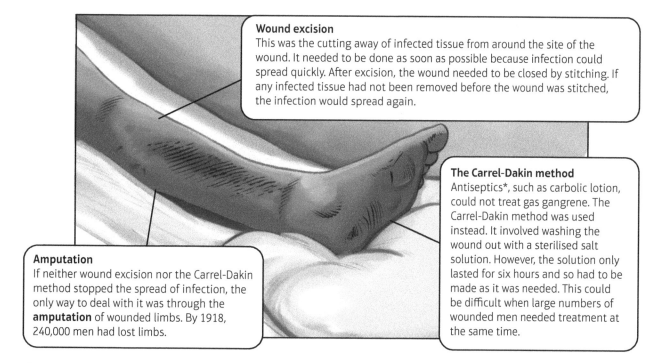

Wound excision
This was the cutting away of infected tissue from around the site of the wound. It needed to be done as soon as possible because infection could spread quickly. After excision, the wound needed to be closed by stitching. If any infected tissue had not been removed before the wound was stitched, the infection would spread again.

The Carrel-Dakin method
Antiseptics*, such as carbolic lotion, could not treat gas gangrene. The Carrel-Dakin method was used instead. It involved washing the wound out with a sterilised salt solution. However, the solution only lasted for six hours and so had to be made as it was needed. This could be difficult when large numbers of wounded men needed treatment at the same time.

Amputation
If neither wound excision nor the Carrel-Dakin method stopped the spread of infection, the only way to deal with it was through the **amputation** of wounded limbs. By 1918, 240,000 men had lost limbs.

Figure 5.9 The main techniques used to prevent infections from spreading.

Source A

From the diary of B. C. Jones, 1915–16. Jones served with the Royal Field Artillery in France from the start of the war until he was wounded in 1915.

7 December. A German shell hit the dugout of our telephone pit. I remembered no more until I woke up in Bethune Casualty Clearing Station Number 33, where I find I have been severely wounded. Left hand blown off, left arm ripped up 12 inches. Scalp [head] wound 6 inches, wound on over side of knee (left) 5 inches.

9 December. Operation on upper arm for gangrene (successful).

12 December. I remain here for 8 days then removed to St Omer by hospital barge, very comfortable. I am then removed by train to Étaples. I am sent to England on the Hospital Ship. Return to Nottingham where I am in bed until the end of February.

3 June 1916. I am eventually transferred to Brighton where I am operated on and re-amputated*. Awaiting Roehampton for artificial limb.

Source B

From Ward Muir's *Observations of an Orderly*, published in 1917. Muir was a Lance Corporal in the RAMC and worked in a hospital in London that received patients from the Western Front at the end of the chain of evacuation.

The majority of stretcher-cases... reach us in a by no means desperate state, for, as I say, they seldom come to England without having been treated previously at a base abroad (except during the periods of heavy fighting). And it is remarkable how often the patient refuses help in getting off the stretcher on to the bed. He may be a cocoon of bandages, but he will courageously heave himself overboard, from stretcher to bed, with a wallop which would be deemed rash even in a person in perfect health.

Activities

Study Sources A and B.

1 What conclusions can you draw from the fact that the soldier in Source A needed to have a limb re-amputated when he returned to England?

2 With a partner, make a list of enquiries you think Source A and B would be useful for.

The Thomas splint

In 1914 and 1915, men with a gunshot or shrapnel wound to the leg only had a 20% chance of survival. These wounds often caused compound fractures where the broken bone came through the skin, causing major bleeding. Broken femurs (thigh bones) were especially dangerous.

The splint* that was in use at the start of the war did not keep the leg rigid. By the time the wounded man arrived at the Casualty Clearing Station, he would have lost a great deal of blood and was likely to be in shock*. He might already have developed gas gangrene infection in the wound. This reduced his chances of surviving an operation to the wound.

A way of improving the survival rate for men with this type of injury was needed. In the late 19th century, Robert Jones had worked with his uncle, Hugh Thomas, who had designed a splint to stop joints from moving. When the war broke out, Jones worked with disabled soldiers in a hospital in London and started to make use of his uncle's **Thomas splint**. As a result of its success, he was sent to France in December 1915 to instruct medical practitioners on how to use the Thomas splint. The survival rate for this type of leg wound increased from 20% to 82%.

Key terms

Re-amputated*

A second operation to remove any further infected tissue and to neaten the original amputation.

Splint*

A framework used to stop an injured limb moving.

Shock*

When the body starts to shut down due to loss of blood.

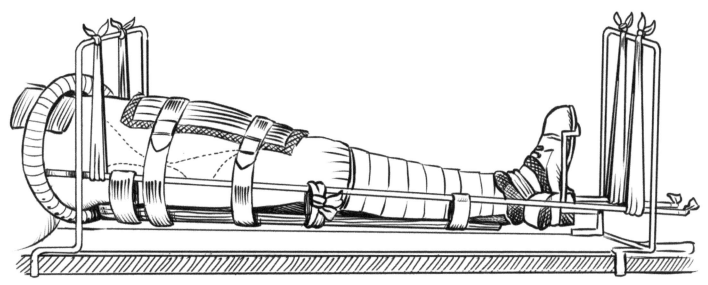

Figure 5.10 The Thomas splint.

The use of mobile x-ray units

X-rays were used from the start of the war. Their main use was to identify shell fragments and bullets in wounds, which, if not removed, could cause infection.

The use of x-rays was a success story, but there were some problems with using them on the Western front, as shown below.

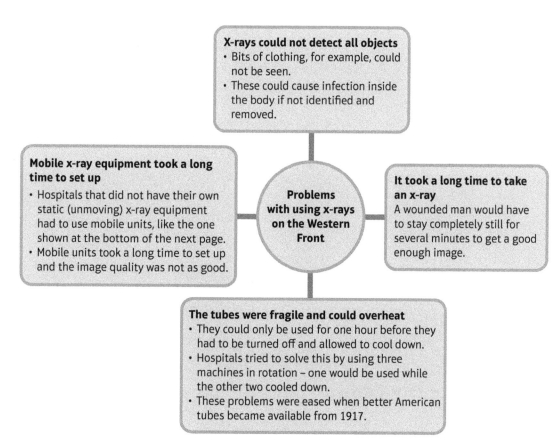

X-rays could not detect all objects
- Bits of clothing, for example, could not be seen.
- These could cause infection inside the body if not identified and removed.

Mobile x-ray equipment took a long time to set up
- Hospitals that did not have their own static (unmoving) x-ray equipment had to use mobile units, like the one shown at the bottom of the next page.
- Mobile units took a long time to set up and the image quality was not as good.

Problems with using x-rays on the Western Front

It took a long time to take an x-ray
A wounded man would have to stay completely still for several minutes to get a good enough image.

The tubes were fragile and could overheat
- They could only be used for one hour before they had to be turned off and allowed to cool down.
- Hospitals tried to solve this by using three machines in rotation – one would be used while the other two cooled down.
- These problems were eased when better American tubes became available from 1917.

Figure: Problems with using x-rays on the Western Front.

Source C

From *Radiography and Radiotherapeutics*, by Robert Knox, published in 1917. This was a textbook on the use of x-rays written by a British doctor.

The need for portable [movable] outfits in connection with the war has led to a great development in the provision of motor wagons containing complete x-ray apparatus [equipment] with all accessories. The mechanism used for driving the wagon, i.e. the motor is coupled with a powerful dynamo* which delivers a continuous current.

Key term

Dynamo*

Machine that turns energy into electricity.

Exam-style question, Section A

How could you follow up Source C to find out more about x-rays on the Western Front?

In your answer, you must give the question you would ask and the type of source you could use.

Copy out and complete the table below. **4 marks**

Detail in Source C that I would follow up	
Question I would ask	
What type of source I could use	
How this might help answer my question	

Exam tip

This question involves a four-stage process. The example shows you what to do at each stage.

- **Pick a detail.** For example, 'a great development in the provision of motor wagons.'
- **Question I would ask.** How many x-ray vehicles were used in 1917 on the Western Front?
- **Type of source I would use.** Military records showing the number of x-ray vehicles being used in 1917 on the Western Front.
- **How this might help answer my question.** The data would show whether the numbers increased and whether this was a 'great development'.

Source D

A photograph of a mobile x-ray unit, taken in 1917. Notice how the equipment has been laid out.

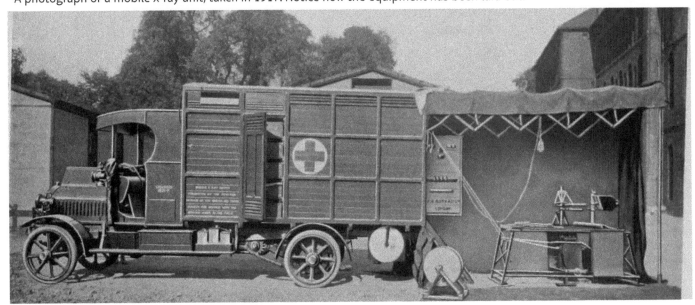

The Base Hospitals and some of the larger Casualty Clearing Stations had static (unmoving) x-ray machines as part of their equipment. Those that did not have them could call on a mobile unit (see Source D). There were six mobile x-ray units operating in the British sector on the Western Front. A tent was attached to the back of the van with a table where stretchers could be placed. The x-ray machine was set up next to this table and linked to the engine of the van, which was used to power the x-ray machine. The equipment for processing the x-ray films was set up inside the van.

The blood bank at Cambrai

Stored blood was used in 1917 at the Battle of Cambrai. Before the battle, Oswald Hope Robertson stored 22 units of type O donor blood in glass bottles. He built a carrying case for the bottles using ammunition boxes which he packed with ice and sawdust. During the battle, he treated 20 severely wounded Canadian soldiers. Some of the blood had been collected 26 days before use. None of the soldiers he treated was expected to survive. In fact, of the 20 wounded men, 11 survived.

Robertson's work at Cambrai was the first time that stored blood was used to treat soldiers in shock, demonstrating its potential to save lives. During times of heavy fighting, there were not many men healthy enough to donate blood at the Casualty Clearing Stations. Therefore, the availability of stored blood made a huge difference to men's chances of survival.

Blood transfusions

Problems

- Without blood transfusions, patients often bled to death from wounds or during operations.
- Blood had to be used immediately – otherwise it would start to clot – so the donor and patient had to be in the same place.
- Not being able to store blood meant there were always shortages.
- Not all transfusions were successful. The patient's body did not always accept the donor's blood because sometimes they were given the wrong blood type.

Solutions

- From 1915, Canadian doctor Lawrence Bruce Robertson developed blood transfusion techniques at the Base Hospital in Boulogne. Many of his patients recovered. By 1917, blood transfusions were used at Base Hospitals and Casualty Clearing Stations.

- Geoffrey Keynes, a British doctor in the RAMC, designed a portable blood transfusion kit. It could be used to provide blood transfusions close to the frontline.
- Keynes added a device to the blood bottle to control the flow of the blood. This helped to stop it from clotting.
- In 1915 it was used in CCSs and saved countless lives.

- Chemicals were discovered that allowed blood to be stored:
  - In 1915 sodium citrate was added to blood. This allowed blood to be stored for up to two days.
  - In 1916 it was found that adding citrate glucose solution allowed blood to be stored for up to four weeks.
- The discovery that type O blood could be safely transfused into anyone reduced the risk of rejection.

Figure: Blood transfusions

The attempts to deal with increased numbers of head injuries

About 20% of all wounds in the British sector of the Western Front were to the head, face and neck. This was the part of the body that was least protected in the trench warfare of the Western Front. This type of injury could be caused by both bullets and shrapnel.

Brain surgery

Injuries to the brain were very likely to prove fatal at the start of the war, for several reasons.

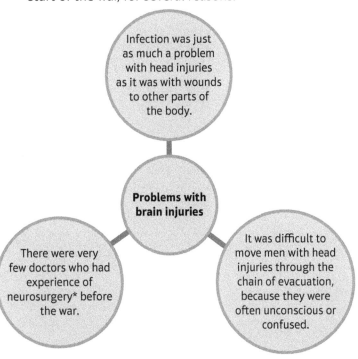

Infection was just as much a problem with head injuries as it was with wounds to other parts of the body.

Problems with brain injuries

There were very few doctors who had experience of neurosurgery* before the war.

It was difficult to move men with head injuries through the chain of evacuation, because they were often unconscious or confused.

Key term

Neurosurgery*

Surgery carried out on the nervous system, especially the brain and the spine.

There were rapid improvements in methods of treatment.

Harvey Cushing, an American neurosurgeon, developed new techniques in brain surgery on the Western Front. He used a magnet to remove metal fragments from the brain. He also used a local anaesthetic* rather than a general anaesthetic* when operating. He had noticed that the brain swelled during general anesthetic, increasing the risk of the surgery. In 1917, Cushing's survival rate was 71% compared to the usual 50% for brain surgery.

Observation	New methods for treating head injuries
Men who were operated on quickly were more likely to survive.	Specific Casualty Clearing Stations were chosen as centres for brain surgery.
It was dangerous to move men too soon after an operation.	Patients remained at the Casualty Clearing Station for three weeks after surgery.
Injuries that looked fairly minor could be hiding more severe injuries.	All head wounds were always carefully examined.

Key terms

Local anaesthetic*

Keeping a patient awake during an operation, with the area being operated on numbed to prevent pain.

General anaesthetic*

Putting a patient to sleep during an operation.

Irrigation*

Washing with water or other liquid.

Source E

From *A Surgeon's Journal 1915–18*, by Harvey Cushing, published in 1936. Here he is describing the conditions under which he is working during the battle of Passchendaele on 19 August 1917.

My prize patient, Baker, with the shrapnel ball removed from his brain, after doing well for three days suddenly shot up a temperature to 104 last night about midnight. I took him to the operating theatre, reopened the perfectly healed external wound, and found to my dismay a massive gas infection of the brain. I bribed two orderlies to stay up with him in the operating room, where he could have constant thorough irrigation* over the brain and through the track of the missile [passing a warm saline solution along the path taken by the shrapnel to prevent infection]. No light except candles was permitted last night.

Plastic surgery

The development of plastic surgery was largely the work of a New Zealand doctor called Harold Gillies. He was an ENT (ear, nose and throat) surgeon. He was sent to the Western Front in January 1915. Head injuries that might not kill, could cause severe disfigurement*. This led Gillies to become interested in facial reconstruction* – how to replace and restore those parts of the face that had been destroyed. As he had no background in this type of surgery, he devised new operations to deal with problems as he saw them.

Source F

Four photographs documenting the facial reconstruction of a soldier whose cheek was extensively wounded during the Battle of the Somme (July 1916).

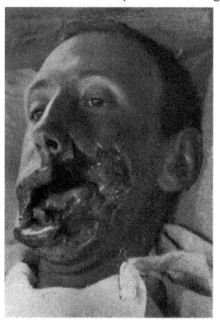
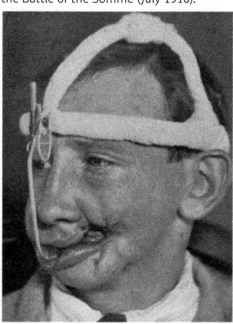

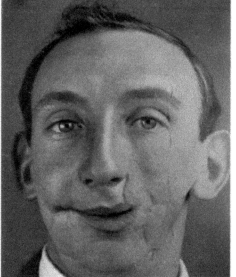

Activities ?

Study Source E and answer the following questions:

1 Give one reason why Baker was Cushing's 'prize patient'.
2 What happened to make Baker's temperature rise?
3 Use Source E to list two problems facing surgeons on the Western Front.

Key terms

Disfigurement*

A wound that changes the look of the body.

Reconstruction*

To rebuild damaged areas.

Source G

A photograph showing the work of Harold Gillies, 1916.

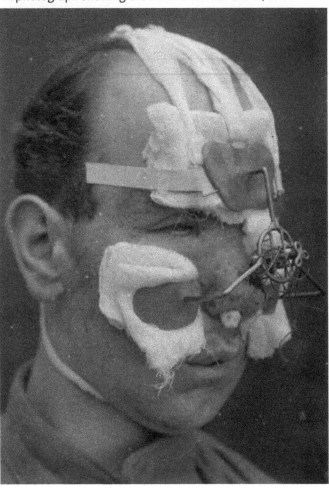

The complex operations and recovery that were required in plastic surgery could not be carried out in France. Men who needed this surgery were returned to Britain.

THINKING HISTORICALLY   Evidence (3a)

The value of evidence

Read Source H, then work through these tasks.

1 Write down at least two ways in which Cushing's memoir is useful for explaining injuries on the Western Front.

2 Give Source H a score for how useful it is for explaining injuries on the Western Front on a scale of 1 to 10.

3 What if the source was used to answer the question: 'How is Cushing's memoir useful for explaining the work done by surgeons and doctors on the Western Front?'

   a Write down any ways in which the source is useful for answering this new question.

   b Write down any limitations for answering the new question.

   c Decide how useful this source is for answering the question on a scale of 1 to 10.

   d Can you think of another enquiry for which this would be a useful source? Write it down and score the source on a scale of 1 to 10.

Source H

From *A Surgeon's Journal 1915–18*, by Harvey Cushing, published in 1936. This work is made up of extracts from the journal* kept by American surgeon Cushing during the war. Here he is describing his first impressions of medical treatment on the Western Front soon after his arrival in France on 2 April 1915.

It is difficult to say just what are one's most vivid [memorable] impressions: the amazing patience of the most seriously wounded, some of them hanging on for months; the dreadful deformities (not so much in the way of amputations, but broken jaws and twisted, scarred faces); the tedious [long and boring] healing of infected wounds with discharging sinuses*, tubes, irrigation and repeated dressings. Painful fractures are simply abandoned to wait for wounds to heal, which they don't seem to do.

Key terms

Journal*

A type of diary.

Sinus*

A passageway - usually used to describe passageways through the face that connect with the nose.

172

Activities

1 Make a list of the improvements in medical techniques that occurred on the Western Front.
2 Divide this list into those improvements that were made by the medical profession and those that were caused by other factors (such as the nature of war, or science and technology).

Summary

- Many new medical techniques and ideas were tried to meet the needs of those wounded on the Western Front.
- The Thomas splint was responsible for a dramatic decline in the number of deaths of men who received leg wounds.
- Mobile x-ray units enabled surgeons to see where shrapnel and bullets remained in the body. This reduced the number of deaths from infection by gas gangrene.
- The first use of stored blood in blood transfusions was at the Battle of Cambrai.
- Harvey Cushing developed new methods of brain surgery.
- Harold Gillies developed the effective use of plastic surgery for men who had suffered severe facial injuries.

Checkpoint

Strengthen

S1 List the different medical techniques used to treat the wounded on the Western Front.
S2 Give one reason why the blood bank at Cambrai was so important.
S3 Give two things you can learn about plastic surgery from Sources G and H.

Challenge

C1 Look at your list of improvements in medical techniques (Activity 1 above). Which of these improvements do you think was the most important on the Western Front? Explain your answer to a partner. Do you agree with each other?

If you are not confident about any of these questions, form a group with other students, discuss the answers and then record your conclusions. Your teacher can give you some hints.

Recap: The British Sector of the Western Front 1914–18

There are three questions in this section of the exam paper. This recap section is structured around the demands of the three questions.

- The **Two features quiz** is designed to help you prepare for the first question, which requires you to remember details about a topic in this section of the course. However, this isn't the only time you'll need to remember details in the examination, so make sure you have a clear knowledge and understanding of all topics. When you are answering questions about the sources, you need to use your knowledge of the period.

- The **This source is useful for** table helps you prepare for the second question in the exam, which gives you two sources and asks you how useful they would be for a particular enquiry*.

- The **What is the question?** table helps you prepare for the second and third questions – in both of these questions, thinking about the enquiry is vital.

- Finally, the **All about the details** table helps you think about the types of source and how they can be used for new enquiries.

Key term

Enquiry*

Planned investigation.

Two features quiz

For each topic below, list as many facts or features as you can. Aim to have at least two features for every topic.

1 The trench system
2 Stretcher bearers
3 Ambulances
4 Trench foot
5 Gas attacks
6 RAMC
7 FANY
8 Dressing Stations
9 Casualty Clearing Stations
10 Base Hospitals
11 The underground hospital at Arras
12 The Thomas splint
13 Blood transfusions
14 The blood bank at Cambrai
15 Plastic surgery

This source is useful for

Sources	Enquiry	The Historical Context	One way in which each source is useful
B (page 147)	What were conditions like in the trenches?	Trench warfare on the Western Front lasted for most of the war and conditions in them varied…	Source B is useful because it shows what a trench looked like.
H (page 172) *or* F (page 161)	What were the problems involved in caring for the wounded on the Western Front?	*Give two problems experienced by medical professionals on the Western Front…*	Source H is useful because it says… or Source F is useful because it says…
C (page 159)	What was the attitude of the soldiers to the medical treatment that they received?	*Give one positive and one negative detail about treatments available on the Western Front…*	Source C is useful because it says…

What is the question?

Source	Enquiry it would be useful for (and why)	Enquiry it would not be useful for
A (page 154)	How medical care in the frontline was carried out – the ways in which emergency first aid was used to keep men alive.	What happened to wounded men once they were moved further back in the chain of evacuation.
A (page 147)	*What aspect of the Western Front does the source show us?*	
C (page 155)	*What is the author describing?*	
C (page 168)	*What technology is being described?*	

All about the details

Source	Detail	Question I would ask	Type of source I would use	How this might help answer my question
B (page 166)	'They seldom come to England without having been treated previously at a base abroad.'	To what extent were stretcher cases treated on the Western Front before being sent to England?	Medical records, and testimonies from those working on the Western Front.	Source B only has a narrow view of treatment on the Western Front. Muir worked in England, and so does not know exactly the types of treatment 'stretcher cases' were given on the Western Front.
G (page 151)			*Select one from: medical records, newspaper reports, photographs, journals and diaries, diagrams, battle report, politician's speech.*	
A (page 138)				

Preparing for your GCSE Paper 1 exam

Paper 1 overview

Paper 1 is in two sections that examine the Historic Environment Study and the Thematic Study. Together they count for 30% of your History assessment. The questions on the Historic Environment section of the 'Medicine in Britain' paper are in Section A and are worth 10% of your History assessment. Allow about one-third of the examination time (25 mins) for Section A, making sure you leave enough time for Section B.

History Paper 1	Historic Environment and Thematic Study			Time 1 hour 15 minutes
Section A	Historic Environment	Answer 3 questions	16 marks	25 minutes
Section B	Thematic Study	Answer 3 questions	32 marks + 4 SPaG marks	50 minutes

Section A: The historic environment: The British sector of the Western Front, 1914–18

You need to answer Question 1 and Question 2. Question 2 is in two parts.

1 Describe two features of... (4 marks)

You are given a few lines to write about each feature. Allow 5 minutes to write your answer. This question is only worth 4 marks and you should keep your answer brief.

2 (a) How useful are Sources A and B for an enquiry into... (8 marks)

You are given two sources to make judgements about. They are in a separate sources booklet so you can keep them in front of you while you write your answer. Allow 15 minutes for this question, to give yourself time to read both sources carefully. Make sure your answer refers to both sources.

You should **ask yourself the following questions about** the sources.

- What useful information do they give? What do they say or show? Check the question and only give details that are directly relevant to that topic.
- What can you infer? What do they suggest?

You must also **evaluate** the source.

- Use contextual knowledge and the provenance (the nature, origin and purpose of the source) to weigh up the strengths and limitations of each source.

Make judgements about the usefulness of each source, giving clear reasons. These should be based on the importance of the content of the sources and should also take account of the provenance of the source.

Analyse	Evaluate
• Useful information • What does it suggest?	• Contextual knowledge • Its strengths and limitations

╋

2 (b) Study Source... How could you follow up Source... to find out more about... ? (4 marks)

You are given a table to complete when you answer this question. It has four parts to it:

- the detail you would follow up
- the question you would ask
- the type of source you could use to find the information
- your explanation of how this information would help answer the question.

Allow 5 minutes to write your answer. You should keep your answer brief and not try to fill extra lines. The question is only worth 4 marks. Plan your answer so that all the parts link. Your answer will not be strong if you choose a detail to follow up, but then cannot think of a question or type of source that would help you follow it up.

Paper 1, Question 1

Describe **two** features of Casualty Clearing Stations. **(4 marks)**

Basic answer

Casualty Clearing Stations were as close as possible to the frontline. The wounded were divided into three groups in the Casualty Clearing Stations.

The answer has identified two features, but has not supplied any supporting information.

Verdict

This is a basic answer because two valid features are given, but there is no supporting information. Use the feedback to rewrite this answer, making as many improvements as you can.

Good answer

Casualty Clearing Stations were close enough to the frontline to be able to deal quickly with the wounded, but far enough away to have some protection from shelling.
A triage system was used to divide the wounded into groups in the clearing stations. Those who were not likely to survive would only be made comfortable, but not treated.

The answer has identified two features and describes them in more detail. The location of the Casualty Clearing Stations is described very clearly. The system of sorting patients is given its technical name and an example of one group is described.

Verdict

This is a good answer because it gives two clear features of Casualty Clearing Stations and gives extra detail to make the descriptions more precise.

Sources for use with Section A

Source A

From Harvey Cushing's *A Surgeon's Journal 1915–18*, published in 1936. This work is made up of extracts from the journal kept by Cushing, an American surgeon. Here he is describing the conditions under which he is working during the battle of Passchendaele on 19 August 1917.

My prize patient, Baker, with the shrapnel ball removed from his brain, after doing well for three days suddenly shot up a temperature to 104 last night about midnight. I took him to the operating theatre, reopened the perfectly healed external wound, and found to my dismay a massive gas infection of the brain. I bribed two orderlies to stay up with him in the operating room, where he could have constant thorough irrigation over the brain and through the track of the missile [passing a warm saline solution along the path taken by the shrapnel to prevent infection]. No light except candles was permitted last night.

Source B

Photograph of a mobile x-ray unit taken in 1917.

Paper 1, Question 2a

Study Sources A and B on page 178.

How useful are Sources A and B for an enquiry into the treatments that were available for wounded soldiers on the Western Front?

Explain your answer, using Sources A and B and your own knowledge of the historical context.   **(8 marks)**

Exam tip

Consider the strengths and weaknesses of the evidence. Make sure you link to the enquiry question. Include points about the following.

• What does the source say or suggest that is relevant?

• What is the provenance (the nature, origin or purpose) of each source and how does this affect how you use it?

• How does the information in the source fit with your contextual knowledge?

Basic answer

Source A is useful because Cushing tells us that there were operating theatres where the wounded could be taken to be operated on at any time.

Some useful information is taken from the source and the information is relevant to the topic focus (how wounds were treated). The answer suggests an inference – 'operated on at any time' – but does not really explain how this helps us to understand how wounds were treated?

The answer does not make use of any contextual knowledge about how wounds were treated in order to evaluate Source A.

It also does not consider the provenance (nature, origin or purpose) of Source A and whether this makes it more or less useful.

Source B is useful because it is an actual photograph of a mobile x-ray machine that was used on the Western Front during the war to find shrapnel in the body. It is reliable because we know that these machines were carried around in vans and set up wherever they were needed. The photograph shows how the x-ray machine was linked to the van and the machine got its power from the van.

The answer considers both sources. The comments on Source B show that there is information that can be taken from the photograph. Contextual knowledge is added to show that the photograph is reliable. It would be stronger if the answer considered whether the source being a photograph made it more or less useful.

Verdict

This is a basic answer because:

• it has taken relevant information from both sources and has attempted to answer the question

• it has added in some relevant contextual knowledge for Source B.

• it has not used the provenance of the sources to evaluate them.

Use the feedback to rewrite this answer, making as many improvements as you can.

Paper 1, Question 2a

How useful are Sources A and B for an enquiry into the treatments that
were available for wounded soldiers on the Western Front? **(8 marks)**

Good answer

Source A is useful because Cushing tells us that there were operating theatres
where the wounded could be taken to be operated on at any time, even at night.
There were staff available to keep watch on patients, although they had to be
bribed to do this.

> Some useful information is taken from Source A. The answer suggests an inference (what the source suggests) – 'operated on at any time'.

Source A is also useful because Cushing was a surgeon who carried out operations
during the war and was at Passchendaele – but it is also not useful because this
journal was published nearly 20 years after the end of the war. He is describing
brain surgery and this was only one type of surgery. Other types of surgery were
needed for other injuries, such as arm and leg amputations.

> Comments are made about the author of the source and when it was written. The answer shows an awareness of other types of operation from contextual knowledge, but this could be developed further.

Source B is useful because it is an actual photograph of a mobile x-ray machine
that was used on the Western Front during the war to find shrapnel in the body.
It is reliable because we know that these machines were carried around in vans
and set up wherever they were needed. The photograph shows how the x-ray
machine was linked to the van and the machine got its power from the van. It
only shows one x-ray machine, so this makes it less useful.

> These comments show that there is information that can be taken from the photograph. Contextual knowledge is added to show that the photograph is reliable.

Verdict

This is a good answer because:
• it has commented on both sources
• it has used some contextual knowledge in the evaluation of both sources
• it considers the provenance (nature, origin or purpose) of each source.

Paper 1, Question 2b

Study Source A (see page 178).

How could you follow up Source A to find out more about the treatments that were available for wounded soldiers on the Western Front?

In your answer, you must give the question you would ask and the type of source you could use. **(4 marks)**

Basic answer

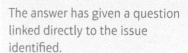

Detail in Source A that I would follow up:

After doing well for three days a massive gas infection set in.

Question I would ask:

What other treatments could be used to deal with infections?

What type of source I could use:

Army medical records.

How this might help answer my question:

They would describe the other types of treatment for infections.

The question is loosely linked to the detail to be followed up.

The type of source is not specific enough. The explanation of the type of source is repeating the question, rather than explaining how the source might answer the question.

Verdict

This is a basic answer because the explanation of the question is not developed. The link between the detail to follow up and the question is weak. Use the feedback to rewrite this answer, making as many improvements as you can.

Good answer

Detail in Source A that I would follow up:

After doing well for three days a massive gas infection set in.

Question I would ask:

How effective were the different types of treatments for dealing with infections like gas gangrene?

What type of source I could use:

Army medical records with data on the survival rates of men who had different treatments for gas gangrene such as irrigation, and amputation.

How this might help answer my question:

It would help to see if one of the treatments that was used on the Western Front was more effective than the others.

The answer has given a question linked directly to the issue identified.

A specific type of source is identified. The explanation is linked back to the question for follow-up and the type of source chosen.

Verdict

This is a good answer because connections between the source details, the question and the follow-up source are securely linked.

Answers to Medicine Recap Questions

Chapter 1

1. To test someone's faith or punish them for sin
2. Galen and Hippocrates.
3. Blood, phlegm, black bile, yellow bile or choler
4. They had to become imbalanced
5. Answers could include the position of the stars and miasma
6. A spice-based mixture that could contain up to 70 ingredients, which was used as a cure to many diseases
7. *Regimen Sanitatis*
8. An alternative to a doctor or to mix remedies
9. 1,100
10. One million

Chapter 2

1. Answers could include Jan Baptiste van Helmont, William Harvey and Robert Hooke
2. Thomas Sydenham refused to rely on medical books when diagnosing a patient's illness. Instead, he closely observed the symptoms and treating the disease causing them instead
3. The printing press
4. *Philosophical Transactions*
5. The science of looking for chemical cures
6. Syphilis had spread quickly in bath houses, making people scared to use them

7. 300
8. Either a pest house, or nowhere. They were kept at home, quarantined for 28 days
9. William Harvey
10. Answers could include prayers or quarantine.

Chapter 3

1. Movements such as the Enlightenment made it fashionable to seek answers to questions about the world
2. Spontaneous generation
3. Pasteur's Germ Theory encouraged other scientists to look for alternatives to spontaneous generation
4. Microbes that caused tuberculosis and cholera
5. Treatments for everyday diseases, such as syphilis and tuberculosis, were not successfully developed until after 1900
6. Crimean War
7. Ether and chloroform
8. Answers could include providing clean water to stop the diseases that were spread in dirty water; disposing of sewage to prevent drinking and washing water from becoming polluted; and building public toilets to avoid pollution
9. 1798
10. The Broad Street pump in Soho

Chapter 4

1. Franklin, Watson and Crick
2. 2000
3. More powerful microscopes
4. 1956 and 1968
5. Answers could include blood tests, x-rays, and progress in genetics
6. Hata, Salvarsan 606; Gerhard Domagk, Prontosil
7. Hospitals, General Practitioners (GPs) and dentists, (otherwise known as primary care), additional services, such as the ambulance service and health visitors and hospitals managed by regional hospital boards
8. Answers could include diphtheria and polio
9. Fleming, Florey and Chain
10. Surgery, transplants, radiotherapy, chemotherapy

Index

Note: Page numbers followed by *f* represent figures.

A

abscess*, 123
Advanced Dressing Station (ADS), 159–160
agar jelly*, 71
alchemy*, 27, 27f, 42
ambulance wagons, 159
amputate/amputation*, 81, 153, 165f
anaesthetics*, 68, 80, 81–82
anaesthetist*, 92
anatomist*, 52
anatomy*, 19, 43
antibiotics*, 32, 108
antibodies*, 107
antimony*, 50
antiseptics*, 68, 79, 165
antiseptic surgery*, 81, 82–83, 83f
apothecaries*, 27f, 52
apprenticeship*, 52
aseptic surgery*, 83, 142–143, 142f
asylum*, 91

B

bacteriology*, 73, 117
barber surgeon*, 18, 18f
barge*, 151
Base Hospitals, 162–163
Battle of Arras, 149
Battle of the Marne, 146
Battle of the Somme, 149
Battle of Ypres (First) 148
Battle of Ypres (Second) 148
Battle of Ypres (Third) 150
biochemist*, 119
biopsies*, 101
Black Death (1348), 12, 32–35, 33f
'Blighty' wound, 162
blood, storage of 144
blood-letting/bleeding, 24
blood transfusions*, 110, 144, 169f
Blundell, James, 144
British sector, of Western Front, 137
    map of, 148f
    medical problems on, 153–155, 153f
    significance for experiments
        in surgery and medicine, 165–172
Brodie helmet, 147, 154
bubo*, 62
bubonic plague*, 32
    see also Black Death (1348)

C

capsule*, 109
Carrel-Dakin method, 165f
Casualty Clearing Station (CCS), 160
Catholic Church, 12, 13, 14, 18f, 40, 26, 26f
cesspit*, 93
Chain, Ernest 117–121
chain of evacuation, 158–60
chemotherapy, 124

chloroform, 81–82
cholera, 72, 88, 91–95
community care, 56
compound*, 107
constitution*, 50
contagious disease*, 14, 56, 114
cowpox*, 84
Crick, Francis 102
Cushing, Harvey 170, 172

D

diabetes*, 104
diagnose/diagnosing*, 15, 16, 20, 72, 101, 105, 111, 143
dialysis, 111
digestive system*, 24, 42
diphtheria, 72, 87, 89, 113–114
dissection*, 18, 18f, 19, 52, 52f
dissolution of the monasteries*, 55
DNA*, 102, 103f
Dressing Stations, 159–160
Dysentery*, 26, 26f, 49, 49f

E

enema*, 23
The Enlightenment*, 69, 74, 74f
epidemic*, 41, 74, 74f
ether, 81
    excision, 165f

F

faeces*, 27, 27f, 91
famines*, 13
Fast*, 63
Fertiliser*, 150
Field Ambulance, 159, 160
First Aid Nursing Yeomanry
    (FANY)*, 158–164
Fleming, Alexander
    and discovery of penicillin, 117–118
Florey, Howard, 119
Franklin, Rosalind 102

G

Galen, 17-20, 44
Gangrene*, 82, 153–154
gas attacks, 154–157
gas gangrene*, 154
general anaesthetic*, 170
genetics, 101–104
genome, 102–103
Germ Theory, 70–72, 71f, 87, 101
GP (General Practitioner)*, 110
Great Plague, 61–64, 61f

H

Haemophilia*, 103
Haemorrhage*, 154
Harvey, William, 58–60, 59f

heaven*, 23
hell*, 20f, 21
hereditary diseases*, 101
Hippocrates, 15, 17-20, 44
Holy Roman Emperor*, 55
Hooke, Robert 42, 47
horse-drawn ambulances, 151
hospitality*, 29
hospitals, 29–30, 29f, 55, 76-77, 110, 162-163
    impact of Florence Nightingale in, 78, 79f
Human Genome Project, 103, 104
humanism*, 44
humanist*, 52
humoural treatments, 23–25
    blood-letting/bleeding, 24
    purging, 24–25
hypodermic needle*, 109

I

immune system*, 107
incense*, 19
infection, 81
    and aseptic surgery, 142–143, 142f
    managing, 82–83, 83f
    treatment of, 165–172
    wound, 154
inheritance 102
infectious*, 73, 79
inoculation*, 84
insulin*, 109
irrigation*, 170

J

Jenner, Edward 84–88

K

Koch, Robert, 71–72

L

laissez-faire*, 87, 88
laxative*, 24, 25
leeches*, 24
Leeuwenhoek, Anthony van 42, 46
leprosy*, 14, 56
lethargy*, 23
lice*, 153
Lister, Joseph 70, 82-83, 142
local anaesthetic*, 170
lung cancer, 122–126, 123f

M

magic bullets, 107, 107f
Main Dressing Station (MDS), 159–160
malnutrition*, 13
mass production*, 109, 120
mastectomy*, 103
medical chemistry*, 50
Mendel, Gregor 102

miasma*, 19, 41, 69, 92
miasmata*, 101
microbes*, 69, 71, 101
micro-organisms*, 45
mortuary*, 162
motor-powered ambulances, 151
MRSA*, 112

N

National Health Service (NHS), 110–111, 110f
neurosurgery, 170
Nightingale, Florence, 78, 79f

O

observations*, 43
orderly*, 159

P

pain, and management 81–82
paralysis*, 14, 114
Pasteur, Louis, 70, 87
  see also Germ Theory
Penance*, 30
penicillin, 108
  development of, 117–119, 120f
  mass production of, 120
  use of, 121
pest houses, 56
Petri dishes*, 71
phlebotomy*, 24
phosgene, 154f
physician*, 15, 20f, 21, 43, 27f, 62f
pilgrim*, 55
pilgrimage*, 22
plastic surgery, 171–172
pneuma*, 58
polio, vaccination campaign against, 114
pomander*, 62
posy*, 34
printing press*, 20f, 21, 45–46
Prontosil, 107–108
prosthetic limbs*, 111
psychological*, 150
Public Health Act, 1875, 87–89

public vaccinators*, 85
purging*, 24–25, 41

Q

quack doctors*, 62
quarantine*, 34

R

radiation*, 122, 143
radioactive*, 123
radiology department*, 143
radiotherapy, 111, 124
Renaissance 40-45, 59
regimen sanitatis*, 26f, 51
Regimental Aid Posts (RAP), 159
remedies*, 23
Roentgen, Wilhelm 142
Royal Army Medical Corps (RAMC)*, 158–164
Royal Society, 46, 46–47f

S

sepsis*, 82
septicaemia*, 108
shelling*, 150
shell shock, 150, 153, 155
shock*, 80, 166
shrapnel*, 153, 154
side effects*, 82
Simpson, James, 81
sins*, 14
slums*, 88
smallpox*, 84
  vaccination, 85, 86
smog*, 114
Snow, John, 92–95
spontaneous generation*, 69, 71f
staphylococcus*, 120
sterilise*, 142
suffocation*, 154
supernatural*, 15, 22
  as Black Death's treatment, 34
  explanations, causes of disease, 13–15
  treatment, 22–23
Sydenham, Thomas 42, 44–45
syphilis*, 50, 51, 62, 107

T

Theory of Opposites, 17, 17f
Theory of the Four Humours, 15–20, 15f, 16f, 18f
theriac*, 28
Thomas splint, 166, 167f
Thompson's Cave, 162, 163f
tithe*, 13
transference*, 49f, 62
trench system, 146–147, 147f
triage, 160
tuberculosis*, 71, 108
tumour*, 108, 123
Tyndall, John 70, 74

U

urine*, 20

V

vaccination*, 84
  development and use of, 87, 87f
  differing opinions about, 85
  national campaign, 114
  smallpox, 84–86
Vesalius, Andreas, 52, 54f
virus*, 112

W

Watson, James, 102
workhouse*, 91
wounds
  'Blighty,' 162
  rifles/explosives, 53
  Wilkins, Maurice 102

X

x-rays, 101, 106f
  development of, 142–143, 143f
  usage on Western Front, 167, 167f

Y

Ypres Salient, 148–151, 148f, 149f